The Emerging Alternative to Western Brands

1. From Istanbul to Indonesia

JOHN GRANT

LONDON   MADRID
NEW YORK   MEXICO CITY
BOGOTA   BUENOS AIRES
BARCELONA   MONTERREY

Published by
LID Publishing Ltd.
6-8 Underwood Street
London N1 7JQ (United Kingdom)
info@lidpublishing.com
LIDPUBLISHING.COM

A member of:

www.businesspublishersroundtable.com

Printed in Great Britain by T J International Ltd.

ISBN: 978-1-907794-43-8

Design: Faizia Khan and Teodora Sararu
Typeset by e-Digital Design Ltd

CONTENTS

This Book Was Made With…

This book was *Made With* many brilliant, helpful and generous people who formed my case story interviewees, my advisers, experts and reviewers – and also the team around me in the publishing and design process. For giving their time, ideas and support, I would like to thank all the people I spoke to and whose ideas either feature in this book, helped my research and background understanding, or who made introductions to others I should speak to – including Peter Gould, Jon Bilal Wilson, Jobeda Ali, Majdi Yasin, Kevin Gould, Sara Ansali, Sanjay Nazerali, Farah Pandith, Ibrahim Al Zubi, Zahed Amanullah, Timur Savcı, Enis Orhun, Serdar Erener, Sedat Kapanoğlu, Sina Afra, Nevzat Aydın, Alemşah Öztürk, Oğuz Savaşan, Haluk Sicimoğlu, Mehmet Demiray, Anil Altas, Gulay Ozkan, Ayca Apak Tonge, Karen Chekerdjian, Demitri Saddi, Fadi Bizri, Tala Hajjar, Nada Debs, Bokja, Amira Solh, Kamal Mouzawak, Fawaz Al Zu'bi, Randa Ayoubi, and Fadi Ghandour. Thanks too to those other people whose work I have admired from afar and whose ideas and interviews I have quoted; I hope we will meet in the future! A huge special thanks also to Warren Singh Bartlett for showing me around and making introductions in Beirut and really stretching my ideas and understanding – this would have been a very different book if we hadn't met (and not in a good way!) – and likewise to Askin Baysal for all the help and support in Istanbul. Thanks too to Paul Skinner, Gulay Ozkan and Ramon Olle for reviewing the early draft and raising so many helpful pointers, questions and ideas. Also to Afia Fitrati who not only conducted all the interviews with her Hijabster friends and contacts in Indonesia, but also gave so much helpful input, enthusiasm, insight and ideas on the whole thesis and subject matter of the book.

Thanks to Martin Liu for taking me back on as an editor five books after he started my writing career and for all the support, advice and feedback. Thanks, too, to Sally Evans-Darby for editing the manuscript and to the whole team at LID for the enthusiasm and impressive professionalism. And thanks to Faizia Khan and Teodora Sararu for creating not just a book cover, but a whole MW brand world and visual language.

Thanks to Faizia, too, for providing the inspiration to write this book in the first place, and for being my muse and wiser, funnier, better-looking other half.

And thanks in advance to the reader, as the project of this book will continue to be *Made With* their own thoughts and ideas. You are invited to get in touch and comment on my blog at www.madewith. info, where you can also see some of the many hundreds of other cases and stories which I discovered while researching this book and did not have the space to include in the final draft.

Another fine Grant & Grant Industries production,
dedicated with much love to my son Cosmo

INTRODUCTION

INTRODUCTION

This chapter covers: the rise of emerging markets. Their potential to create tomorrow's lifestyles, concepts and brands. The Interland as a case in point, straddling a rich and plural cultural heritage with its arms wide open to the West. Ten reasons why this region might prove particularly promising. The main features that make a *Made With* brand different.

What 9/11 told me was that there was no way that globalization was going to be Americanization in the future nor should it be. In order for globalization to advance, it had to be accepted by more people; but not by imposing the dominant American social and philosophical beliefs and structures. [1]

Jim O'Neill, Goldman Sachs

Jim O'Neill introduced his idea of the *BRIC* economies (Brazil, Russia, India, China) two months after the 9/11 attacks on the World Trade Centre in 2001. He told the *Financial Times* in an interview some years later[2] that the attacks had shaken his whole worldview into realizing that non-Western powers would define the twenty-first century. O'Neill chose Brazil, Russia, India and China because they had large populations, underdeveloped economies and governments open to embracing globalization. He launched the BRIC idea in *Goldman Sachs Global Economic Paper #66* in late 2001. In 2005, O'Neill went on to coin the term *Next 11* for the other main emerging markets coming up behind the BRICs: Bangladesh, Egypt, Indonesia, Iran, Korea, Mexico, Nigeria, Pakistan, the Philippines, Turkey and Vietnam. (Presumably he called them the *Next 11* as it was slightly harder to come up with an acronym – VEMBIPPINKT?).

A decade later, emerging markets have outpaced all of Goldman Sachs' originally optimistic-looking predictions. In 2013, Ernst & Young (quoting IMF data) claimed that emerging markets will overtake the developed economies' share of global GDP in 2014.[3] EY estimate that emerging markets account for 70% of the current growth in the world economy. They also highlighted a shift in investment plans among 750 executives they interviewed; beyond BRICs into markets like Indonesia and Turkey, whose GDP growth since 2001 matches that of China and India.[4]

Emerging markets used to be known for hosting the West's textiles and electronics manufacturing, constructing new infrastructure, for call centres, heavy industry and their natural resources. With their economic growth, they then became an important place for Western companies to sell, as well as source from. Now there is a growing recognition that the companies that grow up in these home markets may go on to become global challengers. A 2013 Boston Consulting Group report identified 100 companies from emerging markets that are now fast growing internationally:

> In the past five years, these companies – many of them little known in the West – have added 1.4 million jobs, while employment at the nonfinancial S&P 500 stayed flat. Their average revenue was $26.5 billion in 2011, the most recent year for which figures are available, compared with $20 billion for the S&P 500. In the same year, they purchased more than $1.7 trillion of goods and services and invested more than $330 billion in capital expenditures.[5]

There are some interesting brands in the list: Natura Cosmetics (a client of mine) in Brazil, one of the most enlightened (eco, social and visionary) and beautiful brands in the world; Lenovo, who famously bought the IBM PC division and Samsung's key rival in smart phones; Tata, the $100 billion Indian group built on "family, ethics and hard work" with their famous low-cost Nano car.

What about O'Neill's other claim, that these changes will lead to a globalization where Western "social and philosophical beliefs and structures" no longer dominate?

Could countries outside the West be the source of brands that are built differently than those in the West, drawing on other cultural heritages and visions of modernity? I am not talking about anti-Western brands, but rather post-Western brands, signposting new global cultures in the twenty-first century.

When I first met Nick Hahn (then director of new strategies at Coca-Cola, Atlanta) in the late 1990s, I told him that they faced three broad challenges in the next century:

1. What will happen to Coca-Cola (who bottle "The American Dream") if the US fades?
2. How will you appeal to the growing quarter of the world's adults who avoid alcohol?
3. What will you sell when people won't drink refined sugar (or chemical substitutes)?

Answering these sorts of questions could lead to new global brands. Perhaps a tea-based drink from China? Or a salgam from Turkey? Arguably, this had already happened with Red Bull, originally *Krating Daeng* (which translates as red bison), a "tonic" popular with truck drivers and labourers in Thailand. I subsequently went to Africa with Nick to explore what it could be like to invent a new soft drink there: one that suited local tastes, was affordable, didn't require fridges and created local jobs.

This book takes on the prejudice that emerging markets are just playing catch-up when it comes to brands. It points instead to a multitude of ideas demonstrating that when modernity, creativity and a newfound confidence are combined with a rich non-Western cultural heritage, the result almost cannot fail to be fascinating. I am not claiming that this is a mature trend, however. And unlike the consultancy reports I quoted, I am not very interested in financially driven corporates; I am more interested in creative and entrepreneurial people, in their process and potential. There are some big successes in this book in cultural and commercial terms. But overall, it is still early days.

This book concentrates on just one part of the emerging world – the Muslim countries. These lie in that vast area which I will describe as the *Interland* (between the West and the East – historically home to the Silk Routes). It includes some countries where over 90% are Muslim, such as Egypt, Saudi Arabia, Turkey, Jordan and Pakistan – and others which are more mixed (at 50 to 60%) such as Lebanon, Nigeria and Malaysia.

There could be other books written about emerging brands from India, Brazil, Africa and China. Rather than one "non-Western" modernity, it seems likely given the diverse starting points that we will see a number of alternatives, each with roots in different worldviews, drawing on different cultures. I chose the Muslim region because it is one of the fastest developing, most creative and most richly endowed with cultural heritage, and also because it is by far the most undervalued and overlooked.

But while the Muslim countries have been undervalued culturally, it is hard to ignore their economic momentum. According to Pew,[6] one in four people alive today is Muslim and the Muslim population is growing at double the rate of other populations. The Organization of Islamic Cooperation (OIC), an association of 57 countries with significant Muslim populations, has a combined GDP of $7,740 billion; 13% of the world economy. These countries' total exports at $1,392 billion exceed those of the EU member states. The long-term average annual GDP growth across all OIC states is 6%.

The Interland region is diverse but with some strong ties, common roots and shared values. Historically, many of these countries were interlinked not only by faith and trade, but by the great civilizations of the Ottomans, Mughals, Safavids and Abbasids, which in their golden ages were thriving centres of world culture, infused with ideas and innovations from every corner of the globe.

However, one thing to stress at the outset is that by no means was every case study in this book made by Muslims. (A few I know were by Arab Christians or Malaysian Chinese. In most cases, however, I wouldn't even know.) Nor should they be understood as "Islamic brands" in the halal or sharia sense. Nor as an ethnic niche. These are world-class brands in various fields, which all happen to come from a certain part of the world. If I wrote a book about the creative sectors in London, I wouldn't restrict myself to those born in the UK. A 2005 study by Stanford Law School among American engineering and technology companies found that "25% of the nation's start-ups and 52% of those in Silicon Valley were founded by immigrants."[7]

Also, a paradox at the heart of the book is that Islam is (contrary to its perception in the West) one of the most plural, open and culture-neutral religions and cultures; in China it is Chinese, in Britain it is British, in Saudi it is Saudi Arabian, in Malaysia, Malay. It is a culture defined by its neutrality, flexibility, and its openness to absorbing and adapting. Its long and flourishing cultural, artistic and scientific history was enabled by its ability to take in influences and developments from other cultures, without ever losing its core sense of itself – the unity or *Tawhid* at the heart of the Islamic vision. Thus its architecture took on the city planning of the Assyrians, the domes of the Byzantines… but they made something wholly new out of these, that was wholly their own. The only culture that has come close to this might be the West. For instance, the 1920s Art Deco movement fused sleek Machine Age modernism with influences from ancient Egypt, classical Greece, Africa, China and Japan.

But *Made With* is not the same as Art Deco, which sought to reinvigorate through importing exotic foreign influences. The pioneers you meet in this book mostly have one foot in the West and one foot in their own culture. Novelist Elif Shafak quotes Rumi in saying that this mode of creating is like being a compass; with a sharply rooted point embedded in your own culture of origin, but

15

also able to traverse a wide circle that draws you into a universal humanity. It is the ability to own and blend the two worlds, neither of which feels "other" to the creator, which is responsible for their brilliance and breakthrough global relevance. In Shafak's case, what this "blending" means is writing in Turkish or English first, getting it translated, then rewriting in the second language, then shuttling back again. So calling these cases "Islamic" would belie the fact most of these are East-West blends (or in some cases East-East). And yet again (in another sense), that blending is part of the essence of Islam.

This Interland region could be – as Jon Wilson and I set out in a paper for *The Journal of Islamic Marketing*[8] – "the next Japan". That is, it could be a prolific source of differentiated and yet universally appealing brands. Like Japan from the 1960s to 90s, this would be the result of a rich heritage and distinct culture of business and society, attached to still-living traditions and customs – combined with a wide open modernism or futurism; a society of avid adopters, confident creators, embracing technical and media possibilities.

Japan, one small nation, gave birth to Toyota and Honda, Canon and Panasonic, Issey Miyake and Shiseido, the Sony Walkman and Playstation, MUJI and Pokémon. Just imagine what a population more than ten times its size, situated in some of the world's fastest-growing economies, could do by remixing their much vaster cultural resources with the latest developments, markets and innovations.

To avoid describing everything in the book as "Islamic" and instead to capture its plural mentality, I refer to this region as the Interland. I will explain in Chapter 1 that while the West's defining myth is that of a *frontier* – of conquests and expansion, of progress, of a break with the past – the *Interland* starts with a different mental geography – that of being in the middle. In Beirut, I was told it is the "bellybutton" of the world. This is an ancient image, as cities from Delphi to Antioch used to have an Omphalos or bellybutton stone, signifying their claim of being at the centre of the world. In Turkey, they say they are the "bridge" between Europe and Asia. Others say that they are on the Silk Route. Or a place where West meets China and India. They see themselves as geographically in-between East and West. And also culturally in-between. The Interland is also in-between heritage and modernity; in-between individuals and community; in-between many polarities that divide the West. It's a culture of and, not or.

The Interland is a big chunk of the non-Western global economy. Six out of Jim O'Neill's *Next 11* are Muslim majority countries (and Nigeria, being 50% Muslim, could be counted as a seventh). Just outside the *Next 11* is Malaysia, 28th economy in the world and nearly doubling in GDP every decade; a world leader in high-tech manufacturing and microchips. Meanwhile, firmly established with oil and gas wealth and increasingly innovative are Saudi Arabia, the United Arab Emirates (UAE), Algeria and Qatar. Saudi Basic Industries Corporation, developing oil-based chemical products, is one of Boston Consulting Group's *global challengers*; doubling in output over the last decade and becoming world leader in a number of sectors. The Saudi Government now has ambitious plans to make their nation 100% supplied by renewable energy; with 54 Gigawatts of solar PV (more than half the total global capacity that exists today).

The Muslim majority world also has demographics on its side. A high proportion of the populations are in their teens to late 20s, and so entering their economically productive years, which is a well-known factor in the success of other economies such as Brazil. This generation is tech-avid (UAE and Saudi have the highest smartphone penetration in the world) and a new middle class has grown up with global influences, the internet, travel… to be what Ogilvy Noor describe as "The Futurists":

> The *Futurists* tend to be under 30. This 42% of the Muslim population command disproportionate influence… responsible for shaping branding and marketing for the generations to come. So who are these *Futurists*? They are twice as likely as the

17

Traditionalists to say that "religion gives me a sense of identity". It is this sense of purpose that differentiates them from global Gen Y populations. They are proudly individualistic unlike the *Traditionalists* who seek belonging and social harmony. The *Futurists* are driven by success and progression. They believe in an Islam that is flexible, that allows them to find their own path, balancing their sense of self within the realms of the Ummah or society. The *Futurists* are inarguably the first generation of educated, world travelled and tech-savvy Muslims. They use the knowledge of the world and their experiences to improve their lives and those around them. They are tomorrow's catalysts, confident in using their knowledge and skills to bring about a positive change in their worlds.[9]

Serdar Erener (Turkey's most famous adman – interviewed in Chapter 4) echoes this in saying that the future of Turkey is "more modern and more Muslim". It's a paradox if you hold a Western view that modernity somehow entails a loss of personal religiosity and cultural traditions. Many in this book argue that they can take the conveniences of modernity on board without compromising their values or beliefs. It can lead to some clashes and inconsistencies, but also some trends and innovations that resolve or rise above these; for instance, the fashionable *Hijabistas* in Chapter 6.

Another factor in the emerging markets paradigm is rapid government and institutional change. With the Arab Spring sweeping through the Middle East, following earlier similar changes in countries like Indonesia, that certainly seems the case. And there is no doubt that it has galvanized and inspired creativity and entrepreneurship in the region. But then again the actual Arab Spring countries such as Egypt and Tunisia seem stuck into a long transition process. And others such as Iran and Iraq are both facing challenges that hardly (yet) betoken an opening up to the world and flowering of social potential. What we can definitely see is the will to change in the population. Not in the direction of "becoming like the West", but rather becoming more free to fulfil their potential, and be more themselves.

That's all very well for those countries. But what if you are sitting in London, Madrid, Sao Paulo or Shanghai? Why read this book?

1. Because – as Jim O'Neill realized – the West and the spread of its brands, culture, media and influence will not continue to dominate the world scene in the way that it has for the last 100 years. And emerging markets, by virtue of their growing prosperity, confidence and momentum, are starting to develop powerful challengers and alternatives. Some of these will be in the Western vein. But others will be born in non-Western aesthetics, mind-sets and values. So you could read this book because you want to get a glimpse 10, 20 or 50 years up that road.

2. Because – as Brazilian politician and Harvard professor Roberto Unger argues – globalization is unlikely to mean convergence, in the old Global MTV Generation view. It is more likely to be a patchwork of diverse cultures, each able to each trade from its strengths. As Unger put it in a recent speech to the UN, "the world is labouring under the yoke of a dictatorship of no alternatives". And what we need more than ever before is diverse local experiments. This is naturally how things do develop – just as the EU has not resulted in a common type, but rather continues to look to the French for flair, the Germans for engineering and the Swedes for logistics. Hence you could read this book for a "travel broadens the mind" effect. To escape the sameness and narrowness that comes from every marketing book covering the same few iconic brands. To encounter possibilities beyond what you meet in the West.

3. Because you have learned to distrust the *MORE OF THE SAME* school of trends. They didn't see the internet coming. Nor the fall of communism. Nor many other sea changes. As a result, you have learned to pay more attention to the fringes, outliers and genuine

19

alternatives that are emerging counter to the mainstream. It is plausible that with hurtling economic growth and social change, with such a young demographic, with new openness to ideas from outside and such a wealth of natural and cultural resources, this region could flourish again. But what almost makes this all the more convincing is the negative stereotyping of the region; being portrayed as culturally, politically and creatively backwards. This is a travesty, as you will know if you have travelled in this region. Hence you might read this book to explore a potential "Black Swan", like those challenges I threw down to Coca-Cola 15 years ago.

4. You may recognize, either from personal experience or a knowledge of history, that this *Interland* region – stretching across the old Silk Routes of Eurasia – has one of the richest stores of cultural resources in the world; a 1000-year history of architecture, design, textiles, literature, geometry, calligraphy. Just look at what Japan has remade from its cultural heritage. Then multiply that by ten. So you could read this book as mind food, rich in cultural inspirations and delights.

5. Because alternatives are usually born out of a pair of opposing factors: first, some separation from the mainstream (hence actually being alternative). And second, having creative flexibility, openness and the ability to pick and mix. To continue with the Japanese example, it was their combination of an island mentality with their avid adoption and remixing of Western trends that made them such a potent source of brands (where other nations simply absorbed Western brands and over time created their own versions, the Japanese genuinely created new kinds of brands).

Most subjects in this book are insiders to both the West and their own traditions. Like Sina Afra, a former senior executive at eBay Europe who then started one of the most successful e-commerce companies in his home country of Turkey. You will see from Afra's interview in Chapter 3 that Markafoni is in some ways a very

Turkish company and brand. But it is not reinventing the wheel or playing catch-up. It is recognized as one of the leading e-commerce companies anywhere. One that has gone on to launch successfully in other markets as distant from Turkey as Australia.

6. Because necessity is the mother of invention. We in the West – even in recession – have the decadent luxury of playing at entrepreneurship, creating brands and jobs. Outside a few oil-rich states in the Gulf, the *Interland* is at a stage in its development where this is a must. Otherwise the demographic bulge will naturally turn to the unrest, depression and bitterness of a wasted generation. Many of the people you will meet in this book do see their work – not only as a joy, a vocation, their life's work – but as a kind of social duty. Their work reflects upon and improves the community around them; their family, city, country or region.

7. Because cultural change happens most naturally in the places where people's lives are at an inflexion point. Shakespeare's England. Tolstoy's Russia. Early Hollywood's America. These were times and places where history was in the making. America gave birth to global brands at a time (from 1900) when immigration, industrialization and rapid improvements in education, health, media, technology and welfare were transforming the lives of its population. Compare that to now when the prospects of the American middle classes have been stagnant (at best) for 30 years. And then look East to countries throughout the Interland where the average income is doubling every ten years and the pace of change is almost dizzying.

8. Because the world is getting flatter. There is still protectionism. But it is much less effective in the globalizing economy and information age. Many of the old advantages of the leading nations no longer apply. In fact, nation states as a whole are increasingly irrelevant in a transnational economy. A smart kid anywhere can design and code the next killer app for mobile phones or the internet. And if they get stuck, they can talk to another smart kid

21

the other side of the world, who has done something similar. And the advantage the region has in also *actually making things* allows them to compete in less intangible markets. Turkey has been the leading manufacturer of TVs sold in Europe for the last 10 years. It won't be any surprise if the "iPad" equivalent of 10 years' time is Turkish too. Investment is flowing into the region, as global wealth seeks emerging market growth. And there is something to be said for the more cultural factors in all of this, the emerging market work ethic, ambition, confidence and optimism.

9. Because the Western model is broken. For one thing, there are profound concerns about Western brands, consumerism, the environment and social values. Many in the sustainability world believe that these are only symptoms of a deeper alienation; from nature, human nature, communities and any kind of a moral compass that would enable us to value economies based on wellbeing. Because we are uprooted by our version of "progress", the dogma of the blank slate, the illusion of endless growth. Yet clearly brands do have a power and influence with global populations. Is there a way to create a better version? There are candidate brands that do this in the developed world; like Fairtrade, MUJI and eBay. But it is interesting to explore whether innately non-Western approaches can add something that we have been missing, or help them avoid repeating some of our mistakes.

The crisis is not only external. Within the branding world there also is a deep anxiety that the classic model may not work anymore. That brands are increasingly ephemeral, less trusted, less believed in: that they are increasingly hard to construct with authenticity or any enduring appeal. Leaving most brands propped up by promotional tactics. And the few that really "have it" (in my experience) tending to become edgy to the point of superstition about "jinxing it". It's a crisis of faith.

The problem at the base of Western culture is that there is no base. In the West, we have so vigorously uprooted ourselves from traditions that we scarcely believe in anything. At best, we suspend disbelief. Perhaps for the time length of a movie. Or for the season of an aesthetic, technological or intellectual fashion. As Nietzsche might have said (if he were a contemporary of Stephen Hawking), we have put a black hole at the heart of our society: a big nothing at the heart of economics, social sciences, sceptical materialism.

In our parents' time, people believed in the providential powers and rational ordering of scientists, economists and other experts. "If we can put a man on the moon!" they used to say. But a century of overreaching, techno-rationalism and hubris have made us increasingly distrust these sources; the 1930s scientists that told us not to pick up babies because it was unhygienic; the 1980s and 90s economists who claimed to have found the "secret" to lasting society-wide prosperity, be it *Monetarism* or *New Growth Theory*; the industrialized farming now linked to human health risks from BSE and bird flu to agrichemicals that cause birth defects, and dead zones in rivers and seas.

The loss of the temporary relief provided by rational pseudo-scientific advances has left us alone with the profound nihilism articulated by Friedrich Nietzsche. This produces anxiety, distraction, restlessness – and quite possibly the urge to consume to fill the emptiness. As sociologist Anthony Giddens (former president of the London School of Economics) put it in *Modernity and Self-Identity*:

> To live in the "world" produced by high modernity has the feeling of riding a juggernaut. It is not just that continuous and profound processes of change occur; rather change does not consistently conform either to human expectation or to human control. The anticipation that the social and natural environments would increasingly be subject to rational ordering has not proved to be valid.[10]

23

All this leaves us to cling onto is currency – the value of being "of the moment". The West is a society of fads. There is plenty of innovation that results from the energetic scramble to stay out of the black hole. But very little lasts. And this void at the heart of the West results in the spectacle of a politics that only believes in electability, a media that only believes in being viewed or liked, an economy that only believes in growth. And for businesses it creates unsustainable cycles of hype and obsolescence, with the new new thing being overpriced and overrated – and then rapidly becoming either out-of-date, or just a big fat disappointment. "Gales of creative destruction" may be the capitalist way, but there is a difference between stimulating gales and the destructive super-storms that make it impossible to create lasting value.

What consumers in the West seem to crave and value most is authenticity, humanity, genuine exchanges and experiences. Some brands do provide these. But few escape the currency trap. Most outgrow their authentic phase (when two founders you could relate to ran the show), or see their audience move on as they are overtaken by fresher brands able to tempt away fickle young influencers. There are some emerging models that I have grouped in my previous books under the heading of *New Marketing*. But most of these do rely on the currency of new media and innovation. Even the surge of concern about all things eco in 2007 seemed to go just as quickly out of fashion.

10. Because the examples are great. What gave me the confidence to write this book is the many case stories I have gathered here (and the many more that I found in my research) from outside the West that demonstrate that the newfound confidence in emerging markets is not misplaced. They can create great brands. They do so with a different mind-set, process and contents. The results are authentic and show greater staying power, depth and meaning.

This book aims to do two things:

First, to tell the inside stories of these brand ideas. Hence I have based the book upon interviews with creatives, entrepreneurs, innovators and commentators drawn from across the *Interland*.

Second, to articulate an underlying pattern. I have written this book on the assumption – a hypothesis –that these brands represent a challenge to the Western type of brands. That they offer an alternative.

The three key features that make these brands "new and improved" compared to their Western counterparts are:

1. A turn away from the personality-based egotism of Western branding (Hence *Made With*, rather than Made By).
2. A turn away from either-or distinctions, towards the power of "and" (East and West, Heritage and Modernity, Individual and Collective…).
3. A genuine rootedness and meaning, connected with tradition and community (not an endless alienated dance of empty signifiers around a big nothing).

You do find some brands in the West that these same criteria could be applied to.

And just as I would admit there are some *Made With* examples in the West, I equally would not claim that all of the *Interland* thinks this way.

In previous generations, there was a polarization into conservative "Fundamentalist" rejecters and elite but abjectly "Westernized" accepters. Now a growing group in the current generation – Ogilvy Noor's *Futurists* – are finding a middle way. They see no essential conflict between the mosque (or other traditions) and the mall. These two just take up different places in their lives, at different times.

A middle way for a creative person requires a deep-working knowledge and experience of both sides. Otherwise it is like *Chinoiserie* (one culture aping another's styles without any understanding of the internal history, context and meaning). Because of which, it is little

25

surprise that the *reverse brain drain* from Europe and the USA is a significant part of the story.

I do not want to make the West too simple or some kind of straw man. I live and work here and it has its own interest and trajectory. "The West" is just a convention I am using to point to some developments outside that zone. There is no essential core that I'd recognize in my own fields of work, only a much looser ragbag of conventions and trends, often centred on clusters and communities. "The West" I described above is not the same as the West of *Slow Food* or *Linux*. And it is much more of an Anglo-Saxon "West"; one that readers in Mediterranean countries may struggle with too.

"The West" is only here as an intellectual convenience, to see the wood for the trees. It does have a kind of giant overshadowing presence in the regions I conducted my interviews in. But even if they talk about it in their more philosophical moments of reflection, people don't create or work at that level – it's way too big and abstract.

The potential is a new strain of brand joining the world economy. One that I think has many qualities to recommend it. It will not replace Western branding, but more likely could prove an interesting supplement. What it offers to anyone starting their own business, creating brands or projects – especially those reading this who are based in the Interland and searching for role models – is a fresh stream of inspiration, one that comes at things differently, points to new possibilities.

The stories speak for themselves. And they are diverse. Some are practical feats of engineering problem-solving. Some are subtle, symbolic and artistic. Some are intimate. Others are public and collective. Saying they are "all the same" is not the point of this book. Rather, I just want to point to some consistent threads – consistent with where they are from and in how they create brands.

My summary of this consistent thread of difference is in the title: Made With. There are a number of ways of reading this title and each has some relevance:

- *Made With* = rather than Made By

  Too much ego in Western branding has a price.

  You may be admired if you succeed in a society where envy is key to glamour and charisma, but you suffer a loss of empathy, goodwill and fellow feeling.

- *Made With* = Making and community

  A passion for making. The care, attention and commitment with which things are made – whether a chair or a business process – is one outstanding theme of the stories in this book.

  And a passion for community; for the collective, context and collaboration.

  The two together represent an overcoming of the alienation that keeps makers separate from markets. Creating socialized markets of shared enthusiasm. Or helping people understand how their food is grown, their furniture or indeed (see *Little Bits* in Chapter 2) how hi-tech devices are made.

- *Made With* = Combination

  What separates this generation of case stories from their predecessors in the same region may be their ability to integrate, reinvent, make their own, drawing on diverse sources that are all "native" to the creators; East and West, Heritage and Modernism… This makes them the result of fusion; having, as they say in botany, "hybrid vigour".

- *Made With* = Bridging

  The ideas are often from cities, countries and regions that regard themselves as forming an intermediary between the East and the West, or indeed the Middle East and the further East (of China, India and South East Asia). It means having an added dimension or broader view, as being on a bridge between two worlds allows you to see both sides. And to select the best from both.

- *Made With* = "And" (not either-or)

  The cultural roots of the region include a deep appreciation of the power of "and-", rather than the either-or oppositions that ensnare the

27

Western (Cartesian) mind-set. This approach refuses to accept simple opposites, and prefers either nuanced compromises or creative leaps to resolve a contradiction. Both of these ways, but particularly the second, can produce strong brands with a potential global appeal.

- *Made With* = **Love**

  The emotion that goes with this concept of "and-" is love; as opposed to power, recognition, status, distinction, competition and other registers that divide us. This love is not the "romantic" exception that haunts Western cultures but a passionate involvement in life, vocation, relationships – which makes you feel alive. Love may be featured by Western brands, but it is by comparison a fractured love, a compensation for being alone, a non-material version of comfort eating. All too often it is also an empty promise, a feeling that evaporates after the purchase is made. Not a commitment, as one of our interviewees put it, to "bring a smile to the home". The *Interland*'s totalizing version of love is inexhaustible; it made Rumi a bestselling poet in the West and holds the potential to create an endless stream of strong global brands.

- **Made With = Confidence to be "Us"**

  There is a feeling behind all the conversations I had in the writing of this book of it being "our time" and perhaps "our turn". That while the West may have run out of track, this *Interland* is just getting up to speed. Most would say that it is early days, that they aren't yet sure of their global identity or role. But living in countries where the average prosperity doubles every decade, where there are thriving clusters and business ecosystems, and growing ranks of role models, it is hard not to feel on the verge of a new era. That is the truth of emerging markets: not just their growth, but their growing confidence and ambition.

One of my counterpoints in writing this book was my experience in other emerging markets, notably Brazil.

I would say that there are some similarities – for instance, the rootedness in living traditions, in family and community, and a more holistic, less Anglo-Saxon view; the sense that everything is one interconnected whole; the tendency to be emotional, visionary and intuitive rather than reductive. But you could not say that the Brazilian culture is against personality, icons and ego. Rather, there is an equally developed other modernity that belongs to Brazil. And there are Brazilian factors you do not find so widespread in the Interland; the New World utopianism, the wisdom of the Indians, the closeness and bounty of nature, the sensuality and body culture.

I hope to follow this theme of emerging market alternatives, and write another volume called *Made With Brazil*. Or perhaps a series: *Made With China*, *Made With India*, *Made With Africa…* I do see exciting brands coming from those too. For instance, Nando's (a client of mine in the UK) have a refreshingly South African approach to food, people, experiences, socializing and business. They're unlike anything else I've come across. And hugely successful – growing to be number three in the restaurant market and also rated one of the best big companies to work for in the UK.

For the present book we are looking into just one region with huge potential. So much so that I could never hope to fully do it justice. An account of the brands, creativity and entrepreneurship from a region covering a quarter of the world's population that is based on so few case stories will never be exactly definitive, or exhaustive.

The point of this book is to provide some fresh inspiration for those working in the Interland region, those who might be entering that world, and anyone anywhere who has creative and entrepreneurial aspirations and wants to explore new ways of doing things. The key usefulness might prove to be the detail of one particular case, quote or idea. Or it could be a more general shift. A change in what you think is possible. Giving you broader horizons and fresh confidence to explore them. And as many examples in this book show, that attitude can change everything.

29

THE INTERLAND

THE INTERLAND

The West sees itself as a frontier, progressing in time and space. The Interland doesn't see itself as a mirror image of this. But as a bridge (mediator, translator and synthesizer) in-between East and West, heritage and modernism. A land of "and" (not either-or).

If you look at ancient sea traffic, the Mediterranean emerges as the obvious centre of world history… an organizing force, drawing diverse people into one another's narratives and weaving their destinies together to form the germ of a world history, and out of this came Western Civilization…. If you look at overland traffic however, the Grand Central Station of the world was the nexus of roads and routes connecting the Indian subcontinent, Central Asia, the Iranian highlands, Mesopotamia and Egypt. This eventually became the Islamic World…. A portion of it is called the Middle East, but that phrase assumes one is standing in Western Europe. Therefore, I prefer to call this whole area from the Indus to Istanbul, the Middle World.

Tamim Ansary, Destiny Disrupted[11]

The West, despite its name, is clearly more than a geography. As an idea to work with (and against), let's start with a hypothesis. The West is a set of cultures governed by a single common myth, that of progress over a line:

The Frontier.

It is simplest to explain this myth in its American context. And there is some justification for centring our exploration of the West here. America is not just the place where the most global brands have come from. It is also the latest and most "advanced" version of the Western ideal, for better and worse. And the place that most people outside the West seem to mean when they refer to "The West".

And America is the society of *The Frontier*, par excellence.

33

The Frontier is a line. A line between here, us, now – and "the beyond". It could be spatial – as in the line charting the leading edge of the settling (or conquering?) of America. It could be temporal – marking the leading edge of scientific and technological progress from the Enlightenment. It could be aspirational – as in *Star Trek*, projecting beyond the moon mission into "Space, the Final Frontier".

The Frontier is an invitation, a finishing line for those competing for prominence.

The structure of the Frontier myth is profoundly either-or, us and them. It is a discontinuity; a break with the past and present, a leap into the unknown. And it is the line that defines progress. Inside this line of progress is order, achievement, merit. Outside is pure potential – chaotic, primitive, unsettled and almost nothing. Or seen as nothing of value. Or shrouded in the fog of uncertainty that hangs over the future.

The Frontier idea shapes how we see history, with the present being that line of progress. The past is established territory; the future is a place yet to be conquered or explored.

The Frontier idea shapes how we see knowledge, as a moving Frontier of discovery and adjacent possibility. Stretching to limitless horizons.

The Frontier idea shapes how people in this culture see themselves. As self-made, self-reliant, the makers of their own destiny, true frontiersmen – individuals seeking to surpass limits, go further.

Mixed in with this idea of an ever-moving line of progress is the idea of a break with the past. Old ideas, artefacts, traditions can have nostalgic or cultural value. But they are seen as less advanced. And of less value. The pilgrims and settlers of North America were out to make a *New World*, not a new Europe. Their descendants are a society of pioneers, always restless, always onto the new thing.

It was just after the Wild West frontier stage of American history that the modern brand was born. The earliest modern brand was Coca-Cola, invented in 1892. At that time the literal (Wild West) Frontier was disappearing as a reality, but was growing as a myth. Wild West

Shows toured the USA (and Europe) recounting this heroic recent past, mixing history with a wily blend of exaggeration, embellishment, spectacles and showmanship. They gave rise to a prototype of modern celebrities; real-life frontier heroes like *Calamity Jane* and *Buffalo Bill*, complete with dramatic backstories and sharpshooter skills. They were the Hollywood idols of their time, with 10 million attending shows. And as the Wild West Shows faded, the Hollywood Western was born, a popular genre in the silent movie era, right through to the 1960s. This is still the subject of recent remakes such as *No Country for Old Men*, *Blackthorn* and *Django Unchained*.

George Lucas borrowed extensively from the Western genre in creating *Star Wars*, along with The Heroes Journey, a supposedly common format to all epic hero stories, as mapped out by Joseph Campbell. Soon this storytelling format was the staple of Hollywood screenwriter courses and books. These theories became widely transmitted and influenced subsequent films such as *The Lion King* and *The Matrix*. Although, you could argue it was just formalizing a pattern that went back to those Wild West Shows.

In this view, every story must have a lone hero, someone who the audience identifies with, who goes through trials, who struggles and overcomes dark forces. In Campbell's version, the hero is someone willing to sacrifice himself for the greater good – a point less emphasized by the Hollywood happy ending. America didn't invent the hero, but it did take it to new extremes; Captain America, Luke Skywalker and Indiana Jones.

This heroic individual of American Frontier history found direct expression in brands like Marlboro and their iconic *Marlboro Man*, featured in advertising from 1955 to 1999. And less literally in the sporting heroes employed by Nike. These were not just sports stars, but iconic rebels – many of them African American. Nike hence stood for a fusion of "cool" (rebellious individualism) with godlike heroic competitive success. Today we see the same myth played out

35

in examples like the Red Bull *Stratos* project, taking extreme sports to new heights of human endurance, with an Austrian skydiver taking a record-breaking 39-km leap from the very edge of the atmosphere.

Historian Frederick Jackson Turner claimed that the Frontier was America's foundational experience; turning European settlers into egalitarian, rugged, individualist Americans – a breed apart. By the end of Turner's lifetime in the 1930s, his *Frontier Thesis* had become official American history, as taught in the majority of its universities, at which time Franklin Roosevelt appealed to his electorate to reclaim a "nationwide frontier of human want and fear"[12]. And later, John F. Kennedy developed the *New Frontier* as his trademark political brand, as set out in his inauguration acceptance speech of 1960:

> We stand today on the edge of a New Frontier – the frontier of 1960s, the frontier of unknown opportunities and perils, the frontier of unfilled hopes and unfilled dreams... Beyond that frontier are uncharted areas of science and space, unsolved problems of peace and war, unconquered problems of ignorance and prejudice, unanswered questions of poverty and surplus.[13]

A few years later, Gene Roddenberry pitched a new TV show called *Star Trek* to the Hollywood studios as "a Wagon Train to the skies". A thought carried over into that famous voiceover at the start of the show: "Space, the Final Frontier".

Joseph Campbell's book, *The Hero with a Thousand Faces*, is a deeply good read and is inspired by James Joyce, Carl Jung and others. It should perhaps be separated from the formulaic Hollywood uses to which it has been put. Neil Gaimon, whose work contains many mythic themes, points out that if this is the decisive form that authentic stories take, then you don't need a manual, they will just come out that way:

I got about half way through *The Hero with a Thousand Faces* and found myself thinking if this is true – I don't want to know. I really would rather not know this stuff. I'd rather do it because it's true and because I accidentally wind up creating something that falls into this pattern than be told what the pattern is.[14]

Some have claimed that far from being an essentialized universal myth, *The Hero with a Thousand Faces* is in fact just the founding myth of America itself writ large. As Lawrence and Jewett put it (in 1977 – decades before George W. Bush declared a "War Against Terror" and seemed to cast himself in this role):

A community in a harmonious paradise is threatened by evil; normal institutions fail to contend with this threat; a selfless superhero emerges to renounce temptations and carry out the redemptive task; aided by fate, his decisive victory restores the community to its paradisiacal condition; the superhero then recedes into obscurity.[15]

Modern brands like Coca-Cola, Nike and Facebook were born out of this kind of American Dream and the rugged individual that came with it. It perhaps seemed natural in this culture to equate brand value with standing apart from the crowd. And it was the America of 1950s Madison Avenue that handed down most current theories of brand – like the idea of "brand personality" (from Martineau, Ogilvy and others).

The energy, freedom and scope of the Western Frontier myth is dizzying, exhilarating. It promises an eternal blaze of glory and discovery. Perhaps (techno-futurist Ray Kurzweil tells us) we are accelerating towards a *singularity*; a tipping point event when our technology will take on a kind of life, intelligence and destiny all of its own?

Just as this myth is intoxicating, like any drug it had to have its comedown. There is a real sense today of having reached limits, or running out of anywhere to progress to. The pure Western endless progress myth has given way since its heights to a darker self-doubt. The first shadow was cast by mechanized World Wars. Then came the atom bomb. Then climate change and limits to growth. And now the West has an internal crisis of economic confidence. It seems like a gambler that has run out of luck. And the current slump is perhaps made all the more stark by the manic depressive media combining global bad news with spurts of fresh hyperbole.

The West found its *Wild West* frontier in America – the line between the "civilizers" and the "savages". The older boundary (what the West lies westwards of) was that between Europe and "The Orient" of the European imagination. A Europe whose unshakeable sense of superiority led them to assume that *West is Best!* – even when meeting empires more advanced with longer histories and richer cultures, like the Ottomans and Chinese.

Edward Said made it his life's work to deconstruct this Western idea of the East. In *Orientalism*, Said described how the Western colonial fantasy needed an "Orient" which was (as figured in art, history and culture) irrational, weak, untrustworthy, feminized, eroticized; in contrast to the rational, masculine, civilizing West. Said was a Palestinian Arab, born in Jerusalem, educated in Cairo before heading to America, where he settled for the rest of his life. Said did not write about the actual East. Rather he wrote about the West's idea of the East. A long time before 9/11 (in 1980), Said described the West's view of "Islam" in terms that seem almost prophetic now:

> So far as the United States seems to be concerned, it is only a slight overstatement to say that Muslims and Arabs are essentially seen as either oil suppliers or potential terrorists. Very little of the detail, the human density, the passion of Arab-Moslem life has entered the awareness of even those people whose profession it is to report the Arab world. What

we have instead is a series of crude, essentialized caricatures of the Islamic world presented in such a way as to make that world vulnerable to military aggression.[16]

Across the interviews I conducted in researching this book, I've come to agree with Said that the "East" is itself a Western construction. The people I met with have a different mental model of their geography. One that sees their world not in terms of a line or frontier separating two divided zones, but rather a circle, a zone of inclusion, being in the middle of things. I call this alternative mental geography:

The Interland

The Interland could be described as a literal geographic region – Tamim Ansary's Middle World. A region stretching from Morocco, Egypt, Turkey and Lebanon all the way to Indonesia, Malaysia, Pakistan and Bangladesh.

But it's not just geographical. Rather, it's that anywhere in this region people seem to position themselves at the centre of things; as a "bridge".

In other words, they saw themselves not as "East" at all – but rather as in-between:

Between East and West

Between Tradition and Modernity

The refusal of choosing between such polarities, and the preferences for bridging, seemed to extend to many other ways in which they saw themselves as "and-" cultures (rather than either-or cultures). For instance:

Between Individual and Collective

Between Art and Technology

Between Economics and Society

In Turkey, I was told that they are the bridge between East and West. That you can cross from Europe to Asia just by crossing a bridge. That the two sides meet here. And hence the culture reflects this, making new combinations from these components.

But Mehmet Demiray, an anthropologist and author of reports

39

called *The Mind of Turkey*, told me that this idea was actually common across a huge region, with each country teaching its primary school children they were unique in this same bridging way: in Egypt, Morocco, Tunisia, East Europe and also further East.

Slow food activist Kamal Mouzawak told me Lebanon was a microcosm; like a model, prototype or blueprint for the rest of the world. And he illustrated this by saying that almost every climate on Earth existed there, from mountains to beaches, from lush plains to deserts. He also described Beirut as "the bellybutton" of the Mediterranean, an image used since ancient times to describe the centre of the world.

Interviewees from Dubai and Turkey told me about the East-West fusions resulting from a "reverse brain drain". This, I was told, brought an open-minded generation, educated in Western ways back to the region. And that while these returnees had kept a connection with their culture, families and communities, they also brought not only new ideas, but a more dynamic and open approach to business.

I read that Malaysia (an Islamic state, but also a peaceful democracy with a history of pluralism) was unique in being "like a mixed salad" – mixing ingredients and ideas from Chinese, Indian as well as indigenous and Malay Muslim sources. Creating hybrids, but with clearly distinguishable ingredients.

But it can't be that unique when they even use the same analogy in Lebanon (which is hardly known for its peaceful pluralism). Except here they described it as "like Tabbouleh" (an Arabic salad); while you can taste each ingredient, you could never remove one and have it still be a proper Tabbouleh. Also because it's chopped so finely you could never separate them anyway in practical terms. Just as Lebanon minus any one minority would not be Lebanon.

The impulse to create new cultural hybrids can be found in every city in the world. But it may mean something more to be living and working in a culture that shares a collective myth and self-identity of bridging and being in-between (rather than of going beyond). A land of "and-" rather than either-or.

This idea of being in-between and absorbing influences from all around is not new to this region. It has long been something of an *Interland*, criss-crossed by trade routes that also brought trade in ideas, craft techniques, languages and customs. This was the historical position of the Islamic world. The genius of its golden ages was down to its ability to trade – from China to Spain, along the great Silk Roads – not only in goods, but also in ideas. For the first time, under the patronage of the Abbasid caliphs, all the intellectual advances of the world were translated into one language and combined by the same minds. Islamic mathematicians, for instance, were the first to combine Greek geometry with innovations from India, such as the invention of the number zero, and from China such as their algebra used for astronomy.

The intellectual and economic strength of these periods came from being in the middle. Being able to combine, trade and multiply. To do this well requires confidence and openness. The old Middle World had these in abundance. But then it became insular for a while when overrun by the Mongol invaders. Later came another syncretic flowering in the Ottoman (Turkic), Mughal (Indian) and Safavid (Persian) Empires from the 16th to the 18th centuries. Before these too were overrun, this time by the colonizing countries of the West. Leading to the insular attitude that today we call "fundamentalism". The suspicion is that all over the region, the confidence is returning now. That the awe or hostility the West once inspired is fading. That countries like Turkey are finding their mojo again, and that the old self-confident mixing of their own heritage with imported ideas from all over is back on the agenda.

Along with this plural culture of mixing and trading with other cultures comes a much greater emphasis on collective values. Not being a heroic lone stranger like the cowboy who rides into town, but being part

41

of a greater whole and continuous community of hospitality, peace and acceptance. What the Islamic tradition calls the Ummah; a single global brother- and sisterhood. The dream of the Islamic cultures is based on unity, and a widespread cultural harmony and collectivity is a part of this.

This is, in most of the countries we will be exploring, a civilized and ornate culture – far from puritanical – and hugely fond of worldly goods. Yet there are very few statues, portraits and icons in this culture historically. As we will explore in the next chapter – given that Western brands start and end with the heroic individual icon – this is almost bound to give rise to a different approach to creating brands.

The communal spirit of the Interland countries has been given a new impetus today by the internet. The generation I interviewed were some of the first to go digital (some by virtue of working in Silicon Valley or studying at MIT, rather than the local boom which came later). The direct influence of these possibilities is seen in this book, in the formation of *e-nabled* clusters. The internet has seen a return to the ideal of cosmopolitanism (being a citizen of the world). And this seems to represent a view that is closer (for instance, in being plural and mixing cultures) to that of the *Interland*.

And this – take note – opens up huge potential. If the global internet generation is moving on from the *Frontier* myth to something more like the *Interland* position, this would have huge implications for the character of future global brands, and for the potential acceptance and adoption of new brands emerging from the Interland.

What we will meet in this book is a group of cultural creatives and entrepreneurs, who embody this open, remixing, expansive, synthesizing *Interland* mentality. This is not the only trend in this region. But it is the one that describes their emerging-ness (as opposed to the old binaries of accepting or rejecting the West).

If I wanted to write a book about Islamic brands, I would have to select a smaller proportion of the examples I had met, and even these might not thank me. Few of them set their store out as being "Islamic", even if they incorporate some of the implicit or explicit heritages into their work. Most, whether they are Muslim or not, are drawing on broader influences from the West and elsewhere. As I spoke to more people, I realized that labelling them as Islamic designers, (or -entrepreneurs etc) was too narrow. It suggested that religious beliefs directly and linearly shaped their work (as if we could label America's retailers as "Christian", and its cinema as "Jewish").

There are undoubtedly subtle connections – for creatives above all – between the culture they come from, their ethos and mythos, and their creative productions. But it is not a connection to be made too simply, nor to the exclusion of all other influences.

I do see (most of) the cases and creatives as profoundly influenced by the legacy of 1000 years of one of the most developed, integrated, nuanced and beautiful cultures the world has ever known. Even if not influenced directly by the traditions, then by the atmosphere and milieu; by a certain subtlety of language, poetry, arts and crafts. And even if not by those heritages, then working within one great productive mental model – of seeing yourself as working in an Interland, and being open to the bridging possibilities of AND, rather than the restrictions of EITHER-OR.

One influence that did come up a fair bit was Sufi – the mystical side of Islam. But saying that some creatives in this region are inspired by Sufism is a bit like saying some of their equivalents in California have been influenced by Buddhism.

Firstly, it is true (Steve Jobs being a notable example).

But secondly, it does a disservice to both the religious spirit and also the creative output to describe them as essentially connected, as if one simply "caused" the other.

Sufi thinking itself is quite subtle about where religion stops and human agency starts. In a Sufi story, a sage complains to God that there are beggars and cripples on the street and yet God has done nothing for them. "I did do something," God replies. "I sent you!"

43

MADE WITH (NOT MADE BY)

MADE WITH (NOT MADE BY)

A new kind of brand is emerging which is both modern and yet non-Western. The typical Western brand is all about authorship, personality and identification; Made By- (and for) the ego. The Interland brand is born out of an ethic that distrusts the ego, having a tradition of unsigned art, avoiding icons. Brands in this region are *Made With*; less ego, more authentic, subjective; holistic rather than based on social distinctions, rooted and collective. Western brand strategy is reductive, Interland brands are better understood as stories.

The economic growth we have seen in non-Western countries over the last ten years is enabling the emergence of a new generation of humanity, both modern and non-Western, whose stories I am sure will soon feature regularly in the literature we read. [17]

Orhan Pamuk

If this new generation of humanity in the emerging world is drawing upon non-Western traditions, how will this affect the way they create brands? I will argue across this chapter that a key difference is that these non-Western brands rely far less on the notion of authorship. That Western brands push ego to the fore – they are *Made By*. Whereas the approach in the *Interland* could be better described as *Made With*.

Orhan Pamuk, Nobel Prize-winning author, once described the Turkish language as "the sound of a thought unfolding". His books are suffused with the atmosphere and texture of life outside the West. At times, the details and descriptions may seem incidental. But Pamuk's point is that it is precisely this level of detail that can be most revealing of a whole different approach to life; one that is "both modern and non-Western". With *The Museum of Innocence*, Orhan Pamuk took the highly original step of producing not only a novel but an actual museum, in the Beyoglu district of Istanbul. Both the book and the museum commemorate objects from everyday

47

life in that city from the 1970s onwards. As Pamuk explained in an interview with *Newsweek*:

> Toward the late 1990s, with my novel and the museum firmly on my mind, I began to buy a large number of objects from the handful of shops that constituted this flea market at the time. Instead of writing about the objects – the teacup, the pair of yellow shoes, the quince grater – that my novels' characters used, and then going to look for their physical counterparts, I performed the opposite, more logical process: I went shopping first, or I took, from friends who still conserved them, old furniture, miscellaneous paperwork, insurance papers, various documents, bank statements, and, of course photographs – "for my museum and my novel" was the excuse – and wrote my book based on all these things bought and acquired.[18]

Pamuk's is a fascinating creative process. It is born out of a primary commitment to the real – to the experiences of everyday life – rather than the heroic imagination of the author. Of course many fiction writers do "research" the minutiae of a period, or setting. But few authors see the real details as so core to their work that they would then open a museum as a natural counterpart. I see Pamuk's process as like joining the dots. It is a kind of bowing towards the world, submitting your creative ego to a greater reality and faithfulness to how things are. This is a theme that you see in art across the *Interland* region. In the Middle East, photography has become one of the key forms of art, perhaps for this reason. In Beirut, the leading strand in all artwork is (I was told) archiving the details and events of their civil war. Later in the book we will meet a Turkish artist who makes network maps to show how the world works. Most Malaysians grew up on the cartoons of *Lat* with his brilliant evocation of the *Kampung* (village) life of his own childhood. Pamuk's books bring you closer to the life-world that he evokes. And in this he reminds me of Naguib Mahfouz, the Egyptian author, who could make the eating of warm pastries or the stifling complexity of its civil service so evocative of the old Cairo that you almost feel jostled by it. Brands are not art or great literature. They are commercial and shallow by comparison. But they draw from the same influences. And often, like Pamuk's everyday artefacts, they can be close to the texture of life on the ground.

The point of his museum, Pamuk tells us, is to commemorate the way that previous generations would buy and exchange objects as part of an art of communicating, through "looks, gift-buying, meaningful silences". And Pamuk sees the potential of museums such as his to be archiving not just one local history among many, but "emerging humanities" outside the Western World.

How are these "emerging humanities" different?

Pamuk's phrase (especially the "meaningful silences") suggests a kind of reticence. When Westerners gaze into many of the societies I am writing about, they see veils. And while according to some, that says more about the West's prejudices (it's not like we walk around naked), it also points to an intriguing focus on the issue of modesty. Which is a core value (as we will see later in the book, through interviews with some of the leaders of the hijabi fashion scene) that the women wearing veils do themselves refer to.

What if brands came from a modest society? And one that valued collectivity over standing out? In societies where reticence is central, then allusion comes forward in communication. That's not to say that communication is thwarted, nor that brands are muted. But rather that they speak a more symbolic language: one more reliant on implication. Another way of saying this would be that they are more "poetic".

Kevin Gould was one of the first people I interviewed when researching this book. Kevin is an award-winning British food writer, entrepreneur and chef. He has been travelling around Turkey and across the region for 30 years and I knew (from our own dealings) that he had a strong connection with not only the food, but the local cultures, religions and traditions. I'll leave the points he made to me as direct quotations – as you will see, Kevin has rather a way with words:

In the Islamic world, modesty is generally valued over confidence. You have a dichotomy at least – (the word) Islam means submission and the greatest Muslims were always the most humble.

Their language, way of speaking, persuading is indirect.

The Turkish language is very poor in words, so you have to stretch it to describe anything. They say the Eskimos have 50 words for snow. In Turkish they have one word for snow but would make it work in 50 different ways.

This is a culture of being really good at talking. Like the storytellers of the Souk in Damascus. The language itself has its own power and art. In the West you can say "words are only words" but here words have what Jabir called a "weight".

All over the Islamic world, it's what you don't say that is what is understood. It's all about implication and allusion. The Western way of iconography in branding is very overt. The East has a more internal meter. When they copy the American way of marketing, it's clumsy, learned behaviour.

Their incredibly beautiful work in traditional forms was all about the space between words, images, languages.

In Turkey, it's neither a matter of anarchy and the shock of the new, nor imitation of the West – it's about hip people who deeply understand their own cultural history and are able to pick selectively among their own traditions.

How might this modesty and allusion manifest itself when it comes to brands? One key way is the idea and status of authorship. The creatives of our Western societies are celebrated for their work, be they architects, designers, chefs or entrepreneurs. And personalities in general – celebrities as we would say today – account for a large part of our culture and media coverage. That's just how things are, and how they have been since the Renaissance. But what if a society wasn't like that? If ego were distrusted? If icons, portraits and statues were not the natural mode of art? If your greatest poet (Rumi) did not glory in personalities and power struggles (like Shakespeare), but wrote things like this:

> Sever the chains of the ego. Set yourself free and witness the bright essence of your inner being. Discover within your heart the wisdom of a prophet without books, without teachers, and without prudence.[19]

Another of Orhan Pamuk's books goes to the heart of this difference between the traditional Western and Islamic cultures – the cult of the author, artist, heroic creator. *My Name is Red* is a complex postmodern (self-aware) historical murder mystery set among the miniaturists of the old Ottoman Empire. One of the artists (this is not a spoiler – you learn about it in the first chapter) is the murderer. In the investigation, by another artist, each suspect is asked questions designed to reveal his attitude to art. The very first question concerns authorship:

> Has he come to believe under the sway of recent customs as well as the influence of the Chinese and the European Franks that he ought to have his own style? And does he attempt to prove this by signing his name somewhere?

The theme of authorship and individuality is woven throughout *My Name is Red*. Characters are generally known under anonymous names like Red and Black. And in the narrating of the story, Pamuk passes the authorial voice between the various characters, major and minor; but also variously a corpse (the murder victim), a coin, Satan, a dog and the

51

picture of a tree. The picture of a tree makes a telling point about the way that images are used within the Western and the non-Western world:

> Painting in the new style requires such a talent that if you depicted one of the trees in a forest, a man who looked upon the painting could come here and if he so desired, correctly select that tree from among the others. I thank Allah that I, the humble tree among you, have not been drawn with such intent. And not because I fear that if I'd been thus depicted all the dogs in Istanbul would assume I was a tree and come and piss on me: I don't want to be a tree, I want to be its meaning.

This is the benefit of leaving behind the conceit of individualism; you then draw closer to the universal meanings of things. By being yourself, rather than a "type", you paradoxically become more fully human. And the same, we will see, goes for brands.

The Islamic tradition that *My Name is Red* is set in was profoundly suspicious of icons, portraits and representation – and also of authorship. The miniaturists featured in Pamuk's book were themselves rare exceptions to the rule that in most times and places the artists and craftsmen of the Islamic world created patterns, not representative pictures. And the copyists' pictures such as those featured in Pamuk's story were only to be included (for educational purposes) within private book collections; private illustrations, not public works of art.

How Islamic cultures largely expressed themselves visually (instead of pictures of people and animals) was calligraphy, geometry, architecture and repeating arabesques. These designs expressed profound philosophical ideas like the essential unity (*Tawhid*) of a universe composed of the thoughts of God. But they also avoided iconic art, because of specific spiritual dangers on that path. Titus Burckhardt, author of *Art in Islam*, says there were two main reasons for this: firstly, man created in the image of God, should not be portrayed in a lesser way (a kind of blasphemy by falling short). Secondly, created icons might become worshipped and hence become a barrier between people and God. Hence you see very few statues or examples of representative art in Islamic history, as compared to the Western tradition. It is aniconic.

When you consider that Western marketing people commonly talk about such and such a brand being "iconic", you can see a gap opening up here. And while these brands may be material rather than spiritual icons, they do seem to be worshipped in a way. And identifying with them could well have cultural dangers. What we will see across this book is that refusing to give ego such a central place can result (not in muted brands) but in richer ones. As Pamuk's tree says, when you leave behind showy posturing, you are left with meaning. To repeat this is not an impoverished culture. It is a non-Western culture. Ornate. Fascinated with luxury, craft and grooming. But not as brash, nor self-proclaiming. A culture of allusion, symbol and poetry.

An apt example of just how ego-centric Western culture can be (when viewed from outside) is the artistic device of perspective. Laboriously created, through artificial means, by Renaissance artists. Later included in every photograph, unless treated to some special effect (like panorama or tilt and shift). Art historian Titus Burckhardt points out that the miniaturists (like those in Panuk's novel) had all the knowledge and means to create an illusion of perspective. It was not that they *could not use* perspective. But rather that they would not find anything special about imprinting the copyist's own singular viewpoint, through the imposition of perspective on the picture:

> Perspective which the history of art takes quite wrongly as being synonymous with an objective vision of the world... in no way adheres to things as such, but to the individual subject; things perceived are arranged according to the subject's point of vision.

53

Mathematical perspective brought rationalism and individualism into art. As opposed to this development of modern European art, the Persian miniature represents a normal view of things.

Rationalism and individualism (as we will explore later in this chapter) are the two hallmarks of the ego. Any European painting has a hidden meaning; which is that the most important figures are not those featured in the painting, but rather the artist and the viewer, from whose privileged position everything else radiates. It is a device that unconsciously flatters both the ego of the viewer and the creator. It does so even more obviously within advertising images – signs that we know are created with the viewer in mind, to flatter us and entice. In *Ways of Seeing* (a 1972 BBC TV series, later a bestselling book), John Berger points out that the sheer density and prevalence of visual images and messages from advertising is unprecedented compared to any other society in history. We are so accustomed to these that we barely notice them. It is as if we had become used to living in a world where every surface were mirrored.

A number of modern commentators have suggested that the individual egotism enshrined in Western culture has led to a mass defect of character. Jean Twenge, academic psychologist and author of *The Narcissism Epidemic*, reports a 30% increase in narcissistic traits since 1979 among American students (based on comparing large-scale and long-term surveys). One in four students now exhibit traits falling within the clinical definitions of narcissism, while more than half showed some milder signs of the same syndrome of excessive self-regard. Twenge commented to the BBC:

What's really become prevalent over the last two decades is the idea that being highly self-confident – loving yourself, believing in yourself – is the key to success. The interesting thing about that belief is it's widely held, it's very deeply held, and it's also untrue.[20]

Clearly Twenge's findings could be linked to all sorts of developments, like modern styles of parenting and schooling. But these college kids who see themselves as individual success stories in the making are hard not to relate to the brands, media and fashions they grew up on. It's the underlying story that every brand told them: buy this product and be one of the special people; confident, beautiful, smart, popular. In the words of the advertising for UK newspaper *The Independent*: "It is, are you?"

I will argue that the fundamental proposition of nearly all Western brands is that they are *Made By* (a heroic, aspirational figure), or indeed *Made By* an aspirational type of user (a tribe, audience, or scene that you want to join who adopted this brand and made it their badge). An example of the first would be a fashion label – e.g. *Made By* Chanel. The second would be Harley Davidson (a brand *Made By* Hells Angel style bikers). The distinction is often blurred. Did people aspire to the Apple brand as *Made By* the iconic Steve Jobs? Or did they aspire to be one of the in-crowd of hip, creative industry Apple users? In either case, what is on offer is a boost to the individual consumer's ego. And the call is to identify and imitate. You will be *Made By* what you choose to consume. John Berger, who I quoted earlier, thought that this conceit goes back to the birth of modern painting in the Renaissance: "Oil painting, before it was anything else, was a celebration of private property. As an art-form it derived from the principle that you are what you have."[21]

The *Made By* culture runs deeper than just advertising or painting. The West is fundamentally an *egonomy*. One where value is associated with authoring. At its heart is the pedestal we create for celebrity – the quintessential modern heroes. It is this figure of being a "celebrated" individual – and its fantasy of power, attractiveness, popularity and charisma – that many Western brands tap into. It's perhaps why commercial television became the defining medium for modern brands, because here the (literal) personality could be given full expression.

55

At the centre of this *egonomy* is the cult of the creator:

- Oscar-style awards shows, even for trades like supermarketing
- Lavish features and documentaries about celebrity creators and entrepreneurs
- A media-obsessed media that gives a platform to models, designers, entrepreneurs, architects, chefs – turning them into celebrities
- "Talent" shows where members of the public get a go at playing this role of the celebrated creator or entrepreneur
- Facebook likes and Twitter follows where you can feel part of the entourage (and indeed feel like celebrities with your own friends and followers)

The *egonomy* myth says that it isn't about hard work; it is *talent*, a kind of grace or innate entitlement to be recognized; because of the heroic powers you have been given. Here Jean Twenge is probably right. If you buy into the myth, you might miss the real opportunity that comes from a long slog born out of a deeper, more inward vocation. Real creative achievement comes from years of study, apprenticeship, struggle, hard work. That's not my view, but rather the conclusion of longitudinal studies in the psychology of creativity; comparing for instance the hours of practice by successful innovators like the Beatles with their less successful counterparts.

The signature of the creator is present throughout the "creative industries". "Look at me", the creator is all too often saying through their work, already dreaming of a showcase of awards and plaudits. In the London creative agency (St Luke's) that I co-founded in the mid-1990s, we took the view that this ego culture was unhelpful, because it hitched us to our peers' expectations, rather than really doing things differently. So we decided not to enter any creative awards.

When the signature is absent, and the creator's identity withheld, then it can have a really interesting effect. Look at the fascination that surrounds graffiti artist Banksy because of his anonymity. He refuses to let his art be confused with his own personality. As a result, perhaps, Banksy is more able to create with freedom, tell the truth, connect with the bigger picture, say something real and challenge the status quo. "If graffiti changed anything," Banksy scrawled on the wall near my old office (or rather a mouse caught red-handed with a dripping paint brush is pictured doing so), "it would be illegal"!

Authorship is an essential part of understanding Western brands; the charisma of the creator. This is clearest in the case of fashion and lifestyle brands that are named after designer founders. It also applies quite obviously to the companies of famous entrepreneurs. Today's "Henry Fords" are the stars of *The Social Network* – with their legal suits over the very lucrative question of who authored the idea behind Facebook. This idea of "the author" goes well beyond these brands though, and is described by some as the defining feature of Western culture since the Renaissance. French historian and philosopher Michel Foucault put it this way:

> The coming into being of the notion of "author" constitutes the privileged moment of individualization in the history of ideas, knowledge, literature, philosophy, and the sciences. Even today, when we reconstruct the history of a concept, literary genre, or school of philosophy, such categories seem relatively weak, secondary, and superimposed scansions in comparison with the solid and fundamental unit of the author and the work.[22]

As Foucault points out, it is not just books in the West that are authored, but technologies, sciences, knowledge. Patented Intellectual Property (IP) dates back to Renaissance Venice. Isaac Newton was so hot on getting the credit that he would publish his theories when half-completed in code (so that if someone later made similar discoveries, he could still claim them). Conversely, Western high culture has a horror of copying and plagiarism. Not so much because of the sinfulness of cheating, perhaps, as the loss of authorial status if caught. Western capitalism is about credit in two different meanings of the word. One is financing and speculation (the economic engine since the Renaissance). The other is owning the rights to something, be it a trade route, a piece of software code, or a genetic sequence in a farmer's seed. So you can take the credit and assert economic rights of ownership.

You might assume – surely? – that there were authors before this time. Had Foucault not heard of Plato, or Aesop? But while these are named as writers of their work, that does not mean they shared the individualist conceit of modern authors. As Pierre Hadot wrote about (the Roman philosopher and author of the *Enneads*) Plotinus:

> Today authors lay themselves bare, expressing and liberating themselves. They strive for originality, for what has never been said before. They try to stamp their own personal mark on everything they do. But like all products of antiquity, the *Enneads* are subject to servitudes of a wholly different nature. Here originality is a defect, innovation is suspect, and fidelity to tradition, a duty.[23]

That's not to say their writings could not be a landmark in human thought (which is certainly Hadot's view of Plotinus). It is more the question of an individualist conceit. Are you presenting yourself as the authority who miraculously breaks with the past, is devoid of all taints of influence? Or are you content to draw authority from other sources, which you then interpret in your own way? The authorship question is a matter of degree. It's not that today there are no designers, authors, entrepreneurs or celebrities in this *Interland* region. Nor that there are no Western influences. It's that the culture emphasizes the individual hero less. It places more value on other factors such as tradition (that an individual brilliantly re-expresses) and community.

Authorship seemed the most natural way to introduce the contrast between Western brands and the emerging alternatives in this book. Let's now explore some more detailed contrasts between the two approaches – *Made With* (vs *Made By*):

Made With	Made By
Self	Ego
Meaning	Identifying
Subject	Object
Commitment	Irony
Inclusiveness	Distinction
Holistic	Reductive
Develop with the past	Break with the past
Collective	Individualist
Story	Strategy

Self vs Ego

These terms may be familiar to readers from Western psychology, and in particular to readers of Carl Jung and Sigmund Freud. But they also featured centuries earlier in Sufi writings, where the struggle to escape the confines of the ego ("Nafs") and connect with a fuller, more authentic Self was expounded in the writings of authorities like Rumi:

> In God's presence, there is no room for two egos. You say "ego," and he says "ego"? Either you die in his presence, or he will in your presence, so that no duality may remain.[24]

I have used the term ego throughout this chapter in its (less spiritual and) more modern psychological sense to describe a central factor in Western culture and brands, one less apparent in the *Interland*. So it seems worth exploring it in more depth.

"Ego" is literally (the Latin word for) "I" – the source of the voice in our head. It is what we are conscious of within ourselves. A key discovery of Freud's was that "the ego is not the master of its own house". We think that our conscious, calculating and deciding "I" is what controls our actions. But it actually isn't. This point was reinforced by Daniel Kahneman's 2011 book *Thinking Fast and Slow*, contrasting two modes of thought:

- system 1: *fast, automatic, stereotypic, subconscious, emotional*
- system 2: *slow, logical, calculating, effortful, rational*

Kahneman quotes studies to show that our illusion of consciously, rationally deciding can be easily overturned. For instance, a classic study showed that if you left a dime in a call box, giving the "lucky" gift of a free phone call – and then set up a situation when the subject leaves the booth, like someone dropping the papers they are carrying – then the subject will almost invariably help out. Whereas if you don't leave a dime, then the subject almost invariably ignores the mishap and walks by. Clearly system 1 is working on a principle of reciprocity; an innate human disposition towards repaying good luck. Meanwhile, our ego – system 2 – plays very little part in the decision.

The innate human disposition towards repaying good luck is an example of the operation of the Self. It is not blind animal instinct; it is humanly meaningful, moral, universal and symbolic. This is a part of what Jung's theory of archetypes and the collective unconscious is about; the universal ideas that emerge in response to common human situations. These ideas can emerge at times of stress, blockage and sudden resolution (the kind of experience you might well have in a psychoanalysis) as the dawning of a bigger truth; an epiphany. After this, you may feel almost like a different person. As the French say, you have then reconstituted yourself as a subject. Vocations are a common example; having a feeling that this (job, cause, path) is "what you are here to do". These truths – what Jung called your personal myth – can ground your personality and worldview, becoming fixed points of certainty.

What authors writing about the Self – whether traditional or psychological – mostly agree on is the reward that comes from the disciplined overcoming of your ego; love, wholeness, unity, empathy and interconnection, being less inhibited and constrained, more fully yourself, feeling part of a bigger totality, energized by a deeper wellspring of creativity. From Rumi again:

> When you do things from your Soul, you feel a river moving
> in you, a joy.[25]

In Jung's model of the psyche having two poles (Self and Ego), the examples in this book strike me as being closer to the Self, and Western brands as closer to Ego.

Meaning vs Identifying

Another way to describe the ego is that it is the person we see in the mirror. That was the line taken by psychoanalyst Jacques Lacan. Lacan said that the core emotion of ego is envy. That when as babies we first recognize ourselves in the mirror, we are struck by the contrast between the (more) perfect (than we feel) image that we see, and our own feeling of still being uncoordinated and helpless. It is about identifying with an external image, and yet always falling short. It strikes me that this is the way we react to the perfected images of brands, models and media. The buying of cosmetics, fashion, grooming, diets and body routines could only partly ever fill this gap.

John Berger, the art historian I quoted earlier, said that this prevalence of envy and ego is a perhaps surprisingly recent dynamic in Western visual culture. The net proposition of all advertisements Berger suggested is that we transform ourselves by buying the featured product – and the emotional logic presented for doing so was that we are presented images of characters who are enviable; as "the state of being envied is what constitutes glamour". It hence offers happiness, but not the internal satisfaction of contentment. Rather, happiness as judged by others from the outside. You fantasize becoming – like a model in an advert – one who is observed being happy, envied, but also oblivious to all of these gazes; aloof, apart, above. Berger contrasted this with the attitude of the subject of a classical painting; Mrs Siddens by Gainsborough:

> Glamour is a modern invention. In the heyday of the oil painting it did not exist. Ideas of grace, elegance, authority amounted to something apparently similar but fundamentally different. Mrs. Siddons as seen by Gainsborough is not glamorous, because she is not presented as enviable and therefore happy. She may be seen as wealthy, beautiful, talented, lucky. But her qualities are her own and have been recognized as such. What she is does not entirely depend upon others' envy – which is how, for example, Andy Warhol presents Marilyn Monroe.[26]

One way to react to the ego as image in the mirror is the excessive self-love that Freud called narcissism. I mentioned earlier how some, like academic psychologist Jean Twenge, see narcissism reaching epidemic proportions among American young adults today. When we meet people like this, we tend to describe them as "shallow". What they are missing is the real depths of life. All they care about is appearances; the opposite of which is meaning. People might find meaning in a cause, in falling in love, a vocation, or developing a deep appreciation for design, reading, art or food – relating to it through knowledge and taste; for quality of life, rather than status. That's more the sort of spirit we'll meet in the case stories this book.

Tunisian film director Nacer Khemir has made a series of award-winning lyrical films inspired by Sufi traditions. In a recent interview, Khemir explains the image that inspired his new film *The Prince Who Contemplated His Soul*:

> It is true that the Prince leans over the water, but he does not see his own face, like Narcissus did, because whoever sees only his reflection in the water is incapable of love. The prince

contemplates what is invisible, that is his own soul. We are all similar to icebergs; only one tenth of us is visible, while the rest lies under the sea.[27]

Later in the same interview, Nacer contrasted the outward, narcissistic West with a more inward East, using the examples of the different types of gardens we keep:

> There is nothing like gardens to explain the difference between the East and the West. The Western garden, visible and surrounding the house, on one hand, and the Eastern garden, hidden, thus invisible, in the centre of the house, on the other hand. Whether in Cairo, Grenada, Marrakech or Tunis, this Islamic conception of gardens always prevails. A garden can only be hidden, because it is a place for contemplation and meditation, where the mind escapes. The purpose of the classical Western garden is to dominate the surrounding world, which explains the lines of perspective that lead to the horizon. It is a garden of mastery.

The lack of depth, meaningfulness, inwardness and reflection goes a long way to explain the newfound passion in the West for Eastern imports like yoga and the (2 million bestselling) poems of Rumi. But while it is inspiring to rediscover these "wisdoms", it is something again to grow up with them. That isn't to say all my interviewees were as spiritually inspired as Nacer Khemir. But they did grow up with the same gardens, and the same well of culture to draw upon. Just as Japanese designers grow up with Zen sensibilities and concepts like Wabi Sabi. Even if they are not Buddhists.

Subject vs Object

The *egonomy* – oversaturated with celebrities, images, icons – suffers from the same basic alienation and envy that Jacques Lacan pointed

63

out in the mirror stage. The media images look perfect, coordinated, in control. But that's not how we necessarily feel inside. When we see a model in an advert, we are not seeing another human life with all its struggles and issues. We are looking at an ego construction: a life without issues. It is natural for ego-based brand appeals to work in this way. But then there is also that inevitable disappointment and insecurity Lacan pointed to, already baked in.

A deeper way of working with brands is to delve into your own inward experience of things. What you create then has a subjective quality and meaning. It feels really true to your inner experience. And many times relates to that of the audience too. In the next chapter, for example, we meet a designer who created a toy based on the insight that children love playing under tables. And when people buy a more authentic and inwardly meaningful brand, they don't feel impoverished, but rather enriched. Meeting someone else's subjectivity is the main way that we know we are not alone in the universe. It can bring, as one of our other interviewees says, "a smile to the home".

As a creative or entrepreneur, this kind of more subjective approach comes from fully immersing yourself as a person in what you produce. What would I want? How would I feel? What would I do next? And from an attitude of service; that you would do all of this for someone else – like leaving notes under a pillow to surprise your lover. Somehow it's this attitude; wanting the best for people rather than setting out to exploit; or at least striking a balance between the need to make money and the need to believe in your work... that seems to lead to something so much more authentic.

Many of those interviewed in this book have an attitude of relating to their work subjectively, with their full person, their intuitions. And not letting egotistical ideas, like double-guessing how it might be received, trip them up. Just focusing on the work. Letting originality flow from the work. From patient problem-solving, following it through, rather than the showy shallow innovation of creating difference for effect. Or trying to copy formulae. Or using tricks to gain appeal and market share.

Everything else pales into petty insignificance next to a creative individual who has found their *thing*. The people you meet in these pages often express a sense of vocation. They can start talking shyly, then light up as you get them onto their passions. You get the sense that they wouldn't understand the Western idea of "work-life balance" because they are engaged in something like their *life's* work. Some mentioned the first time they encountered their whole field of work in glowing terms; when they became instantly hooked. And it sounded like falling in love.

Commitment vs Irony

As one coming from outside the *Interland*, it struck to me that a major difference between the creatives I met during this research and the equivalents I work with in the West may be that the former do think of their work as very meaningful. Here in London, the meaning of a chair (or a font, or fashion) might be that it will sell. Or that it's part of a current trend. Or it's your clever creation. It's seldom about new ways of sitting. For that, we have to go back to the pioneering age of modernism, to Corbusier.

In emerging societies in transition, there is this deeper level – being part of a living history and potential future, both for the makers and the audiences. This is a time when history is in the making, not a time of decadence adrift. You do see fusion. But it is not a postmodern witty clash for effect. (Like the famous window display in a 1990s Tokyo store of a "crucified father Christmas".) It lacks the irony and nihilism behind the impulse to "take the piss" like that. The broad point being there is a gulf of difference between living and working in a context where life feels like it does have meaning and a direction – and one which is more nihilistic. Here, being ironic is cool; in the Interland, the key quality is warmth, passion, connection, commitment.

65

To return to my point; while the people you will meet in this book are often funny and playful, they do take their work seriously, and have little ironic distance from it. The same with companies – in societies where creating jobs and improving your own life plus a general feeling of being at a tipping point are so present – you don't get the sense of people working in such an alienated way as to feel "lost in the machine". The companies don't need "vision and values" statements to know they have a purpose.

Inclusivesness vs Distinction

The ego isn't just responsible for self-regard. As Kahneman points out, it is responsible for thinking that is "slow, logical, calculating, effortful, rational". It is the style of thinking that reasons "out loud" in our head, trying to figure things out. Like when you write lists of pros and cons, or you perform mental calculations.

Logic relies upon clear-cut distinctions. A or B. Our rational mind seeks categories, priorities, rankings, tables and family trees. This is a vital part of thinking, especially the kind of book learning you need to pass school exams, sell business plans or write good code. There is nothing at all wrong with either-or categorizing, per se. It is only when excessively applied to the fuzzier areas of life that it can become too much.

The logical categorizing function of the ego and its "look at me" quality might at first sight strike you as distantly related properties of the mind. But they are intimately connected when you look at the functioning of the ego (as psychoanalysts do every day). From perceiving social differences, it is a short step to "us and them". The logical categorizing of the ego and its egotistical self-regard are hence closely related.

Distinction is the apt word chosen for both these functions taken together by sociologist, anthropologist and philosopher Pierre Bourdieu, for the exact reason that it combines definition (dividing people into groups or cliques) and a sense of superiority. Bourdieu's book *Distinction* describes how our tastes can mark us as members of these groups that feel socially "better than others". It could be a taste (like opera) that shows we are educated, are members of the upper class. It could be a subversive taste that makes us part of a cool youth group. It could be our disdain of the petty bourgeois, designer goods and showing off that marks us out as serious intellectuals, and better than the nouveau riches. These days it could be geeky technical adoptions that mark us as an inner-circle, early member of a digital trend.

Most Western brands are grounded in distinction. One soap powder appeals more to middle class "yummy mummy types" (in reality, probably guilty career women, attempting to be like their mothers while not having time). Another soap powder appeals to a functionalist, organized, rational, "notes on the fridge" type mum, one who is on top of schedules, routines – who wants the latest scientific advances, to wash faster, cleaner, with less allergies or at lower temperatures. The lost opportunity in so nailing brand colours to these shallow personas – and both of these are neurotic, in being based upon underlying insecurities – is that there are deeper universal values that they miss. Brands are often so busy competing to stand apart, they ignore truths. What about the almost baptismal feeling of spring-cleaning, or of fresh sheets after you have been travelling? Or the joy of muck and smelly socks? These more inward, less insecure feelings were perhaps what Persil/Omo aimed at with its "Dirt is Good" ads. (Although my own favourite was the Japanese brand of soap powder produced by fashion brand Hysteric Glamour in the 1990s, under the name *Fuck Housework*.)

When you hit these deeper notes in humanity, the result is inclusiveness. Not feeling that we are all the same. But recognizing that we are all, after all, human. What we often find most attractive in others is not their status, but their fullness and frankness in not holding back – even if they aren't like us, they are themselves. It's the same with brands. What we crave in a world of genuine fakes is a bit of authenticity.

Holistic vs Reductive

Most of the people I met were holistic thinkers – seeing the world in patterns and systems of interconnection, beyond simplistic categories like cause and effect. Anthropologist Mehmet Demiray told me that such systems thinking was a characteristic of Turkish business people, the way they plan and operate (and others said similar things in other countries, so I don't think of it as only Turkish).

It is a famously Western thing to be Cartesian and reductive. There is the annoying habit that anyone who has been to business school can have of trying to corral a free-flowing discussion with their grids, models or lists. As if having a clever way of categorizing or explaining something were more valuable than being open to understanding it afresh. Most of the people I spoke to were more instinctive, intuitive and emotional, or more practical (or a bit of both). There were very few theorists. Most told me that they try to evolve their ideas empirically; try something, learn and change. There was talk of observing, trying to get to the realities of a situation with less preconceived ideas. And they often would keep their options fairly open, refusing to specialize or over-define things, in case the context should change.

Another common thread is synthesis. There is an East-West fusion theme running through the book. But it is one of studying, living, travelling, marrying, partnering or otherwise absorbing and internalizing "other" influences, so that they are part of your own make-up. That is very different from when one culture imports and adopts an exotic style out of context. As just one example, I ate in a Beirut restaurant called *Casablanca* that has a fusion of Asian and Lebanese cooking. But the story here was not that of a "mad creative chef" but rather a madly in love chef. He had apparently married a Chinese woman and made it his life's work to bring her food culture and his into a romantic union. Not only is that his private motivation but it is well known by his customers, including the people who took me there and regaled me with this story.

Develop with (vs Break with) the past

The egotistical conceit of modernity (in its Western version) is that 99% of our achievements are our own. It's like the comic book myth of Superman, who crashed to Earth as a baby already having intelligence and superpowers. It's only late in life as individuals that we may start to realize just how much we owe our parents, our teachers, our mentors and friends. And it takes careful reflection to recognize just how much we constantly copy and paste other sources, conversations, images and phrases into our own ideas. Not to mention the debt to our ancestors who invented everything from penicillin to the human uses of fire. As Dewey, the polymath inventor of the library system, put it: the ratio of an individual's contribution to human culture, to their debt to that culture, is comparable to the amount of words a baby adds to a language, compared to the amount of language that babies absorb!

The ego doesn't want to see things that way. It wants to be an omnipotent baby.

A friend of a friend (a photographer's assistant), at whose flat it was my misfortune once to eat dinner, had got it into his head that he was a very creative person; and hence he should be able to apply this same instinctive brilliance to cooking. The result was undercooked salmon, a "sauce" like hot grey milk and some weirdly bitter ("creative") spices and herbs. That is cooking from the ego. Also known as reinventing the wheel. There is a section later in the book about the brilliance of adapting; internalizing the import thoroughly so you really understand how it works, why every piece is in place; and then adjusting it to fit your own local context. You usually end up with something more original (and certainly more workable). It is only egotism that would say: "round wheels have so been done, let's try polygons".

A sense of continuity and acceptance of tradition also opens up a treasure chest of customs, ideas, intuitions. Things that already fit, feel humanized, homely and familiar, have been worked on for generations. And yet they might find entirely new uses, applications

69

and outlets. One of my interviewees in Turkey told me about their ad campaign for a local brand that featured animated babies singing Turkish folk songs. The idea was rooted in an old folk saying – "a baby is the joy of the household". And it was given new life with live action footage of babies, animated to look like they could really sing. The ad was so popular that even after being off air for a year it was still rated in a survey as one of Turkey's most remembered ads.

Made With people don't feel the need to start with a blank slate, be the first, the original, one who has no precedent. By accepting the abundant cultural resources, what has already gone before, you end up paradoxically with something far more original and effective than attempting to start from scratch.

Collective vs Individualist

This is one of my either-or distinctions that betrays a Western outlook. ("The West is individualist, this region is different, therefore it must be wholly collective".) But actually what most people told me was that there was a balance between individualism and the collective. Between self-actualization and the sense of belonging and obligation that comes with community ties. A perfect example in later chapters is the entrepreneurship which is clearly born out of an independent spirit, yet does often seem to have a more collective flavour than its Western equivalents.

Many of my interviews reveal subjects who are comfortable with blending the individual and the collective; for instance, being proud of their work, but also seeking to pass much of the credit onto colleagues, mentors, other sources. The two can also be emphasized to different degrees in different domains – like in the Arab proverb "eat whatever you like, but dress as others do". The great conjuring trick of Western brands is that they claim to magically produce individuality through buying the same phone, trainers or coffee as everybody else. Through not trying too hard to stand apart, the examples in this book are often more individual in the sense of relating to a subjective, personal taste and sensibility, or being less uniform or mass produced, or drawing upon local sensibilities and ways of doing things.

There are few subjects in this book that subscribe to heart-on-your-sleeve ethics or environmentalism. When I brought up such topics (for instance, I remember specifically being pulled up on the word "empowerment"), I was told "these are Western concepts". And I was also told that the codes of modesty are especially strict in this part of the world around doing good – it almost negates your good deeds if you let them be known. Yet most seemed aware of working within communities, giving something back to them; whether creating jobs or adding to quality of life. There is a sense that what you produce ought to have social value (and not be harmful). This is a natural result of taking a bit of pride in your work. But it is also perhaps from the experience of growing up in societies that are less atomized, and where people do feel more held to account by families, communities and society – where disapproval and shame are still strong sanctions. There seem to be more family rituals and observances than we might expect in the West. For instance, one contact told me that he attends a funeral almost every week (because the obligation to attend funerals and pay respects extends to a very broad network). And the extended family is expected to be the first place you turn to for help and support. Family was often referred to as the hub of society, perhaps functioning differently in Arab vs Turkish societies, or other contexts like Indonesia – but always central. That may sound natural, but I would say that in the West we have (outside more traditional regions like the Mediterranean) enthroned youth (and the ideals of that life-stage like establishing your individual identity) as the centre of our society; not the family and its matrix of support and obligation.

Story vs Strategy

Western brands were (you could argue) invented in their modern form to cover up industrial products bereft of humanity and any

71

handmade feeling of care. To inject personality and difference into the lifeless and the samey. With those sorts of brands you can talk about strategy as if it were something separate, deliberate, calculated. The brand is grafted on for effect. Books about these brands are replete with grids, or clever reductive explanations of their "killer application" or trick. Western brands tend to have reductive strategies, in other words. They are drawn to a singular selling point in the minds of the audience, like the perspective lines in Western art. Underneath this brand proposition, it is mostly one monotonous story over and over – that of the individual hero who with the help of this magical brand lives happily ever after. The brand is reduced to a metaphor; a symbol of some quality or value. It is like lifting just the props from a play. (Forget Hamlet with all his human indecision, let's just focus on the skull!) Stories may be used, of course, in advertising to convey this metaphor. But they are fantasies, daydreams. Not to be confused with the real story of the actual product and company, which we know deep down is usually humdrum.

The *Made With* brands are not so easy to reduce. They are better expressed as stories. Stories that involve people (not just individuals, but collectives) rooted in still-living traditions and a different kind of modernity. There may be a leading character in the story. But the point of the story isn't that you want to be an individual just like them. It is rather that you buy into the whole way of life or ethos expressed by the story. It makes sense and brings meaning, enchantment and enjoyment. It humanizes.

We will meet many examples of working from a *Made With* sensibility rather than the Western egonomy approach in the course of this book. For example:

- We will meet one of the Middle East's most famous entrepreneurs – Fadi Ghandour, the founder of Aramex and also instrumental in Maktoob.com – who says he did not know he was "an entrepreneur" for most of his career, and that he finds the heroic myth implied by this term unhelpful for teaching the next generation the very practical skills needed to grow a business. This is something Ghandour is now pursuing across the Middle East region with a programme called CER (Corporate Entrepreneurship Responsibility).

- We will meet a globally successful designer – Nada Debs – who combines traditions from Islamic geometry and ornament with the minimalism from her upbringing in Japan and the functional modernism of her design education in New York. The resulting pieces have a kind of universal appeal. But she says the meaning of her work for herself is that she managed to reconcile the two sides of her own identity; her Arab family (more florid) and her Japanese upbringing (more formal).

- We will meet a social entrepreneur – Kamal Mouzawak – who created "Make Food Not War" (in Beirut). Kamal says it is not much to do with the food, but more about the human projects of contributing, meeting, exchanging – with food as a common ground on which to build a peaceful society. Kamal is one of the leaders of the global Slow Food movement, but clearly what it means to realize this in his local context is different than in Italy or California.

Each of these examples is undoubtedly a strong brand, but they seem more human, more complex and less fake than some Western brands with a painted-on "image". This book is a catalogue of such stories, arranged into seven chapters. The examples within each chapter can be quite diverse. Some are about practical engineering types or e-commerce; some are about artists or artisans; some are about entertainers or educators.

Each chapter collects a different subset of the *Made With* approach to brands. There is a lot of overlap in the examples, but these are clearly separate strategies. Some do have counterparts in the West, others less so. But all have a distinct Made With approach:

Craft With
Networks of artisanal production made relevant to modern markets.

Invent With
Bringing humanity, story, play and involvement to new technology.

Adapt With
Importing, adapting and surpassing best practice from the West.

Fuse With
Synthesising "East" and "West" to create transcendent, universal ideas.

Remake With
Layers of heritage, creating an archaeology of the future.

Emerge With
The power of networks to create awareness, movements, change.

Citizens With
Finding a common ground and purpose in divided societies.

To make it clearer what the case stories have in common, I have written a simple fictional story at the start of each chapter, set in a little city in the desert. It is simple enough to make clear what the other stories have in common. These aren't nearly as artful as *1001 Nights*. But hopefully, as stories, they do retain some of the feeling qualities of the brands and their creators (in a way that lists or diagrams cannot).

And if nothing else, they were fun to write, are easy to read and set the stage for the more serious real case stories to follow.

SEVEN EMERGING ALTERNATIVES
TO WESTERN BRANDING

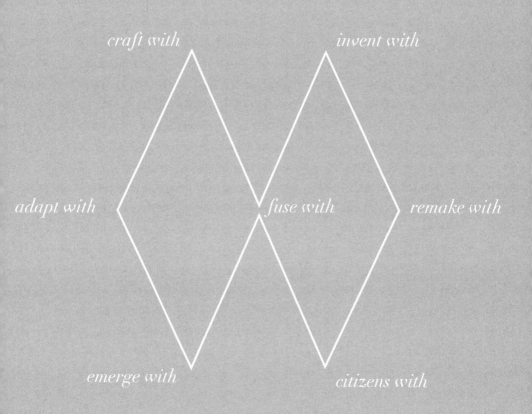

craft with

invent with

adapt with

fuse with

remake with

emerge with

citizens with

1

CRAFT WITH

Networks of artisanal production
made relevant to modern markets

1 CRAFT WITH

Once in a city faraway in the desert, all was not well in the market. The craftsmen who made all the lamps and pots and rugs and cloths and jewellery found that local people were buying there less and less. Perhaps they preferred plastic and metal foreign goods, like they saw in the American films? The market stalls made the goods cheaper. They even started making copies of the imported goods. But this just seemed to make things worse. And as the craftsmen didn't do so well, the other businesses around didn't do so well. And then people bought even less.

One day, a man came to the town. He had grown up there as a boy but then lived in faraway lands making his fortune. He was sad when he saw that the craftspeople had so little work, as he loved all their products that reminded him of his happy childhood.

So do you know what he did? He opened a hotel. It was lavishly decorated with the cloths and carpets, the pots and rugs. The craftspeople had plenty of work here to revive their trades. And they got to make new things in new ways, to fit in with his hotel design that also drew upon ideas and styles he had met on his travels.

The hotel was fabulous and became well known. As tourists came to stay, they would buy crafts from the market to remind them of this charming city. And the local people too, seeing all those crafts in such a stylish modern context, started to be proud of what they made again and started to buy them too.

These stories are about bringing artisanship into the 21st century. Craft is something the Interland was well known for historically. Now, producers with a feeling for craft are creating customized but scalable systems of production and design to revive this for today. Case stories include: Karen Chekerdjian whose designs fuse industrial modernist

79

styles and handmade craft; Timur Savci, producer of Magnificent Century, a hit TV show in 43 countries; Demitri Saddi, founder of .PSLAB that does for lighting what couture does for fashion; and Nevzat Aydin, whose food ordering system has brought modern online search, service and support to one in seven restaurants in Turkey.

What follows are a series of interviews with people who are passionately connected with their craft, their work process, their business. Creating to standards (not of popularity, or recognition, but truth); what one calls "sincerity". Another explains that they had to go after awards to reassure international clients that they met safety and quality standards. An instrumental view. One not over-tainted by ego. In these stories is a first inkling of what might be different when you start outside the West, within a tradition that makes a more vital and living connection with people's work.

I met Karen Chekerdjian in her store in Beirut. She showed me around, explaining that what she sold there was divided into "things we make, and things we love". As we looked around, she told me mainly about the guest products, and not too much about her own. "I don't like to talk so much about my own work," she said shyly.

I think what broke the ice was when I picked up a brass casting of what looked like a flint stone. Turning it over in my hand, feeling its weight, its coldness, its edges, I told Karen that I had once written a paper (studying for a masters in Jungian psychology) about what I called flint think, which was the set of intuitions that we must have inherited from the two million years of human evolution when our ancestors worked on stone tools. Like the feeling a beaver must have for its dams, or a bird for its nests.

"That's exactly what the range is about!" Karen exclaimed. "I would love to read that!" We talked about the brass flint, and how that feeling of working with our hands helps us to "grasp" things. Karen showed me across the other pieces in the *Archetypes* range. She told me that the first one she had designed was the cast of the indent made by a hand. Then she did the flint. Then a hammer (like the ones used by doctors to test reflexes), whose original Karen had found and "never knew what I would do with".

Karen said these pieces were designed to be "tools" for a modern office; working with computers, sitting at a table, and never so much with our hands:

> It's to have something in your office that reminds you. Tools you can get out of the box and put on the table. You feel attracted to touch, to feel the material. They are tools you probably won't use in a literal sense. But they ground you. You feel something. You connect to the earth. Everything today is so unreal, so unrealistic. Tools were the first object that mankind created.

We talked about that same need perhaps being why iPhones with touchscreens had proved so popular. Because they drew on an innately human way of touching an object. "You can give a baby an iPhone…" said Karen.

At another point in the conversation, when she was talking about her early career with high-end design brands in Italy, Karen said "I am not a tool". She was explaining how others around her were much more proficient in technical drawing, or computer-aided design. I thought it was an interesting contrast given the tools Karen had created to humanize office life. The choice was to find yourself and be fully human; or to become mechanized, spiritless, like a machine or tool in a production line. It seemed like Karen had made this choice, long before creating that brass flint.

Karen's passion, she told me, is storytelling. You hear that word a lot around design these days, but – like the tool/tool dichotomy – what Karen meant turned out to run deeper than most (who often mean just an elegant way of selling design). Her dream had been to become

81

a movie director. She had come close to breaking into the movies, but then fate had intervened. So now she put that impulse into her design work. "Every time I start a new project I have to tell the story. The material I use. An encounter. Some random thing that becomes the story of that object." We talk about the way that mass-produced goods that are all the same can become alienating. "I think they have no spirit," Karen says.

All of Karen's designs are handmade. She told me that originally this was simply because she had no choice. When she worked in Italy she had access to high-tech manufacturing. They could make almost anything she could imagine. Back in Beirut, if she was going to manufacture, she would have to work with local artisans. Over time, this had created something unique, and really important to her, "so my curse became my blessing". If she had not come back, she would probably still be designing in identical ways to her friends in Paris and Bologna, part of a system and not developing her own way of working, finding herself in her work.

Not only was it an opportunity for her own design vision to branch out, but Karen saw she could "give the chance for these craftsmen to have a new life". But it had been a struggle, she told me. And it still was whenever she worked with new craftspeople. Karen told me about working with the brass caster, who used to make traditional items for tourist shops. "I told him now you have to forget everything you have done." She pointed to the tray our coffees had come on as an example. They looked completely bare. But when I picked up my coffee later, I noticed there was a single bird engraved at the centre; looking like a French naïve "oiseaux" illustration. Karen's tray had a fish.

For him that was nothing. Usually a tray had to be completely engraved with sentences from the Koran, with drawings, flowers. I wanted no engraving at all. The guy thought I was crazy. It was a three-year struggle to make him follow me.

Now he thanks me for pushing him further, getting him to try new things; to think different.

Karen Chekerdjian had changed her approach too, with that long slow process of collaboration leading to new understanding on her side of working with real materials. Sometimes she had found that her ideas just couldn't work. For instance, her perforated sheet metal screens lacked strength, so were hard to curve well. But more than this, she learned to appreciate imperfections. "I originally wanted perfectionist objects. But when they are hand cut and handmade from wood they are never perfect." She showed me the organic line of a join in the table we were sitting at. This had a surprising advantage, she told me – you wouldn't hear a customer say "I can't buy this table, it's marked". The objects were imperfect to start with. That was just their look. It also was "alive" she said, in the way it would age, the copper getting more "brownish".

I asked Karen about her sense of time, how that comes into her work. She told me that she was very attracted to futuristic themes. She talked about the way the future was portrayed in a recent film *Hunger Games*; the fascinating way that in future cities they have to mix the gleaming technology with a bit of dirt, something gritty to make it real. In her design work, Karen said there was often something about it that looked almost retro and familiar. But when you looked close, you realized that you haven't seen anything like it before. Or that it had been taken to a new extreme, through technical research. She described it as "winking" – something playful in the object, like the pull chain on her mushroom-shaped *Hiroshima* lamp, that felt almost Art Deco until you looked closer. It was a way of "taking you into" the object, starting with the feeling of familiarity, of there "being no conflict", but then drawing you on, into the 21st century.

Karen next showed me a range of children's toys she had designed. It had started with the large oval boxes they came in, made of what looked like plywood. Karen told me they were originally used

83

for sweet pastries that she remembered from her childhood. But gradually that market had gone over to plastic containers. She tracked down one of the last places making them in Damascus (in Syria, just before the war) and she felt she wanted to give it a second life, so on an impulse she ordered some. Given the connection with her own childhood, she decided to create toys to go in the boxes. The first toy set called *Adam's* came about by accident, when a friend's young kid was visiting and Karen gave them some wooden blocks that she uses to hold display placards to play with. These worked great as toys. So instead of painting the blocks, she ordered them in different woods; sycamore, beech, oak, mahogany and ash – and also different shapes – cubes, cones and cylinders and so on. By having much less to them than most toys, they leave more space for imagination.

My favourite toy, though, was *Beit Claire*, the tablecloth at the other end of the table where we were sitting. Hanging to the floor on three sides, it was an off-white cloth printed with thick ochre-coloured lines, in a naïve style, to look like a play house; with the window cut out in a square so you could look out. If you climb under the table, you find that inside the cloth are printed a stove and other play house images. On top are drawn some place settings so that after having your friends over to play, you can have tea together. Karen told me that *Beit Claire* was the result of thinking about "how to get a house into a sweet box". And the inspiration came from remembering how "children love playing under tables".

That's the kind of insight that gives Karen Chekerdjian's work such warmth. The style and materials can be modernist, almost industrial. But there is that spark of recognition when you see someone has had the same idea as you. Like the spark of recognition I got when I picked up the flint. Perhaps most of her customers have that experience with something in the store? Karen is making things in a way that you could describe as the opposite of "alienation". (Could "humanation" be a word?)

Karen Chekerdjian is using storytelling as a structuring intelligence to guide her intensively crafted designs. We next meet someone who used craft and absolute attention to production quality to reinvent storytelling in the previously quite debased medium of Turkish television. In a way, their creative ethic is similar – guided by a strong intuition and putting their own subjective selves at the heart of the creative process. But whereas the largest thing Karen tends to design is something like a retail interior (for her glamorous neighbour, Rabih Kahrouz), our next interviewee makes lavish TV epics that set audience ratings records, and is easily one of Turkey's biggest cultural exports.

Timur Savci describes himself as a serial entrepreneur. I think this is so much more accurate than "TV producer" as he has created new markets, products and genres, often with considerable commercial risk. I met him at his production company *Tim's*. Timur told me that he started out trying to please his parents by studying to be a lawyer. As soon as he entered university, he hated it. Meanwhile, to make ends meet as a student, he embarked on a career as a waiter and also DJ-ing in clubs. He loved these side jobs more than his studies. The café he worked at was a popular social hangout for creative people. One of these was the famous writer Meral Okay, who he worked with decades later on the TV series *Magnificent Century*.

One day, Timur went to see his cousin on the set of a TV commercial shoot. As soon as he saw the set, Timur knew, in an epiphany, that was what he wanted to do with his life. I asked him why and he said: "First it was a very different world. Second there was discipline in it. Everyone had a role and yet it was flexible and relaxed – a bit like waiting the tables. And of course it was very creative."

Timur hung around at the shoot all day. Then at midnight there was a crisis. The commercial was for a brand of detergent, and they needed some fabric dye. Timur volunteered to find some – "Just give me a car" he told them. He succeeded, of course, and the next day the boss gave him a job as a runner. From then until 1998, Timur worked his way up, becoming production manager and then production coordinator

85

in that company, making movies as well as TV commercials.

At that time, Timur happened to become the production manager of a TV series called *Second Spring*. Timur was used to working in commercials and cinema where the production values, art direction, scenarios and stories had a developed quality. Turkish mainstream TV was, as he put it, "Indian style" – cheaply made, with poor storylines and acting, and often made by a famous singer, who also starred in the show. Timur brought a whole different production quality to this show – using a team mostly from cinema, also bringing in expensive lighting and new techniques.

At that time, Timur's main work was still in making commercials, which was much better paid. With a friend, he had started his own commercials production company. They had a couple of golden years of success, making commercials not just in Turkey but also for international brands in Japan and the USA. Then in 2001, there was a huge financial crisis in Turkey and the entire commercials production industry simply stopped. Much worse for Timur's company, though (because of their balance of payments in and out), was that the Turkish exchange rate plummeted. Overnight, they were broke. He couldn't even go and work as a producer for another advertising company because they saw him as a rival. So Timur was unemployed. And he sat around the house, feeling hopeless and depressed for five to six months with nothing to do.

Then the phone rang. Based on his work on that one previous TV show, a production company wanted to hire him as a coordinator for what was (for him) a very low fee. The project at the outset looked quite low-grade creatively. "Like one of those TV productions where a famous singer is the star." But Timur bit his lip. "I had to take the job, because I had to pay my electricity bill."

At first, he just did the production coordination job and kept his head down. Timur couldn't bear to tell most of his friends what he was working on because it wasn't something he could exactly be proud of.

But then before it even aired, the production ran into trouble and he was offered the exec producer job, which he jumped at. Now he could run the show. That TV show was called *Lady of the Ivy Mansion* and to this day it still holds the TV ratings record for Turkey.

Timur first brought a different level of professionalism to the whole production process. And with this, a raft of more advanced production techniques that were familiar from commercials production and cinema, but had never been used in Turkish TV: like commercials-style colour grading and filming with steadicam. Second, rather than shooting the show as intended in a bland location in South East Turkey, he moved the setting to Cappadocia, the area that famously "looks like a lunarscape". Hence following how cinema enthrals its audiences by creating a unique, crafted, visual identity and setting – a life-world that you get immersed in.

At this point our translator Anil broke into the conversation to say how much she had loved the *Lady of the Ivy Mansion*. How amazing it had looked and how addictive it was; how friends used to tape it for her when she was living in London. Anil was fairly typical apparently. 80% of the entire country used to tune into this weekly show.

Another common factor in both this show and his previous TV series, *Second Spring*, was working with that famous writer who used to come to his café, Meral Okay.

Timur explained that most of his subsequent successes were based on being forced to analyze where the gaps were in the industry. He wasn't established enough to survive without being entrepreneurial. His first production after launching *Tim's* in 2006, called *Daydreamers*, broke new ground as the first Turkish drama made for a young audience. Retrospectively, an obvious gap. Turkey is a young country. So why force teens and young adults to sit through shows that were "made for their mothers"?

I asked Timur how he was able to spot what could be a potential hit. He told me that it was mainly instinct. Or more particularly, what he looked for was a quality of "sincerity". What this meant, he explained, was that the feelings portrayed are sincere, that they touch you as real, true, in an intimate way. As if they know the inner you.

I see a connection between Timur's work and Karen's here, even though they work in such different fields. Both bring this subjective quality into their work; of life as it is lived from the inside. The audience feeling that defines such work is *recognition*; you recognize a part of your own inner life, your feelings in it. Like you do when you hear a song and feel that the lyrics must have been written about you.

Magnificent Century, Timur told me, represented a new stage in his career. Now he had money and a track record and for the first time had the freedom to do pretty much whatever he wanted. And what he wanted was to make something big. And different than anything on Turkish TV before. In fact, it would have to be produced for a global audience, from day one, because there was no way that the economics of Turkish television would stretch to the sort of epic production Timur had in mind.

For several years before this, Timur had been talking with Meral Okay about a creative departure for both of them – making a historical drama set in the Ottoman Empire. I asked Timur whether this was part of the growing confidence in Turkey at that time. For instance, in the UK when Merchant Ivory had been making similarly lavish historical dramas for TV and cinema, it was in the context of Margaret Thatcher, Laura Ashley, Paul Smith, British Airways and a general return to British identity. Timur said not at all. It had nothing to do with conditions in Turkey.

I asked other people I interviewed this question and they said the same thing. *Magnificent Century* had, according to adman Serdar Erener, been "a real *Black Swan*". Serdar also told me that far from being a part of the New Ottoman rhetoric from Erdogan's AKP, the show had led to a huge clash with the Prime Minister who publically denounced it: "This man spent 40 years on his horse, conquering," Erdogan had complained, "not sitting around in his harem". Timur also tactfully neglected to mention that his own government had threatened to introduce a law "banning programs that infringe on national values by insulting, denigrating, distorting or misrepresenting historical personalities and events". So it does seem, from what I gleaned, that Timur could justly claim not to have jumped on the *Ottomania* bandwagon, but rather to have started (or at least anticipated) the trend.

And here comes the entrepreneurial catch 22. There was no way on earth that Turkish TV channels would ever finance such a lavish production; especially ahead of the trend that would make it so obvious in retrospect (a hit movie on the start of the Ottoman period followed, and even a Suleiman-branded property development in central Istanbul). So they had to fund it themselves. First they had to spend a year developing the storylines and scenarios. Then there was another lengthy period of research and development, working with academicians and history consultants to get every detail right in the costumes, the sets. So over this time Timur put all the money that Tim's had made in the preceding years into the project.

I asked Timur why they had picked the story of Suleiman and Roxelana (the red-haired foreign wife, who became the Sultan's queen and greatest love). Timur thought it came down to two factors. One was that Roxelana and Suleiman was the archetypal love story, like Romeo and Juliet; one that everyone in Turkey knows. Secondly, other Ottoman shows had looked half-baked and drab, but that period in history was the absolute height of Turkish power. It was a magnificent time, in terms of power, opulence, culture, confidence, success. So the potential was to make everything in the show – every shot, every surface, every costume – magnificent. To create an immersive world of magnificence that the viewer would be enraptured by.

Timur realized just what a risk this strategy was when he visited the sets as they were now completing pre-production. It looked like a scale of production he had only ever seen in Hollywood. It looked, in other words, incredibly expensive. At this point, Timur got the fear. He finally realized why his friends had been telling him he was crazy for the last few years. But he decided – what the hell? – there was no turning back now.

The rest is history. The show was a huge success in Turkey. Audiences were mesmerized. It was picked up in a bidding war for international rights by Gulf TV networks. And if anything, it was an even bigger hit there. It prompted national debates about whether Saudi husbands were as romantic, attentive and "magnificent" as they should be! The show eventually aired in 43 countries. It spread to the Balkans, across the former Ottoman Empire, and even beyond. When I arrived back in London, my Asian taxi driver told me him and his family were going to Istanbul for a family holiday. Did his wife watch *Magnificent Century* I asked? Oh yes, he replied, that was why they were going.

I asked Timur "What next?". He told me that he was developing two projects.

One was based upon a bestselling novel called *Kılıç Yarası Gibi* (*Like a Sword Wound*). He didn't give many details, but I did my own research. It is another historical story, set in the 1920s. And the novel's author, Ahmet Altan, is a controversial figure, who was fired from newspaper *Millyet* for writing an alternate history of Turkey called *Attakurd* (in which he wondered how Turkish people would react if they lived in a Kurdish country that tried to ban the Turkish language). *Like a Sword Wound* is not only about Turkish history, though; it is a complex love story, set in the last days of the rule of Sultan Abdul Hamid, when the Young Turks were organizing their revolution. It sounds in every way a worthy successor to *Magnificent Century*; something like a Turkish *Doctor Zhivago*.

More intriguing still, what Timur told me he believes will be "the next big trend in Turkey" is another show he has in development called *41*. It is set in the present day and concerns people who have supernatural powers; "not like American superheroes" but rather with "immortal love that goes on after death". Timur describes it as "a metaphysical drama", strongly influenced by Sufi sensibilities, drawing on quotes and ideas from Rumi's *Mevlana*.

If you were a chef, a nightclub owner, a gallery (like London's Barbican), a hotel or a wealthy home-owner and you wanted to use light in a way that was totally unique to your space, your brand, that created a unique effect in line with your own vision… then .PSLAB might be the best people in the world to talk to.

If you were an architect trying to source some reasonably contemporary lighting installations to complement the rest of your creative concept and you wanted a flexible supplier who would work to a tight brief (or preferably just supply something similar to what you saw in a hotel once, or in a design magazine) – then forget it. From the view of that sort of architect or designer with fixed ideas, .PSLAB could be a nightmare. You'd see them as difficult to work with and potentially show-stealing.

This would never be a problem in reality because .PSLAB are very choosy and wherever possible they work directly with the end client, not "intermediaries".

.PSLAB seem very careful about how their brand is presented and described, so allow me to quote their website:

> .PSLAB are designers and manufacturers of site-specific lighting products, founded in 2004 with over 100 team members and working out of four bases in Europe and the Middle East including Beirut, Stuttgart, Bologna and Scandinavia. Our work can be found in private homes in London, art galleries in Beirut, restaurants in Rome, hotels in Paris, conceptual boutiques in Antwerp, offices in Berlin and at events and in public spaces worldwide.
>
> We are to lighting what haute couture is to fashion – through a customized project approach we offer a complete service,

91

which has allowed us to build ongoing working relationships with our collaborators. Our creative and technical teams work together on every aspect of product development, from concept to construction giving us the edge at the core of the .PSLAB identity. Our concepts are born out of the individualities of a space and our products conceived for specific projects, custom-manufactured by our artisans in our workshop and hand-finished with minute attention to detail.

I met with Dimitri Saddi, .PSLAB's founder, at their workspace in Beirut. Dimitri told me that they had reached a new stage in their development. He was questioning their whole approach. Previously they had to establish their brand and reputation internationally. And they had succeeded in that: with seven *Red Dot* (global design) awards to their name. In that previous stage of expansion, they had to be ruthlessly disciplined about what they were and what they stood for. And so their work, their brand and all their manifestations had a tightly and centrally controlled identity. The problem was that this ran against their most basic belief which is that each solution is unique and grows out of the context, the need, the client's vision and so on. And if it led to controlling their international offshoot offices too tightly, Dimitri felt that "this is the approach to make another Starbucks".

There were two implications. Firstly, that they would now try relaxing and let each office develop aesthetics that responded to its local market. The second implication was to work even harder to formulate what it was in the process that made them unique: the "who we are in what we do". This shouldn't be confused, Dimitri told me, with other terms like skillset. It was their method of working *together* that had an influence on the outcome. To develop that further would mean to question some of the "invisible boundaries" that people would tread carefully around, but not cross. Dimitri also felt that now they had proved themselves commercially, they needed to be much more selective. "It's not about producing more now, it's about what we want to be part of."

Dimitri Saddi showed me around because he felt that the physical space was a big part of their design philosophy. He showed me the large prototyping spaces that made it possible to do early work with physical materials rather than just on screens. And his next step, he said, was building a kitchen. I thought it was a metaphor at first. That when he talked about "teams cooking and eating together" he was referring to close-knit project work. But no, he really meant a kitchen; with a herb and vegetable garden. Dimitri felt that bringing more humanity, more social rituals into the workplace would help to break down those invisible barriers he mentioned earlier.

It wasn't all about soft competences. Part of their proving phase had been about demonstrating they could work to international standards. They had to gain credibility for electrical safety, and quality control. No easy task as, like Karen Chekerdjian, .PSLAB had been forced by being based in Beirut to work with local artisanal production. This was a blessing in the same way as for Karen, in encouraging them to develop a unique approach. But it was also a challenge when, as Dimitri told me, some of their producers had "Post World War II" type facilities. Whereas their competitors – in Germany – would have suppliers within easy reach with state-of-the-art equipment and controls. To build sufficiently robust quality assurance systems, Saddi told me they had to invest heavily in their production facilities and the lab testing.

I was curious to know in today's jet-set world, and with such strong credentials, why it wasn't possible to run all their operations from Beirut. Dimitri told me that it was because they had to gain the confidence of local clients, work with them closely and collaboratively. "People have to come in and chat, touch the materials." It was a similar point to that of needing, where possible, to deal directly with the end client. He told me it was ultimately about creativity – wherever there are distances, people are more inclined to play it safe, and they won't take risks, even good ones. "The quality of work depends on the quality of the dialogue." That means that their typical client was an up-and-coming brand, one that has a solo owner. They especially liked working with clients who were creative themselves; like a chef or a fashion designer.

Saddi told me he felt that there was an intimate link between the development of the company and "your development as a human being". If you as a leader had hang-ups and barriers, so would the company. If you worked on them and grew as a person, so would the company.

My favourite bit of the tour was when Dimitri pointed out the high industrial yard wall and huge sliding metal door that screened them from the world outside. "You need a barrier between you and the outside world," Dimitri told me, if you wanted to stay authentic: "The real issue now is you get so consumed out there. People jump on you, ravage you, consume you and then move on to the next brand." Being authentic meant resisting that, he told me. And it meant holding fast to your own version of the world, and "not just chasing the money just because there is a market". That's why I suspect .PSLAB had become reminiscent of something more like a working monastery than an office; restrained, cloistered, disciplined, but inwardly flourishing.

Next to Istanbul, another highly designed office. Nevzat Aydin is one of the best-known entrepreneurs in Turkey. Not only because he has one of the biggest internet successes, with a recent investment round of $44 million from US Venture firm General Atlantic, but also for his appearances on the Turkish version of *Dragon's Den*.

Nevzat turned out to be an unassuming man, quietly spoken, charming. He's the first interviewee in this chapter who wasn't dressed in black. A practical business builder with a real sense of humility about him, coming from – he told me – quite an ordinary background. That's why he had taken on the TV appearances; to show by his own example that you could come from any background and create something. In his case, something extraordinary.

Nevzat had come back to Turkey in 2000, after taking an MBA in

Silicon Valley. He knew that he wanted to do something entrepreneurial and had gone there mainly to "breathe the air" and absorb what was happening in e-commerce. His passion for the internet had started much earlier, in 1994, when he had done his undergraduate degree in computer engineering.

> Within the tenth minute I knew I would do something with this. I was just browsing the site of Yahoo. It was all text based. You just hit the return button on links. Immediately I thought "This is going to be huge". And the more time I spent on it, the more I thought that.

One immediate application Nevzat found was that every week there was a national newspaper competition with really obscure general knowledge questions; "And every week I was winning!"

Nevzat says he wasn't a very good student, and hence while he'd have loved to have gone to Stanford, he ended up at the University of San Francisco. But he did manage to get some work experience at big name tech companies. And he witnessed both the upsides, like companies going IPO (making the founders a fortune through selling stock, by making an Initial Public Offering), and also some dramatic dotcom failures.

Returning to Turkey, he rejected his first three ideas – creating the equivalents of an eBay, a Match.com, or a betting site – because all of them would run up against problems with local legislation. Instead, he went for a safer a model and one very close to the Turkish heart; how to order local food online from that delicious but slightly disorganized little kebab place up the road. Perhaps one you hadn't even tried before. The model, he worked out, could include a directory of thousands of restaurants, some information on each, all the information you needed to order, and it would also handle the transaction itself. The result was Yemeksepeti.com (which means "food basket").

He knew that to pull this off, he would need a team. Nevzat figured what he was best at was the creativity, innovation and motivation. There were two other key parts of the business. One was IT. And while he says he is an "okay" computer engineer, he knew a much better one, who was a friend. The other key piece was restaurant relations. The kind of person who could "do cold calling and get a result on the fourth or fifth attempt". Which definitely wasn't him. But again he knew someone perfectly qualified. The three teamed up in September 2000, and by January 2001 the site went live, albeit with only 30 restaurants at the time. For the next four to five years they struggled with limitations. Most customers, for instance, used a dial-up modem and they had to ask them to log off the internet if anything went wrong, so they could contact them by phone.

What Nevzat Aydin thinks they got right from the start (and where comparable sites in the USA went wrong) was the business model. Firstly, they never charged a restaurant except for commissions on actual orders. No fees for membership, or listings, or leads. And they never ever charged the end customer, who hence always paid the same as if they had phoned the restaurant direct. Secondly, they never went in for logistics (and hence only signed restaurants who could already do local deliveries). All they did was take and transmit the order in the fastest, most robust way, and also offered perfect end-to-end support to customers if anything ever went wrong. And looking around his office, there was a large team on the phones doing customer support. I think of it a bit like asking a hotel concierge to organize a takeaway for you.

Over that initial period, they managed to increase their daily orders fivefold, but it still wasn't enough. Then when broadband hit in 2005-6, order numbers went through the roof. Towards the end of 2005, they reached financial break even. Today they process over 55,000 orders per day. Around one in seven of all the restaurants in Turkey that deliver food are on the site. They have launched in Cyprus. And they are launching in three or four more countries in the next six months, using the funding from General Atlantic. Plus they plan many more food-related services in Turkey.

The other key to their success, Nevzat thought, was finding a cooperative model, where everyone wins; the customers, the restaurants and his own company all doing better, functionally and economically.

What Nevzat and his team had done was create something that made existing small businesses more successful – giving them everything they needed to rival the big players like American pizza delivery chains. Their latest venture, Nevzat told me, was taking this even further, into the much more local specialities. Their new model so far only includes 50-100 suppliers that have been handpicked by food experts as offering the best of the unique regional speciality food. Hence you can order the really local varieties of olive oil – or typical dishes such as Gaziantep's baklava or Trabzon's cornbread that you can't find in the big cities. Anil Altas, my translator for Timur's interview (also a writer of books on digital Turkey), told me "even my parents are using this".

Nevzat thought that if he had founded the company in another country, he's not sure it would have got this far. His employees in Turkey had a particular knack for trying things, being practical, making changes. They also really stuck with stubborn problems until they solved them. And they didn't mind adversity, struggle, chaos and setbacks – that was just normal to them. He told me about a Yemeksepeti group ordering feature that had been really problematic, so they had had to remodel it four to five times. But now it was a huge hit with university students and was on track to account for a quarter of all their orders in a few years' time.

Just as well they were adaptable, as everything kept changing so fast. Mobile a year ago only accounted for 1% of their volume. Now it was 5% and will soon hit 20%. And – while the practical, improvisational Turkish entrepreneurial mind-set might cope better than most – things will change even faster in the future. Nevzat told me that he

97

had been watching his friend's two-year-old son using a touch screen and realized that quite soon new generations would be coming up "with visions that we never had".

The model throughout this chapter is one of finding ways to connect the quality of small-scale and high-end craft quality with the design, convenience and service demands of modern consumers. While the service may include your own designs, it's the process, the production flow, the collaboration that is critical.

They all approached this in a way that seemed very intuitive; as if they just recognized the right approach. But that's not to say that it is unthinking. All of them had done lots of analyzing and correcting, fitting their empirical learning to the market rather than blindly chasing after second-hand fads. In an aside, Karen Chekerdjian told me that she had started out making abstract, artsy objects, like round "storage balls" for keeping things in. But she found that people couldn't connect with them, couldn't imagine them in their home. So she started to work instead from really familiar forms, and then let her more artistic side work on the nuances, meaning and intelligibility.

As Karen suggested, this may partly be because they have had to wrestle with the physical making of things and with local limits. Not working with concepts, but with brass. And with stubborn artisans who know how to work with brass. Timur's craftsmen were originally drafted in from cinema, bringing a different dynamic into the flow of TV production; put together less hastily, more carefully constructed.

Discipline was also a key element of all of these stories.

I also think what Timur said about being an entrepreneur is key. They are running their own business and even when dealing with commissioning are making sure that they are wholly involved, taking responsibility for the complete outcome. While Karen talked a lot about storytelling, she also told me at points about her business; about margins, international deals, the problems of getting represented right by galleries.

The complete picture is one of work, as it should be. Not suffering from the division of labour, from client Chinese whispers, from double and triple guessing. You are then completely operating as a whole human being, taking in all of the information (with a team of collaborators) and giving a whole response.

The point that Dimitri makes about having a process, not a preconception, strikes me as incredibly powerful. As does his way of creating the interior of his company as a kind of microcosm, a world apart that can then effortlessly produce more creative, more original work because it isn't too beholden to trends, it is authentically "apart".

Another key theme from .PSLAB is the idea of a creative process as an open and flowing conversation. One that it's important not to have firewalls within – such as the one that can be introduced between client and contractor or through internal "invisible boundaries".

Authenticity is a key part of these stories – or "sincerity" as Timur put it. That's I guess what makes all their products so globally successful too. Because in our own hyper-real societies, authenticity is hard to find, and fleeting when you do. We have so few functioning traditions and customs that we rely on the *new new thing*; fresh, cool, popular, a trend. A year later we see it hanging in a cupboard or parked on a driveway and it feels not so current, not so alive to us. These designers are bringing their own authenticity, vision and resistance: to create the enduring appeal of "instant classics".

If you had to summarize what unites these approaches when it comes to the end product being so appealing, the main connection would be a dedication to craft. And a kind of intrinsic, authentic, quality that comes from a deep and full involvement of the Self. The craft takes on a modern precision, sharpness, quality – but also retains a handmade feel, whether it is Timur's penchant for steadicam, or Karen's love of lines that wobble slightly. But these interviewees are not the craftsmen themselves, wordlessly chiselling, turning and working their material. They are operating on a more semantic,

99

symbolic level. And the key word for that – a word that recurred throughout the interviews across this whole region – is storytelling. Not just the abstract storytelling of an entertainer, but the involved storytelling of a participant in the drama. One, for instance, who has learned their humility and resilience because blocks or setbacks have made them change their plans.

Finally, there is the question of what motivates them to produce such beautiful products, often at great commercial risk, when their markets can have much lower standards. Obviously there is a commitment to their ideas, to what they produce having value: but not through egotism. Rather, because they have developed it with a protective respect, not to be so easily parlayed away by any idiots who don't get it (they all told me stories of such idiots, and how they rebuked them, or walked away).

And it also perhaps comes from an unspoken assumption that the world actually deserves better than the "affordable" lazy mush that furnishes our home, lights our public spaces or fills our TV channels?

Another factor is bringing their brilliance to a humble category. TV dramas; office furniture; kebab shops; lighting. I don't mean for a moment to downplay their work. I thought it was creatively top-notch. But it's even more brilliant because they didn't apply it to a world with the lazy instant glamour of fashion, architecture or cinema.

Bringing humanity to making is a big theme of the next chapter too. Only here it is about how to humanize and socialize inventions (in that otherwise soulless world of the pointless techno gadget)....

100

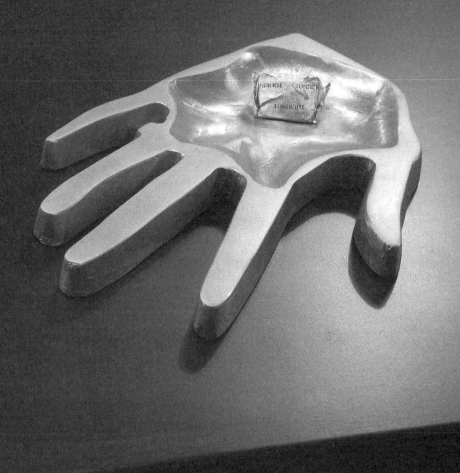

“It's to have something in your office that reminds you. Tools you can get out of the box and put on the table. You feel attracted to touch, to feel the material. They are tools you probably won't use in a literal sense. But they ground you. You feel something. You connect to the earth. Everything today is so unreal, so unrealistic. Tools were the first object that mankind created.”

Karen Chekerdjian

Hands On, design by Karen Chekerdjian Studio, photograph by Nadim Asfar

2

INVENT WITH

Bringing humanity, story, play and
involvement to new technology

2. INVENT WITH

Once in a city faraway in the desert, the hotel owner's daughter felt like a fool. She had persuaded her father to buy her a van, so that she could start a delivery business. All the artisans worked from home and would spend too much of their days trudging around getting supplies, and taking their goods to market. But when the van arrived, it wouldn't fit up the narrow streets. And so it sat behind the hotel gathering dust.

One day, some children were playing behind the hotel. Finding some crates and barrel tops, they copied the van and made themselves a cart. Seeing this, the hotel owner's daughter had an idea. She got the carpenter to make a number of these little carts. And then she got local kids to run errands every day after school for all the craftsmen and stalls. Whizzing around the streets pulling the carts was so much fun that the children were happy to take part. And the town became even more prosperous (if a little perilous for pedestrians in the late afternoon).

These stories are about inventions Made With *a spirit of play and involvement. Instead of focusing on the perspective of the geek or their gadget, they open out to the audience. The Arab region, in particular, is famous for its historical pioneers of science and technology. But there is nothing antiquated about examples like the Beirut DIY scene, Ayah Bdeir, inventor of the* Little Bits, *Sedat Kapanoğlu, founder of Ekşi Sözlük, a top five Turkish internet site compiling competing definitions of everything and everyone, and the inventive Istanbul digital agencies Rabarba, C-Section and 41?29!*

One of the most popular TV programmes in the Arabic region is *Stars of Science*. Airing on 17 TV channels across the Middle East, it has the familiar format of TV talent shows; starting with 7000 applicants, and working up to a final, with viewers voting on the winner. Now in its fourth season, the show has (for this genre) a relatively modest $600,000 prize fund, divided between the top four finalists, with half going to the winner towards their subsequent product launch. And as Fouad Mrad, the show's scientific adviser, told *Wired* magazine, it is all about "proving that Arabs can still invent". *Stars of Science* has nearly half a million Facebook likes, suggesting it not only attracts a large audience, but also a very involved one.

The winner of series one, Bassam Jalgha, developed an auto-tuning mechanism for Arabic scale stringed musical instruments. Three years on, he has formed an electronic prototyping company called Depot Beirut as well as developing his invention called TORK, now due for commercial launch in 2013. Bassam has also been working to develop the local Hackerspace and DIY technology scene. Speaking to Wamda (the entrepreneurship portal for the Middle East), Bassam said:

> A big problem in this region is that there is a lack of support for hardware development. We grew up with the idea that we cannot actually produce, that we have to consume things that come from abroad, and this is wrong. Personally, I'm trying to change that, with my friends. I thought a good idea would be to gather all of the people who work in hardware in Beirut in a single space and try together to promote this culture.[29]

Bassam's comments echo those of Iranian intellectual, Jalal Al-e Ahmad, who wrote about his country's dependence on the West in the 1960s, under the heading of *Gharbzadegi* (which roughly translates as *Westoxification*, *Weststruckness* or *Occidentosis*). Al-e Ahmad, like American historian Lewis Mumford (who coined the term *Megamachine*) saw the West as being like a machine; made up of literal industrial machines and factories, but also the devices in the home, the hospital, army and airport, and all the mechanical protocols and controls of the society and economy. This machine divided the world into "constructors" and "consumers". Iran could not be free of Westoxification, Al-e Ahmad wrote, until it too could become a constructor. Although then he added it would need to struggle with a second syndrome, which is a dehumanizing *Machinestruckness*. The development of an inventor culture is a crucial step in the revitalization of the Arabic countries' identity. That cultural self-identity is an important supporting platform for future innovators to build upon; becoming better able to attract investors, customers and public support. But there is also always the secondary problem with technology of how to humanize it. To avoid the destructive effects on traditional customs, crafts and ways of life. Bassam Jalgha's Arabic instrument tuning TORK is an example of a technology that doesn't disregard, but rather enhances local life; as is his adoption of open public hackerspaces.

This year's *Stars of Science* winner was Khaled Abu Jassoum, aged 27. His invention called *Tahi* is an automated cooking pot, able to mix ingredients, store recipes and cook healthy meals for families from fresh ingredients. A member of his national swimming team, Jassoum said he invented the device mainly to promote health. The runners-up included a (literal) desktop allowing up to 20 students to interact with a computer display projected on a table using virtual touchscreens; and a timed device to dispense medicines at home, saving older people from having to remember what pills to take, and when. What these share in common is the idea of invention for the public good – not just gadgets but improving human wellbeing.

The *Golden Age* of Islamic art, science, architecture and philosophy that *Stars of Science* harks back to happened in the Abbasid Caliphate between (in Western dating) the 8th and 13th centuries. And it centred on the Abbasid capital city of Baghdad. The astonishing intellectual output of this period was the subject of several major international exhibitions in recent years, both originated by London's Royal Society. *The 1001 Inventions* exhibition travelled to New York, Washington, Los Angeles, Istanbul, Abu Dhabi and Qatar. It has attracted over 2 million visitors to date and won multiple awards; not just for its timely and fascinating content, but also for its state-of-the-art interactive storytelling. The show has become a multimedia brand in its own right, having over 22 million video views and publishing bestselling books. The *Library of Secrets* film for the exhibition features Oscar-winning actor Ben Kingsley playing a cantankerous librarian (who turns out to be 12th-century engineer Al Jazari).

The next year, the Royal Society followed this up with another exhibition called *Arabick Roots*, looking at the influence of Muslim sources on the much later 17th-century scientists and philosophers of the Enlightenment. This show has also now moved to Doha in Qatar. The curator of the show, Tim Turkmani, commented:

> The most important lesson I've learned from developing *Arabick Roots* is the meaninglessness of the term *Clash of Civilizations*. When cultures learn from each other, they are unlikely to belittle one another. I now believe that an understanding of science's international heritage is essential for its progress.[30]

It found a ready reception in the Middle East, tapping into a desire to retell their own history in a way that frames present developments. This is exactly how Mansoor Al Khater, CEO of the Qatar Museums Authority, introduced the shows:

> With the Renaissance sweeping Qatar at this time, it is the ideal time for us to highlight the achievements of our forefathers, and remind ourselves and the world what we are capable of. These two exhibitions will encourage Qatar's younger generation to innovate and contribute towards a better future.

Qatar is perfectly placed to be a leader in modern science and technological innovations.[31]

Reviving this heritage and confidence in the ability to invent – whether you think of it as Islamic, Arabic, Middle Eastern, Persian, Turkish… – is a telling development. Confident cultures tend to create confident brands, businesses and inventors, especially when riding on economic success.

What gives these exhibitions about Arabic inventions a particular relevance is the stream of successes of their inventors today. A great example is one of the tutors on the *Stars of Science* show in 2010, Ayah Bdeir. Bdeir is a Lebanese artist-inventor, who has caused a stir by making the design of electrical circuits visual, intuitive and playful. The circuits are made up of colour-coded modules that join together using magnets, which makes prototyping and experimentation literally a "snap". Educated in computing and sociology at the prestigious AUB in Beirut, then taking a masters at the MIT Media Lab, Bdeir is much more than just a technical inventor. While a fellow at an art foundation in New York, Bdeir developed projects that explored the identity of Arab women in playful ways: such as *Arabii*, where the audience could operate a burka veil into different configurations; or *Tatya Haniya's Secrets*, featuring a range of underwear, with a humorous take on a Syrian tradition of hacking electronic toys to integrate them into panties, creating DIY sex toys. The flamboyant underwear featured in this show included panties with large tail feathers flapping like wings, with magnets strong enough to hold workman's tools, with touch and speak lips and with light shows.

Ayah Bdeir also spearheaded the development of an Open Hardware License, subsequently adopted by CERN and Creative Commons, and co-chaired the first Open Hardware Conference. But it was with *Little Bits* that Ayah moved from making art to making a brand, culminating in a TED global fellowship, awards from *Maker Faire*, *Popular Science* and the National Parent Publication Awards, and a $4 million venture investment. And it also became her most successful artwork: *Little Bits* being purchased for the permanent collection of MOMA (the New York Museum of Modern Art).

Little Bits drew on Bdeir's experience of teaching. She realized that the important thing to focus on was the intersection between creative design and electronics. Using the components of *Little Bits*, it is possible to make versions of today's common gadgets, such as mp3 players, using quite a small number of modules. But then you get to understand far better the functions that go into such devices, and also get to invent your own new versions and hybrids. Examples submitted to the *Little Bits* Projects page include an electronic foosball game, robots that paint and create geometric patterns, and a helicopter made from a PET bottle and chopsticks. After the storm surge in New York, the *Little Bits* team held a workshop on the Lower East Side using *Little Bits* modules to help kids understand how the power stations got knocked out. The set is attractive, colourful and invites play and experimentation. Echoing Al-e Ahmad's points about not just consuming the machine, Bdeir told *Wired* magazine:

> Why should you need an electrical engineering degree to design with light, sound, sensors and motors when these are things all around us? We want to make it magical and imaginative, but at the same time powerful. We're looking at electronics the way LEGO looks at structural engineering. Electronics is a universal language – it's astounding. It's important that we encourage kids to get interested in science and technology, and teaching through problem-solving. In fact, it is not just important, it is urgent. Technology shouldn't be something we just consume.

If it achieves the kind of widespread success that it just might, *Little Bits* could become another platform for engaging a whole generation of future inventors. Just like early cheap computers like the Sinclair *Spectrum* inspired the previous generations to create some amazing ideas. And few are more amazing than that of my next interview subject: Sedat Kapanoğlu, creator of Ekşi Sözlük, one of the top five internet sites in Turkey. According to my friends at Kapital Media who introduced me to Sedat:

> Positioning itself as "Sacred Fountain of Knowledge", Ekşi Sözlük is a huge forum based on user-generated content and entries about nearly everything under the sun can be entered in it. Having more than 260,000 "entry" writers as of now, the site is able to shape not only the internet agenda but also overall country agenda. Politicians, broadcasters, publicists, the world of sport, nearly everyone follows Ekşi Sözlük closely and reads entries about themselves with grand curiosity. Ekşi Sözlük is one of the most important idea centres of the country with the community consciousness and identity it created, besides its intimate, humorous, ironic and entertaining content.

The site is based upon competing dictionary style definitions. The paragraph above might form one entry defining Ekşi Sözlük. But then many other users would add their own definitions into the same thread; some factual, some humorous. After the interview, Sedat kindly sent me translations of some typical entries, to give a flavour of what the content is actually like (most entries are much longer than these; these are just some short examples that were easier to translate):

The first entry ever (#1):
Topic: Pick
Entry: a small, plastic, weird object used for playing guitar.

And some of 2011's most "upvoted" entries:
Topic: Liberal Democratic Party
Entry: the party which got three votes in the city I voted in. You sons of bitches there is regional president of the party, vice president, members.

111

I voted. So which party are you voting for, assholes?

Topic: Yildirim Demiroren (football team board member)
Entry: If he got in charge of PKK (terrorist group), terrorism would be over.

Topic: Sex tape scandal of Ahmed Hodja
Entry: in foreign countries they have sex tapes of Kim Kardashian, Paris Hilton. In our country it's Ahmed Hodja, Ali Kirca. What the hell is that?

Topic: Turkish GPS announcements
Entry: "Graveyard ahead. Turn down the volume".

But it's not all just humorous. Sedat told me he had just won a court case over an entry defining a politician with only two words: "Ignorant" and "Bigot" (as I understand it, they won the case because his legal team were able to prove that the individual in question was both of these things). That gives a flavour of the subversive potential of putting a dictionary that gives opinionated "definitions" on any subject into the hands of an avidly enthusiastic and discursive young population.

Sedat Kapanoğlu is a self-taught computer programmer. He first saw a computer (a Sinclair *Spectrum*) when he was ten. His older brother wrote four lines of code, which changed the appearance of the screen. Sedat was instantly hooked. You often read about those sorts of vocational epiphanies in the biographies of high-achieving inventors; a profound sense of fit with what becomes a lifelong subject of fascination. It seems to be a bit like the experience of falling in love. The result in Sedat's case was an intense "accelerating learning curve". He was so into computers that he failed the university entrance exams three or four times, only passing "when I switched to economics". And subsequently he didn't graduate from university for similar reasons. That kind of distracted education didn't prove an impediment for Bill Gates. And actually it was Microsoft that spotted Sedat's prodigious coding abilities and brought him to the

US in 2004, to work on their *Windows* core operating system.

The idea for Ekşi Sözlük first came to Sedat in 1995. "I was writing funny articles that were like pages from a huge imaginary knowledge source. I used to put references in it, thinking it was funny if it contained huge amounts of information. And I thought: what if I could build something like that?" At the time, it was hard to see how he could. He only had access to the internet through university, and the main platform was the BBS (Bulletin Board System). In 1997, the internet became available in Turkey for general users and he started talking about the idea in IRC (Internet Relay Chat) channels. A friend sent him a copy of *The Hitchhiker's Guide to the Galaxy* as a text file, and Sedat realized that his basic idea of a kind of hypertext mega encyclopaedia and fount of all knowledge was not original in itself. In 1998, Sedat was writing articles to publish on the web (in the days before blogging platforms made self-publishing easy) and he became tired of the cumbersome need "to know ftp, markup, html… it was way too much overhead just to upload an article to the web". On February 15th 1999, close to midnight, Sedat started writing some utility code to make the whole process easier. And in just two hours, he had a working programme. He then called friends asking them to try it out. And people started contributing articles. In those days, "we had a manual version of social media – invite by ICQ IRCN. Suddenly in a month we had 300 users contributing. By the end of 1999 there were 1500 or so." And then Sedat says "it got popular beyond my wildest imagination".

Ekşi Sözlük's early success, Sedat told me, was partly that it was unique as a place to write articles and share your content with a community of others; as there was then no Tumblr, Blogger or Wikipedia. The site still has a unique look (one that I'd compare to Craigslist – you can tell this is a real community site, not a corporate one). But its key appeal – and Sedat says what ensured its enduring popularity 14 years later, with 3 million topics and counting – is:

It's completely subjective. It contains mostly opinions, very little facts – and that's one of the best things about the website. All we ask is that it's in dictionary format. We have a footer saying everything on this website is wrong. It helps to make people question what they find on the web. In general, we have got better at receiving, filtering, separating facts and opinions. And our site has been one of the factors in changing society in that way.

Sedat told me that in contrast, his generation had grown up in a restricted society for information, post the 1980s military coup, when "we were made to believe everything we read in textbooks or saw on TV". But then the web had brought another type of dictatorship, with "websites generally governed by people who only wanted to keep people who share their perspective on their website. If you had the opposite opinion to an admin they would ban you". Sedat told me one of the benefits of being self-taught and starting out away from the mainstream of the world's web development communities was he had simply done what he thought was right, without adopting other models:

> I didn't know that was how things were done and I didn't embrace it. Maybe if I knew that was how things were supposed to be I would have chosen to do it too. But I didn't impose any certain perspective. Any political or religious view could contribute – and do so together, in the same place.

The only thing that the site doesn't allow is slanderous remarks about other users.

Despite continuing pressures from the current government over freedom of speech, which made it an ongoing struggle to run a website like this (there are more lawyers in his office than technologists), Sedat told me that it had worked really well. That it functioned "like an oasis". The site was a place where people could write and read criticisms of the government (whereas mainstream media were cautious, being kept "on tight strings"). And whatever the views of those in power, the people of his generation were far less conformist or overawed, were tolerant of criticism of their own views, able to interact with others and make up their own mind.

Sedat Kapanoğlu told me that the most popular topic is politics, it being the only place where people with diametrically opposed views would meet and debate. I asked Sedat for an example of a recent topic, and he told me that a politician in a recent speech had said that he found the use of the word "vagina" outrageous. This blew up into a big discussion, where some said that he was just expressing his own opinion, others said that it was ridiculous, and there were lots of positions taken in-between. With over a third of the whole internet population of Turkey visiting the site monthly, it has expanded well beyond its original catchment of university students, although these still tend to be the most fanatical core contributors to the site.

Ekşi Sözlük had just been Sedat's hobby for eight or nine years. But as the site grew, he found that through banner advertising revenue, the site was paying more than his salary. He then came back to Turkey in 2009 intending to try a whole string of start-ups. But the Ekşi Sözlük site proved so all-consuming that he hasn't had the time yet.

It all sounds like plain sailing, but running a site where radical opinions clash is still a brave decision. Sedat told me that he had received death threats. One individual had been sent to prison for this. But he told me, "You have to be brave to do anything tangible in Turkey." He added that "it's amazing how people get by here, with the bureaucracy, the traffic, ridiculous law suits". Sedat told me that he felt they were finally at a turning point in recognizing and starting to confront this as a society:

10, 15, 20 years ago people would say things were okay, even though they weren't. Now we are aware that there is something wrong. We see the friction in society that causes some people to be treated differently than others. That's a start, at least the

115

awareness is there. And more than anything the internet has been instrumental in bringing this before our eyes.

It also affected how institutions ran, Sedat told me, with the smarter ones learning how to function with transparency. Transparency brought change from government, public services, companies; since what people do in full sight can be very different from what they might be tempted to do lacking this visibility. "Information doesn't start revolutions," Sedat told me, "but it contributes." In particular, by making people better able to read the world, take in information, start to judge the rights and wrongs for themselves, and able to communicate their views.

I asked if there was a particular Turkish character to social media and life online. Sedat laughed and told me that Turkish people love to talk, love to debate, love to get their views known. They also have a prankish sense of humour. There was a *Time* magazine poll, he told me – for "The Most Influential Scientist of the 20th Century" – and Turkish people went overboard, contributing and voting. So much so that Kemal Ataturk (a modernizing president and founder of their Republic, but hardly a scientist) topped the global poll. And there were two other Turkish candidates in the top ten. One had a made-up name that sounded like a rude word in Turkish. And the other was a friend of Sedat's, who other people thought it would be funny to nominate because he was well known for making software bots that flooded online events like this poll. Apart from the mischief, there was genuine national pride mixed up in all this, he said; Turkish people loved seeing their country in the headlines, getting attention from the world. The Bond movie *Skyfall* had been a huge hit in Turkey, just because of the opening scenes set at the Grand Bazaar in Istanbul.

The other thing Sedat told me was quite different from his time in America is the way that the social media always spilled over into wanting to meet in real life. Ekşi Sözlük had started running a few social events that had then snowballed into a summer festival that around 10,000 now attend every year. The entrance is free to anyone who contributed on the site, and each was allowed to bring one friend; there were free bands and entertainments too, but they had to pay for their own drinks.

I wondered if the people's dictionary of everything had started to change the language. Sedat told me an example. The term *ayur vermak* or *ayur* for short (literally meaning "fine-tuning") had come to signify the process of so comprehensively critiquing someone else's previous entry ("like writing a PhD about it") that they would "never feel like ever saying anything online ever again". Sedat said that *ayur* did serve a positive role, which is that it made everyone more careful to say something that wasn't too hasty or stupid.

The Ekşi Sözlük story strikes me as a good example of what an inventor does, as opposed to more commercially minded folk. The hobbyist nature of Sedat's self-taught computing skills – clearly world class as he was later hired by Microsoft – gave him a different approach to developing his site. He naturally set out to create something he thought would be "cool". And every step of the way he took decisions based on what would be most useful or meaningful. It was an open process of discovery and development, with the community playing a big role in its features, etiquette and conventions. Few investors would give money to go and explore and play like that.

And basic looking, populist and playful though it is, make no mistake. This is a seriously advanced application. Remember that this appeared years before Wikipedia or Blogger. And to some extent, it still greatly exceeds them. What Sedat has done is invent a new combination of speaking and writing – with all the advantages of both conversation and documenting in coming to understand stuff. I wouldn't be at all surprised if in ten to 20 years time this sort of exchange and application becomes a mainstay of classroom education.

The spirit of inventing is an amateur one. It's about people following their passions for discovery. There has been a resurgence of what some have called the *Prosumer*, following in the footsteps of the Victorian amateur scientists like Charles Darwin who was a self-taught enthusiast. Let's not forget that the web itself started as a kind of hobby project; originally a means of cross-referencing relationships in the telephone directory of scientists working with CERN, the high-energy physics research centre.

The internet has proved a veritable playground for digital agencies worldwide, three of whose main strategies consist of:

1. Creating game-like campaigns that entice participation
2. Creating content that people love to share around and point to
3. Restructuring the process by which people choose and buy.

In each of these, the marketing model has shifted from communication (sender-message-audience) to inventing (platform-participant-relationship).

The digital agencies I met in Istanbul – despite having some true internet veterans among their founders, often with international experience – came late into all of this, because their markets (both the public and their clients) were late to adopt the internet. But now they are surging ahead both in the way that they approach their inventing – and also in areas like mobile and mobile payments where Turkey has a distinct lead. And they are starting to win international recognition for their efforts.

I was lucky to meet with three of the leading Istanbul digital agencies, and just for fun I will relate the work of each to those generic digital strategy categories:

1. Game-like campaigns.

C-Section describe themselves as a digital-minded agency – they mainly make websites, but do also make TV commercials for clients like Coca-Cola. Their approach is usually interactive and participative. And very "inventor"-like.

I met with founder Enis Orhun who told me that a key to their success had been that they would only produce an idea if they thought it could be brilliant (not just because a client would "buy" it). He contrasted their approach with advertising people and their ideas: "They think they are creative just because they make bits of film just the same as everyone else. But there is nothing creative about that."

C-Section's recent Valentine's Day campaign for Coca-Cola involved a classic Candid Camera style stunt in a shopping mall. A Coca-Cola vending machine had a sign on it saying that to celebrate Valentine's Day it would give free cans of Coke to loving couples. When a couple kissed and cuddled in front of the machine, it dispensed a free can of Coke (as if the machine itself was watching and rewarding them). And their actions and reactions were filmed from the same webcam (on an iPad), which also allowed *C-Section* to remotely trigger the vending machine. This was their local execution of Coca-Cola's global campaign of what they call *Happiness Machines*. Enis commented that making couples kiss in public in a Muslim country was quite a feat. And mentioned that the idea also did well at the Cannes awards.

Another practical joke-based campaign was "Will this be the Year?". If you took part, the system sent an email from you to a friend saying "Hey I found this amazing site that will predict your future". When your friend accessed it using the link you sent, the site would contact you so you could make live predictions in answer to their questions. Obviously because people know their friends well, the answers could seem spookily accurate. And it became a craze, used by 17 million consumers in Turkey and abroad.

Enis started the agency ahead of the (local) digital curve nine years ago, at the age of only 23. Now he has 50 people working with him (and another 50 in a social media agency), and when we met was on the eve of signing a deal with global group WPP. He said their success was mainly down to hiring brilliant individuals; people with the technical know-how to find new possibilities (rather than advertising types who worked only with concepts). Enis also said that the fact he came from a wealthy farming family, and did not have to worry too excessively about chasing client income, had always helped; meaning that they only needed to take clients or make campaigns that could be brilliant.

With most of their clients, they tried to get an innovation budget to conduct original R&D, prototyping ideas to see if they could work. An inventor agency through and through, in other words.

2. Content that people share.

Oğuz Savaşan co-founded *Rabarba* as a spin-off from *Alametifarika* (the agency created by Serdar Erener, who we meet later in the book). Oğuz had been reading in the international trade press about new kinds of creative agency that were digitally focused, with whimsical names like *Glue*, *Poke* and *Perfect Fools*. With the advent of DSL internet connections bringing connection speeds of 3-4Mb/s, it became possible to envisage video becoming a big part of the Turkish internet. "I told Serdar we have good video skills, let's use them to make interactive videos. I'd seen these in *Campaign* [the advertising trade magazine] every week and wanted to do some of these things."

Oğuz told me that Kapital Media conduct a "most respected company" survey among marketing clients every year, and that *Rabarba* came third in the Most Respected Agency category (after two other traditional ad agencies, but ahead of all the other digital agencies). The name *Rabarba* came from the "rhubarb-rhubarb" noise that TV, stage and film extras make in crowd scenes. And they chose that because the agency's core approach was all about creating buzz. The economics were based on creating content so entertaining that people wanted to share it; hence saving all the client money that would have been spent on TV airtime. For instance, when they had hired a popular comedian that Oğuz described as "like the *Seinfeld* of Turkey" to appear in videos for a bank, they got so many views the first morning the campaign was released that it had already paid for itself in media equivalent terms.

Covering all three of our strategies, Oğuz said he was increasingly drawn to working with clients on new digital utilities that clients provided to their customers. For instance, they had been working with Turkcell, the mobile company, on a digital wallet for mobile payments. And he had also developed an iPhone app with several colleagues that had become a hit, with 10 million downloads. The game is called *iSlash* and it is in the same genre as *Fruit Ninja* (where you use the touch screen to swipe like a sword). What they did different was make it also about solving visual puzzles. So that "instead of vulgar swiping you have to have strategy as well as dexterity".

As far as the prodigious success of his agency and the digital sector in Turkey went, Oğuz suspected that apart from "right place, right time", there were three main factors.

First was a stable business-friendly government; "although the government is Islamic, it is also one of the most liberal and most civil we have had – rather than all the previous attempts to design and control the country through military power". It could, he said, seem a confusing-looking mix from outside, because it was getting more liberal *and* more traditional at the same time. Oğuz told me that only in the last week, school uniforms had been scrapped across the country in elementary and high schools. On the one hand, this meant anyone could wear anything they liked. On the other, it meant that kids from conservative families would be able to come wearing headscarves.

The second factor was that the young population were avid, passionate, almost fanatical adopters of new technologies (like iPhone 5) and new applications. So that anything a digital agency like *Rabarba* produced that was popular was amplified into a firestorm of buzz for the brand involved.

Thirdly as ("only") a digital agency, they had often been working out of sight: "Marketing directors were not so much into it because they didn't understand it. So we just got to do what we wanted." This resulted in *Rabarba* catching up with Oğuz's heroes and winning recognition internationally in awards shows like *Eurobest*.

"Mobile is something else though," Oğuz told me. Because here, Turkey had a distinct lead. For five years or more, mobile penetration had been very high and the country's digital community had got into mobile marketing faster, and in some cases further (as with mobile payments). So now they were taking a lead and inventing new applications.

3. New ways of choosing and buying.

Alemşah Öztürk described his latest venture called 41?29! (which is the latitude and longitude of Istanbul) as a storytelling agency. He means digital storytelling – creating meaning out of information – rather than just content that features a story. A key difference is how the audience is involved in creating the story too.

The case study Alemşah told me about that best fits the "new ways of choosing and buying" strategy was their *Game of Your Life* campaign to recruit the best students for OzU (full name Özyeğin), a new university in Istanbul. It wasn't an easy task to attract students, let alone the best ones, to a university that could not point to a track record, or show any case studies of how successful their alumni had gone on to be. So 41?29! decided to create virtual success stories, by getting candidates to play a game predicting how their life and career would turn out in future, based on their answers to role-playing questions (like whether they would skip an early lecture in order to stay at the party a bit later). The choices, experiences and results were posted into that person's Facebook timeline. Only the dates were in the future, not the past (the first time it had been used that way). To make it entertaining, the agency created thousands of pictures, first-person videos and mini-blog posts to create the predicted futures. The final results of the game were saved as a future CV, and a mix of public and jury votes picked the finalists, who came to OzU to pitch in person for scholarships.

250,000 took part, and the university not only got to nab some of the country's top 1000 students (a key objective and a real coup), it also established high awareness and a reputation for being more student-friendly and modern. It's the sort of campaign any digital agency in the world would be proud of. And in fact, it got favourable international coverage, in media like *Contagious* magazine and awards.

It is also a prime example of the shift from communicating to inventing; in this case, a much more engaging 21st century university admissions scheme. And Alemşah said it was also about "not having to shout, or be flash".

Alemşah is himself a good example of the inventor type. He started out teaching himself programming at 16. At 18 he entered university to do computer science, thinking it would help him on his way to designing computer games. But: "I learned that was completely wrong on my first day". By 19 years old, on the back of his pioneering flash animations – using black and white photos to tell simple graphic stories – he was hired by an ad agency to "do some of this stuff for our clients". By 22 he had started one of the first digital agencies in Turkey, with a group of friends, then another which they sold to an agency group, and then finally 41?29! He told me that they were "doing digital strategy for brands; ad agencies don't understand digital". They now had 60 people, worked with many of the top clients in Turkey and had sold a majority stake to WPP.

Alemşah pointed to Turkey (along with Brazil and only a few other countries) having a unique mix of opportunities; with a median age of 26, the biggest mobile Facebook community in the world, tending to be avid consumers "of anything digital", and high credit card penetration. Plus it had only just got going. He said there were still "mental barriers" to be broken in the public's minds, to allow the full potential of the technology to be realized. But in some areas, like mobile, they were already ahead.

More importantly in Alemşah's view "Turkey as a country is all about adaptation". It had an entrepreneurial spirit. And having to struggle to survive in business, the norm was to be agile, fast, hyper-competitive. Plus they were now benefiting from a big reverse brain drain with the booming economy and energy of the country. Suddenly many of his peers were realizing it could be a better place to live than the UK or US. That they didn't have to go abroad to become successful anymore; there were actually better opportunities in Turkey now. But it wasn't about nationalism; "the feeling of being part of a nation is less important" to his generation. Alemşah himself worked between Istanbul and London and felt at home in both places.

Apart from inventing, what do all these examples across this chapter of the new era of inventing in the region have in common? Compared, for instance, to the hard-edged high-tech innovation culture of, say, Shanghai, Boston, Seoul or Helsinki? I would agree with Alemşah that a key element once again is the storytelling. There is simply a bit more subjectivity in these ideas. The *Stars of Science* finalists, for instance (perhaps because they advance through a public vote), are not just wizard technical ideas, they are human and socially positive applications. Some like TORK are culture-specific.

The human element is accentuated by the fact that so many of these brilliant people were self-taught. Or working as professional amateurs. There is something about coming at a field without an exactly groomed model of the current paradigm, how it is "supposed to be", that frees you to improve the model. As when Sedat decided to allow all views, not just the ones that conformed with his own. It was, after all, his hobby, supported by his friends. They could really do what they liked. And if you are going to have a site that thrives on debate, repartee, exchanges, then you don't want everyone to agree. So it is actually a smart design feature.

There is also an art-science crossover in many of these cases. In the West, that is a strict divide. You have to go back to Leonardo Da

Vinci to feel comfortable with them co-existing. But here they mingle freely. Ayah Bdeir is an artist and now the CEO of a technology start-up. Her product still made it as an exhibit at MOMA. Later in the book, we will meet Burak Arikan, a civil engineer turned computer programmer and mathematical modeller who decided that as his highly inventive work didn't fit any conventional framework, and galleries seemed to like it, it must be art.

I also like the fact that many of the most original features aren't the result of trying to be different, but rather the result of fixing flaws, gaps and solving problems – a process of tinkering to get something working.

Few of our subjects set out to be or see themselves as "inventor" in the Western ego-based role. They work through their own intuitions; about what is missing, what people really want. Really getting into the story and seeing the gaps, like the new university that couldn't provide career testimonials. That is totally different to the "what can we make that's more advanced" engineering approach. (What people really wanted from a jet plane turned out to be Easyjet, not Concorde!) It is more like a "thought experiment", as they call it in physics, where you take a human eye view of a ride through the system, process, market or use situation.

This means that what you are making is essentially playful. For the inventors, and also for the users. Nowhere is that more clear than Ayah Bdeir's *Little Bits*. It's perhaps the ultimate invention of this type. It is an invention that encourages and prepares a new generation of intuitive, prototyping, playful inventors.

Play is probably the key creative principle overall for these inventors: access to a childlike state of wonder, enchantment, magical thinking. And taking it lightly. If Sedat had given himself six months to lock himself away and code something that would make millions or be a landmark invention, do you think he could have done as well as when he coded a utility he needed in two hours and shared it with friends? The breakthrough wasn't the publishing tool, though; it is what and how you publish.

There is also a kind of alchemy at work here. A prototyping and seeing what happens; the best ideas often emerging from mistakes or oversights. It is that ability to take a broader view than rational foresight and planning that links back to the theme of creating from the Self (or you could call it instinct and intuition), not just the ego.

It's no wonder, given how the inventors are invested in the work, that what comes out is so life-enhancing – whether tuning an Arabic-scaled instrument, or teaching electronics with something a bit like LEGO, or getting couples to kiss. Why would you create something dull if you weren't one small cog in a corporate R&D environment?

It is also rare to be working on whole human applications in this way. Usually with a project like a car or a telephone exchange, the innovation tasks would be specified and subcontracted. Ensuring that no-one is rethinking what a car or telephone exchange actually is or does. And there is little scope to change the brief halfway through. Hence, for big ideas, look to inventors. That said, our inventors are not just backroom boffins. Most show considerable resourcefulness and tenacity in getting their ideas sold, made, taken to market.

The internet is also like a giant version of Bdeir's *Little Bits*; an inventors' playground. You need serious coding skills to do anything at all fundamental. But there is loads at the more human playful application end that anyone can try. (I, for instance, once hosted a human bee colony on Twitter as part of a London insect and art festival.)

But there is never any need to reinvent the wheel. The Interland is not as behind with the internet as you might think. Although it only really took off in the last five years, they went straight to Facebook, e-commerce and mobile apps. But there was clearly still room (as in many fields) to adapt what was already proven in the West....

> *We have a footer saying everything on this website is wrong. It helps to make people question what they find on the web. In general, we have got better at receiving, filtering, separating facts and opinions. And our site has been one of the factors in changing society in that way.*

Sedat Kapanoğlu, Ekşi Sözlük founder, photo by Gunyuz Keskin

3

ADAPT WITH

Importing, adapting and surpassing
best practice from the West

3. ADAPT WITH

Once in a city faraway in the desert, a family arrived from a distant country with all their possessions on a caravan of fine camels. They set up their home and started a business exporting the goods from the city's fine craftsmen who had a growing reputation abroad. All soon seemed happy and settled except the grandmother.

The hotel owner's daughter made friends with the grandmother and found out what the trouble was. It wasn't that she was homesick, or in any pain. It was the food. She had loved to cook for her family in her old country. But so many of her favourite recipes called for ingredients that wouldn't grow here in the arid desert climate.

The hotelier's daughter persuaded the grandmother to tell her the recipes. And they sat in the hotel kitchen looking through the larders for the nearest equivalents; using mint to replace a herb, or other grains to replace rice. Soon the grandmother was back in the kitchen. And on Fridays she came to cook in the hotel. The townspeople loved her food – so spicy and different – and so her recipes gradually became adopted as part of the local cuisine.

These stories are about how new businesses and innovations are being Made With a highly selective adaptation from the best practice of the West. The heritage of the Interland is importing, combining and surpassing ideas that travelled the trade routes. We meet Ibrahim Al Zubi, a leading sustainability thinker and doer in the region; SEEQNCE and Starch, two types of accelerator; Fawaz Al Zu'bi, former telecoms minister of Jordan; and Sina Afra, former senior exec at eBay, whose Markafoni is a leading example of why many are saying it's Turkey's turn at the internet boom.

131

Our region is unique. A lot of best practices have been absorbed from somewhere else, but the hybrid approach is always the best. Singapore would be the closest comparison. Dubai is setting the example for others to follow.[33]

Ibrahim Al Zubi certainly should know. From his profile I was expecting someone more imposing. But instead I found myself meeting an unassuming but confident young man, casually dressed in a brown polo neck sweater for his flight to Canada later that morning. Al Zubi is the Head of Sustainability at Majid Al Futtaim Properties (MAFP). MAFP develops and manages the shopping malls that the new Middle East is famous for, such as the *Mall of the Emirates* that houses over 500 retail brands plus attractions such as *Ski Dubai*. In total, over 100 million people visit MAFP malls per year. Al Zubi previously worked for the government and is associated with educational campaigns to raise awareness of issues like climate change, as well as spearheading the development of unique and progressive standards. A keen diver, Al Zubi is also a coordinator of United Nations Environment Programme initiatives. In recognition of all of this, he was also made an official ambassador for the *Al Gore Climate Initiative*.

The malls of the Middle East are famous for their gleaming modernity, their luxury stores and their opulence. What is less well known is that construction in the Middle East is taking a lead on sustainability standards. One of MAFP's competitors, Msheireb, has a regeneration project in Qatar that will contain the largest cluster of LEED (green building standard)-certified buildings in the world; a total of 100 buildings all targeting Gold and Platinum status. Besides attention to individual buildings, the whole development is angled to catch a prevailing northwest breeze, creating a comfortable microclimate.

Al Zubi told me that the region has gone from playing catch-up to setting a lead. For instance, MAFP's *Mall of the Emirates* is not only a top ten global mall in business terms, it is also one of the only malls in the world with a LEED Gold award. It helps that the region is booming again, after a hiatus during the credit crunch. But Ibrahim also told me that it is "different than ten years ago". The environmental standards have become perceived as an integral sign of quality. And crucially, they have been adapted to local conditions; since what is "eco" for a building in (cold and wet) Great Britain may not even be relevant in (hot and dry) Dubai.

LEED (from the USA) and the BREEAM standard (a UK equivalent) form a basic international reference point for development in the region. But Middle East governments, Al Zubi explained, have also developed their own standards to reflect local conditions, needs and challenges. Abu Dhabi has developed the Estidama integrated design initiative, one element of which (PEARL) covers environmental standards. Estidama itself is a broader holistic framework covering economic, social and cultural impacts. PEARL is based upon BREAM and LEED but is adapted to a region that has an extreme climate, where temperatures can exceed 50°C. Because of that local climate, greater emphasis is placed on water conservation than energy consumption. Unlike BREEAM and LEED, which are voluntary schemes, the PEARL rating system is being incorporated into national building codes and could in future become mandatory. Qatar has also developed its own standard – QSAS – part of which has already been made mandatory. That's a fairly straightforward account, but Al Zubi warned me against any oversimplification, saying "it takes a lot of research to understand the region properly".

Ibrahim Al Zubi told me that the work of governments in setting these standards had provided a common base for defining quality. He described his time in government as being "more like working for an NGO". As an aside – incidentally – isn't this refreshing? How often do you hear in the West that governments under pressure from powerful vested interests, or in terror of displeasing voters, have failed to set high enough standards? Those businesses who actually want to do the right thing have to compete at a disadvantage with those who cut corners.

Ibrahim told me that governments had applied the standards first to their own buildings. In the United Arab Emirates, "all new government buildings must be at least two-star". This in turn helped create a local green building market, boosting skills and training.

But the other important factor, Ibrahim told me, was private development companies like MAFP being family-owned. This meant that "it is never just profit, or just passion, it is always both". Perhaps, though, he added, we would have heard more of this passion from the region if there had not been a stringent culture of modesty. Al Zubi pointed out that while

> Qatar gave over $11 billion to foreign aid last year, you would never hear them making a song and dance about it. A lot of that kind of thing is not captured. It's one of the things the family companies do right; keeping a low profile. You won't see any annual reports detailing how many orphans we have helped. "Showing what you have done" is not the Muslim way.

The balanced approach to sustainability – including economic measures – is interesting too. In the West (while there are enlightened ideas like "the triple bottom line"), the reality is that businesses generally seek to make the maximum economic success, and then "give something back". Sustainability therefore becomes an afterthought. This has two main problems. Firstly, it is likely to be too little too late; for instance, designing shoddy, wasteful and unhealthy buildings then at the last minute implementing schemes like recycling and lift sharing. Secondly, it misses the economic side of sustainability. Al Zubi pointed out that with 60% of the population under 30 and high unemployment in some countries in the region, creating jobs is actually the number one priority for a family-owned company like his. The mall they are developing in Lebanon will create 2000 jobs in the retail site alone. Also, on the social side of sustainability, Al Zubi told me there had been rapid moves to make sure health, training and worker safety are in accordance with the highest standards – something I am aware the region has been criticized for in the past.

Al Zubi said that the key goal that governments and companies like MAFP are aligned on is the need to foster entrepreneurship. Previous generations could rely on safe jobs in government or corporate-style companies, but the new generation's prospects will depend far more on entrepreneurship. The governments in UAE have committed to awarding at least 10% of all their own contracts to SMEs. And Al Zubi told me that many are expecting a small business and entrepreneurship boom across the region. Access to education and seed funding was improving. The culture and media had become much more supportive. And the new generation are responding. For instance, Al Zubi told me about his recent visit to the *Arab Thought Foundation* conference, where he met many young people (some from Palestine and other poor countries) and was impressed by their energy and ideas.

Boosting this local culture of entrepreneurship, Al Zubi told me that there had been a reverse brain drain, bringing people with education and experience of best practices from elsewhere in the world back into the region:

> In some ways, 9/11 did us a favour. People who would have stayed in the US after a business degree felt less welcome there and felt more comfortable back at home. These people coming back have open-minded ideas, but they still practise some of the religion, I'm sure.

That apparent aside, referring to a balance of open-minded modernism and yet still attached to the traditions and culture, is a key aspect in Al Zubi's work. "It's good that a Western author is looking at all this," Al Zubi told me. He added that he himself had written a good

135

deal in Arabic on sustainability, environment and Islam:

> I reread the Quran and Hadith (the reported sayings and
> acts of the Prophet), researching all the references to the
> environment. There are more than 18 verses talking about
> water conservation alone. There is a Hadith about planting
> a tree. And then there is zakat, one of the five pillars, about
> charities and giving back.

Another example of linking Western best practice with Islamic
wisdom is ProductiveMuslim.com – an online self-help phenomenon.
Mohammed Faris started the site as a university student in 2007.
Originally from Yemen, then growing up in Saudi, Faris had gone to
the UK to study, later returning to Jeddah, where he now works in a
bank. While a student, Faris liked to find tips to help him be productive
in his studies and his life; juggling a degree, two jobs, running the
Islamic society. And so Faris started to read about productivity and
time management. Over time, he noticed that some of the tips really
helped. The original idea of his blog was to be able to share the tips that
he found worked best for him with others, and – as he was so involved
in the community and people kept asking him – specifically with
Muslim readers. This went on for a few months and then it trailed off.
Six months later, he revisited the site for two reasons. Firstly, a reader
emailed him asking why he had stopped and saying how helpful he had
found it. And secondly, as Faris explained in an interview in *Saudi Life*,
another way of looking at the whole thing had occurred to him:

> I realized that instead of trying to take the "Western"
> knowledge of productivity and share it with Muslims, why
> not take the Muslim understanding of productivity and share
> it with the world? This later point hit me like a brick wall
> when I read the Hadeeth … "The early hours are blessed for

my nation." I realized that the Prophet taught us something that every Productivity guru has been advocating: "If you want to be productive, wake up early!"

Faris, by late 2012, had created a thriving franchise with a whole team of contributors to write blog posts. He also does motivational speaking tours – I first heard of him when I was researching Malaysia, where he seems to have a huge following. ProductiveMuslim.com are now developing an ambitious suite of content and services. In a typically organized fashion, Faris lists these as:

1. Websites: ProductiveMuslim.com (and all translated versions), ProductiveRamadan.com, ProductiveAncestors.com, ProductiveMuslimah.com, and AbuProductive.com.
2. Training/Seminars: In-house training for companies/schools/universities, public seminars in countries, speaking engagements.
3. Consulting: Productivity consulting for companies/government agencies.
4. Apps/Software: Productivity smartphone apps + online software solutions.
5. Animations/Merchandise from animations: Sponsorship for our animation, licensing fees, and selling of related merchandise.

This is an impressive achievement for someone who was studying and now has a day job. Testimony no doubt to the effectiveness of the tips and techniques that Mohammed Faris promotes. All the same, I think even he would be quite impressed by the productivity of my next interviewee's organization.

"We do have lots of pride," said the smart and self-possessed young man sitting opposite me. "What I meant is that we have no qualms." The location of this conversation was the funky but functional office of SEEQNCE, an internet accelerator in downtown Beirut. Fadi

137

Bizri, one of the founders of SEEQNCE, was correcting a suggestion ("pride?") I had made as he was struggling to find the right English word. I had been asking Bizri about the recent arguments in the pages of *Tech Crunch* after some accused the internet industry in the MENA region of producing nothing more than clones of successful models from the West. Fadi Bizri explained what he meant:

> You have to separate the glamour from the realities. We are five to ten years behind the West. If the model works here, we are not dogmatic; if it can work over here with the right adaptation, we are all for it.

What Bizri was saying is in line with the whole "less ego" theme. The hero myth of entrepreneurship – me, my talent and my big idea – could be an impediment to the real business of starting and running a great business that delights customers, solves problems and creates satisfying stable work.

And Bizri is right. There is a myth. And it's far from reality. In my experience of the gold rush days of the original internet boom, originality was the last thing on anybody's mind. If investors this month were looking for *B2B*, then that's what every business plan would offer. Investors like this sort of plan because they are backing something the consensus says will work. How much more this could be the case when the business plan is launching in a country where e-commerce, content streaming and social media are new, but the model is already proven elsewhere. Isn't that the absolutely obviously right thing to do? Not reinventing the wheel, but reapplying it. What kind of an idiot would try to make polygon wheels because "round wheels have already been done"? On the other hand, you might need different tyres for different roads.

SEEQNCE had started out by helping an online streaming media start-up called Cinemoz.com get off the ground. Cinemoz's founder and CEO, Karim Safieddine, had previously worked at Miramax in the USA, and was familiar with models like Hulu.com which were valued at a billion dollars. "If it worked there, why not here?" Karim reasoned. The SEEQNCE team helped him get it running on the ground, hired a team, found funding, got an office and got it operational. Cinemoz launched in late 2011. It is now making steady progress and has launched some new and original features, like an agreement with Facebook allowing users to share scenes from content they are watching. It also outgrew SEEQNCE within nine months, leaving that team casting around for what to do next. Cinemoz is currently valued at £7.5 million, which isn't bad for a media start-up in Beirut, launched using a $200,000 loan by a 27-year-old.

Next the SEEQNCE team decided to import another proven model into Lebanon: the accelerator. Learning from the early dotcom experience of huge investments in unproven teams and models, taking years to build and mostly doomed to failure… Silicon Valley's *Y-Combinator* created a common sense alternative. Nearly 50 promising teams are given a small amount of money in internet terms (around $18,000) and three months to get their company, website and pitch ready. It culminates in a demo day, when the start-ups pitch to an audience of venture capitalists. Famous alumni include Scribd, AirBnB and DropBox. The total value of companies created by *Y-Combinator* was estimated in 2012 (by Forbes) as $7.8 billion.

What the SEEQNCE team of five founders, all with experience of the internet sector, liked about the *Y-Combinator* model (and that of similar programmes such as *Tech Stars*) was the "element of speed and urgency", Bizri explained. But as he and his team worked through the details, they realized that it would not work in Beirut. Almost everything that *Y-Combinator* has on tap in Silicon Valley is seriously lacking in Lebanon. For a start, leaving aside ongoing security worries, there simply wasn't a pool of wannabe entrepreneurs. So Fadi told me that if SEEQNCE launched and said "please apply, start-ups" there would be silence. Most talented tech, creative and business people tend to leave Beirut at the first opportunity. Not least, Bizri told me, because they could earn five times as much abroad. (Bizri should know. After taking a master's in Canada, he had worked in London at a print-on-demand internet start-up.) Those talented individuals who did stay tended to get snapped up by big companies. (Like Maroun, another member of the SEEQNCE partnership who had worked as a systems engineer for the local TV station.) And there were few precedents for leaving your safe job and branching out into tech start-ups. The culture was entrepreneurial in developing and exporting service businesses, and in the creative industries, Bizri told me. But not dotcoms. For investors, there was not enough happening to be confident that investing was a good idea; which led to not much happening.

Bearing in mind these challenges, the team of five partners at SEEQNCE "did a lot of overnights" and came up with the SEEQNCE programme. This "overnight" thing is a part of their ethos. As I arrived there were people getting up, putting away sleeping bags, stumbling around looking for coffee or a toothbrush. The office is purpose-designed and looks a bit like the *Big Brother* house, only in office form. It is complete with colour-coded rooms for different functions, and glass desks you can draw upon with pens (because "you are never going to have enough whiteboard space"). Bizri drew out the words "three phases" on the table for me, and proceeded to write a list that would explain how they mapped out their new process.

Three phases
1. outreach
2. selection
3. acceleration

For outreach, they spent two to three months "blasting out" the message in social media, talks in universities, plus media appearances on TV and in print. The message was that there was this really cool new programme, all you had to be was over 18 – you could be in a current job, or a student, you could be abroad – and you could apply either as a developer, a designer or a business person. They set a target of getting 300 applicants. And after creating a lot of buzz, they actually managed to get 436.

The selection process also took three months (so by now they were already running to double the whole time length of *Y-Combinator's* programme). They used exercises where individuals were matched into teams, and one-on-one interviews. There were social nights on the roof (more of this later). And they gradually narrowed down from 436 hopefuls to 100 strong individuals. From here, SEEQNCE increasingly encouraged candidates to try out as teams. Some had come to the programme with ideas, others not. Those abroad worked virtually through Skype, so "you saw a lot of teams huddled around laptops talking with absent members". Near the end of this phase, the candidates were asked to get into their final teams. At this stage there were 16 teams (48 people) left. SEEQNCE then ran a 48-hour hackathon, where candidates had to build a complete working idea, including the website, and pitch it. This was to an audience of 600 people including investors, who were also there for a big fancy party on the roof of the SEEQNCE building, called *Night of the Start-ups*. They had even printed funky retro event posters, designed to look like a 1950s B-Movie horror film.

Night of the Start-ups took place on August 25th 2012. It was a culmination of the six-month process begun in March. The winning teams then had a month to get their affairs in order – quit a job, get a year off college, even move over from Cairo in one case. Then the accelerator programme proper started. And eight real businesses got stuck into six months of development, with more overnights along the way. By month two, Fadi told me that all the start-ups had a beta site. By the third month, three of them had made some income from real customers. If two of the eight succeeded in achieving a $1-million valuation, he said, then they would count the programme a success.

The eight start-ups vary in their extent and type of adaptation. Some are being built for the local Lebanon market, at least as a test bed; others in English for Europe (so clearly not clones). In fact, Bizri told me that he'd recently been at *Le Web* in Paris and not only did the start-ups he came across not seem especially advanced compared to those at SEEQNCE, but the general levels of energy and commitment seemed pretty lame compared to their own batch. They might be five years behind America, but he suspected that they were not far behind Europe, if at all.

One of the SEEQNCE start-ups is a dating site for the conservative societies of Saudi Arabia and Kuwait. Obviously that was going to require a bit more work than just making an Arabic language clone of match.com! Bizri said the first thing was getting that team to research their intended market (mostly through chat rooms): what features would people want, what had worked and not worked in the past, what local customs and rules would they need to apply? Bizri pointed out that this was an example of how the "Arabic Web" market of 400 million-plus users could be a "mirage", this "one market" ranged from Beirut (ultra-liberal) to Riyadh (ultra-conservative). There were common factors too, though; notably the avidity of their tech adoption with "smartphones through the roof". And it was easier to appeal across the region in games, apps and entertainment.

The SEEQNCE start-ups were now on a countdown to their own demo day. Bizri felt that the essence of the model they had imported was actually the insight that to promote entrepreneurship, you need to be entrepreneurial yourself. More conventional ways of education would be "like trying to teach basketball using PowerPoint slides". Over the next year, the team are hoping modestly to expand their catchment from eight to ten start-ups. To fundraise to cover five years, rather than just one. And then to start franchising their model throughout the region.

Traditionally, young people in the more affluent sections of the Middle East population have tended to focus on getting a good degree and then a safe job, either in government or for an established company. There hasn't been a culture of entrepreneurship. But one country that realized early that this might need to change was Jordan. I met with Dr Fawaz Al Zu'bi, the former Jordanian telecoms minister and now chairman of a venture investment company, to learn how the initiatives put in place ten years ago had accelerated Amman, Jordan to being what some call "The Silicon Valley of the Middle East".

The first big moment of public excitement had come with Yahoo's acquisition of Maktoob.com, based in Amman. Maktoob was the first platform to provide email and other services over the internet in the Arabic language. Rather satisfyingly (given its subsequent huge success), Maktoob in Arabic means both "writing" and "destiny". They received a $5-million venture investment from Abraaj capital, and were later bought by Yahoo for $164 million. It was the first stellar "dotcom" media deal in the region. Fawaz described how this event created a wave of excitement.

Maktoob also groomed hundreds of veteran technologists and entrepreneurs, now ready to start their own dotcom success. Maktoob's founder, Samih Toukan, has started another internet group called Jabbar, originally composed of Maktoob group acquisitions that were left outside the Yahoo deal. Toukan told the *Financial Times* recently that he estimates Jabbar is now bigger than Maktoob.

What Maktoob and other success stories had done, said Al Zu'bi, was confirm the promise of entrepreneurship to government, and also the nation's parents. Jordan, he told me, along with Palestine, spent the highest proportion of per capita GDP on educating their children. With this tended to come a weight of expectation. Children would feel pressure in their career after all that investment not to let their parents and community down. The new phenomenon of entrepreneurship was starting to transform expectations away from a traditional path of seeking safe government jobs. The world has become much tougher anyway, Al Zu'bi said, so the notion of safe jobs was now an unsafe one. But there had to be a shift away from seeing failure as unacceptable to viewing it as permissible to try, fail and try again.

Nowadays, Al Zu'bi told me, the idea of entrepreneurship had finally taken hold of the public imagination. His company had invested in *Oasis 500*, a tech start-up accelerator and seed fund quite similar to SEEQNCE, only bigger, with a target to launch 500 start-ups in the next five years. Fawaz said they had been surprised by the response, with over 800 applications from start-ups that wanted a place there. But it had been a long path to get to this point.

Fawaz told me that his company had originally invested in *Oasis 500* for deal flow. This is what investors call exposure to a stream of promising plans and start-ups, so that they can select the best from a bigger pool of candidates. They also get early indications of trends. And keep an eye on promising young talent. It also helps them become visible as a potential investor. Thus far, everything I have said is familiar "best practice" from the West. But, as so often in this chapter, this also needed to be adapted carefully to work in the region.

Through getting involved in *Oasis 500*, Fawaz and his team realized that while the start-ups they were meeting had good basic education and sound plans, they had precious little understanding of how tech entrepreneurship actually worked in the real world. So they created a 90-day programme called *Launchpad*, taking their start-ups on an experiential tour of the East and West Coast start-up scenes in the USA. In the past nine months, they have taken five companies on this tour. The main objectives were learning from other start-ups in the same space and also seeking out early partnerships and commercial deals. These, Fawaz told me, had short-term benefits to the businesses, but also provided ongoing access to the latest thinking, technologies and talent after the tour was over. Al Zu'bi's team also used these tours to showcase their promising start-ups to some potential future investors, raising their profile.

Another piece of the *Oasis 500* jigsaw puzzle has been creating a network of angel investors. Formerly, Fawaz Al Zu'bi told me, people in the Arab region tended to put their money into tangible assets like real estate. They might occasionally have invested in their own child's business idea. But the notion of "investing in the creative power of the human mind" had been almost unknown. Through the *Oasis 500* programme, 220 high net worth individuals had come to the events where graduating start-ups pitched their ideas and started investing their own money. This, he said, had created a huge buzz throughout the community. A bit like *Y-Combinator* again. But in Jordan, the angel investors programme needed recruitment, education, community and development. They don't have 20 years of experience, like they would in the US.

I asked if there was any danger of a backlash. After all, as he and I both knew, tech investment is risky; especially in the early stages; and especially for angel investors who may be less clued up on relevant technology, legal, commercial or competitive issues. Fawaz agreed a backlash was possible. He said there were signs in only the last few months that this was starting to happen. But Al Zu'bi thought this was probably a healthy sign; leading to "a steady state" where some angel investors dipped in occasionally, and others became "much more committed and involved".

Dr Fawaz Al Zu'bi, Chairman of iV Holdings (an early stage venture investment company), is something of a entrepreneurship veteran in the region. He was originally a successful private sector entrepreneur himself. After studying for a PhD in fluid dynamics in the USA, Fawaz had started out installing some of the latest drip irrigation technologies on his family farm. Seeing how well this worked, neighbours started asking them to order this for them too. And soon they had so many orders it made more sense to manufacture within Jordan. The resulting company Adritec went on to become the biggest player in drip irrigation and related services in Africa and the Middle

East, with subsidiaries in Jordan, Syria, Morocco, Tunisia and Greece.

Then, in June 2000, Al Zu'bi took up his position in the government as Minister of Post and Communications. By 2002, he had helped reposition this as the *e-Ministry*, with responsibility for driving Jordan's participation in the booming global knowledge economy. He told me that when he came into his post, the entire IT sector in Jordan had revenues of only $50 million. Now, they had more than $1 billion. The mainstay of their strategy had been IT services that could transform the Jordan economy; in banking, health, education, real estate and business process efficiency. These commercial applications, Fawaz said, were hardly "sexy", nor what he would call "innovation". They had developed a US outreach fund to identify and import promising technologies and companies in these areas. Generally what these businesses had in common was addressing inefficiencies, rather than expanding capabilities. But they had made what was now possible start to happen. Because a modernized infrastructure in internet, credit cards and mobile phones then created the market for secondary services, with a big enough addressable home market to draw upon.

When I asked about the difference between this and what the US government might do, Al Zu'bi said there was no comparison. America would want to create 100 companies per year with a $1-billion valuation. In his country, even after ten years, they had created only one of any size. It was "not in its infancy now, more in its adolescence". But it would continue to be tough: "When we say nine out of ten won't make it, we are not kidding."

There were also incredible stories that you wouldn't usually hear in Silicon Valley. One of the *Oasis 500* founders, Fawaz told me, was a Palestinian refugee who, while a student, decided to translate *Harry Potter* into Arabic for his friends. He had sold over 1000 copies for a nominal price before he got a letter from the publishers about infringing their copyright. (Al Zu'bi thought that coming from a refugee camp, you perhaps had more excuse than most not to know about such things.) He continued in the area of publishing and translating, now going legit, and employed 13 people, six of whom were his own brothers and sisters. It's a great story that touches on how entrepreneurship is different in emerging markets – that it can mean utterly transforming life chances and communities.

The Jordan situation had improved, Al Zu'bi told me, with "entrepreneurship creating a pipeline of companies" but still "a lot of handholding has to take place". The end customer markets were still slower to take up innovations, investors were still wary of such intangible businesses, and it was still difficult to exit, either within the financial markets or to find a trade sale (a buyer in the form of a bigger IT company). But it was a long way from the starting point 12 years ago.

Jordan's King Abdullah II was the driving force behind the whole initiative, Fawaz told me. The new king's idea was that rather than civil servants to make this work, they would need to bring in the private sector. Al Zu'bi himself was recruited for that reason. And the whole programme was developed in close partnership with the private sector. Inviting them to say "this is what we need from government". As a result, there were sweeping reforms to the laws around investment, company types and shares that Al Zu'bi told me were unique in the Arab world (and actually in several details even ahead of the UK). They also liberalized the telecoms industry; affordable mobile and bandwidth being identified as a key enabler of everything else that could follow. The net effect of all of this was "transformative".

So the apparently unlikely location of Maktoob recipient of the Arab world's first "Facebook style" media deal in Amman, Jordan was far from coincidental.

Where Amman is known for technology (and also gaming, animation and creative production), Beirut is the cool capital of the Middle East, home to creative designers, architects, chefs and artists, as well being one of the region's centres of excellence for creative services like advertising. While I was there, I came across a scheme

147

called *Starch* created to help up-and-coming fashion designers. The scheme runs a competition for select talented designers. They then have a year-long apprenticeship, culminating in their work being offered for sale in Starch's boutique store in Beirut's Saifi Village. Starch co-founder Rabih Kayrouz is one of the only two fashion designers from the Arab region to be included in the official Paris couture fashion show calendar. Having worked for both Dior and Chanel as a designer in Paris, Kayrouz had returned to Beirut in 1997 initially just to help a friend with a wedding dress. Starch launched in 2008 and Kayrouz told *The Daily Star* that:

> Too often in Lebanon, people are content with sitting back and complaining about the problems in society. But we do nothing ourselves, we just sit there with our coffee, filling the restaurants. So it's our duty, if we want to make a change, to be part of that change. And, it is natural that in any business, if you love your work, you want to spread it.[34]

Tala Hajjar was working with Rabih Kayrouz when they first set up the scheme together. I interviewed Tala by email and I'll report it here in Q&A format:

Q. *What is your own background, how did you come to be involved in Starch?*
A. At the time when Rabih and I set up Starch, I was working with him as his marketing manager. I initially studied fashion design with a specialization in fashion marketing. I decided to continue down the path of communication and marketing because that is truly where my heart is!

Q. *What is the essence of your own brand? Why "Starch"?*
A. *Starch* is really all in the name: a raw basic component

that is crucial in many industries. It is hardening, it is raw, it is pure, and it's a start!

Q. *What is/could be Starch's proudest moment?*
A. We have had quite a few of those proud moments! Especially when you realize a Starch designer's own success. When you witness their growth and feel you were able to contribute to launch the designer's career. Many have reached success in not just necessarily sales and press, but also awards, international exposure and international fame in a relatively brief time. It definitely puts a smile on our faces!

Q. *Beirut has a troubled history – what would you say are the effects of this, positive and negative?*
A. I think the turbulence of the Lebanese history has made the Lebanese so courageous and entrepreneurial. They don't calculate too much, they just throw themselves out there, *carpe diem* being really their way of living, no time to waste! "We'll see what happens" kind of attitude. Sometimes you wonder how a system functions in such a loopy environment, but it does. It encourages people to just do! As opposed to plan forever until it's time to execute. Lebanese don't plan, because either way, you never know what's going to happen. As for the entrepreneurial bit, and putting aside that a Lebanese by DNA is a trader, the Lebanese love launching their own thing, leading, playing their own game.

Q. *How is Starch different than retailers sourcing from talented degree show graduates?*
A. To begin with, Starch is 100% non-profit. We don't seek to make any money out of the foundation or the designers.

Another important difference is that retail is only one part of the many services we provide at Starch. That almost comes in last. Our help starts from developing the collection, branding and communication, collaborations, workshops. We inject many, many elements into their year at Starch. It is an incubator with the sole purpose of launching these designers and in parallel contributing to our growing design scene.

Nina Curley is editor-in-chief of *Wamda*, and spends her time between these two centres of entrepreneurship, Jordan and Beirut. She likes both, she told me, although she said that Beirut's nightlife can make Amman seem like a suburb. Wamda is a platform for entrepreneurship across the Middle East and is broad in its coverage both geographically (taking in other hotspots like Tunisia and Egypt) and in terms of industry (covering retail and other offline entrepreneurs). What they mean by being a platform is that they not only run a high traffic blog on the start-up sector – to this extent they could be regarded as adapting the *Tech Crunch* model. But they also drive the whole education and inspiration agenda, with events like *Mix n' Mentor* (which Nevzat Aydin of Yemeksepeti had told me was the best event he went to in his life). And Wamda also has a fund that invests in start-ups itself. Nina explained to me that compared to equivalents in New York (where she hails from), the fact that they do all of this rather than specializing in just one area was a result of taking into account the much lower knowledge base and development of the ecosystem. When reporting on the Wamda blog, they have to mix the sort of analysis and trend news that outsiders to the region would look for, with very basic "instructionals" like "how to pitch your start-up". I asked her about trends and besides the obvious ones (education, translation, connected health, mobile payments and marketing), she told me that internet start-ups targeting women was a hot theme in the region at the moment.

Meanwhile in Istanbul, Gulay Ozkan, who was previously a Silicon Valley mobile technologist, is now coaching future entrepreneurs in Turkey. Gulay has developed an award-winning training programme called *Courage to Create a Business*, which she teaches as part of the MBA course at a number of universities. Gulay told me that the course is based upon design thinking (as taught at Stanford) and it is very different from the usual project-based entrepreneur programmes that help you develop and write a business plan. Instead, Gulay says that their starting point is seeing that entrepreneurship is a kind of "lifestyle". So they use techniques from drama coaching (Gulay has a background in both engineering and drama) to help students discover their own creative and entrepreneurial skills. Gulay Ozkan puts a particular emphasis on diversity, as her website explains:

> In this programme, diversity is taken as one of the pillars of creativity. Therefore, all details are arranged to enrich diversity. There is a 50% quota for women. There are students both from engineering and the social sciences. In project teams, the groups must contain women and students with different backgrounds.[35]

I asked Gulay, who also consults and mentors tech start-ups in Turkey and other emerging markets, how entrepreneurship here was different to the USA. She told me that they were still too dependent on copying processes without fully grasping their meaning, and that these hadn't had time to become innate. As a result, Gulay said, they didn't have the mind-set she would meet in America that "it's your company, you can do anything you want". She said when she taught at the university she told students that it was possible to "build the world in our terms, that it can be green and ethical and diverse". But that she found in general that "in emerging markets, people are not aware of this power, they tend to follow the old capitalism". On her course

151

for MBA students, they start with understanding the ecosystem and very real constraints they will face locally, before then moving to self-discovery and only then on to ideas:

> We focus on realities in the entrepreneur's country. We don't believe in the "lone hero" entrepreneur. Larry Page and Sergey Brin would have not been able to found Google in an emerging economy. Being an entrepreneur in an emerging market and an advanced market are two very different things. Teaching entrepreneurship in an emerging market by its very nature is not the same as teaching it in Silicon Valley.[36]

Another expert who teaches digital entrepreneurship is Anil Altas who wrote a book (*e-ticaret Satista Tsunami Etkisi*) on the digital media boom in Turkey, and is currently writing another book aimed at students who are interested in how to make money from and start a career in the internet. Anil spent 14 years working in e-commerce roles for various companies including Tchibo, and was recently made country manager of Zanox, the affiliate marketing network. Anil told me that there was a lot of interest in this topic. But I had to bear in mind how recently it took off ("we only got Facebook in 2007") and how fast it was developing and changing. The key promise of the internet, she felt, that so attracted the new generation was the freedom it offered. Within a Turkey family, community and government had tended to discourage kids; "don't talk too much, don't look at that". And it was not very easy to travel into Europe and other places. But the internet opened up a whole world. Now the new generation were embracing this freedom. Many more were keen on travelling and keeping in touch with other citizens of the world. Altas said when she went to the university, she saw students who really wanted to see and do something different, to be innovative. "Nobody wants to work in a bank anymore."

The question for brands is not just how to adapt a business model, technology or product and service – but how to adapt culturally. Haluk Sicimoğlu, Chief Strategy Officer at Alice BBDO, shared a quote that he uses in presentations when we met in Istanbul – from a poet who brought Islam to Japan:

"Things of the West stay here if they are of value."

When it came to modernity, Turkey, Haluk explained, was ambivalent. It had suffered from the imposition of a stern Westernized modernity, following the 1920s secularization by Ataturk. And that had followed the shame of its period of late Ottoman decline as "The Sick Man of Europe". As a result, Sicimoğlu told me that for developing brands to appeal within Turkey, the ideal lies between the two: not completely modern and copied from the West (because why not then just buy the "original" – like a BMW?), nor too traditional, because that signifies backwardness, but finding ways to reframe tradition in a contemporary way. One brand that gets this right, Haluk told me, is Hiref – functional modern glassware, inspired by Anatolian traditions. This same formula also helped to create Turkish brands that worked well internationally – such as fashion designer Rifat Ozbek – being rooted, but relevant.

The current Erdogan (AKP) government, Haluk Sicimoğlu told me, seemed to understand this whole dichotomy and have the ability to appeal to its people through the essential aspirations that belied apparent differences. They understood that "whether you are wearing a veil or a miniskirt, you want to lead a comfortable decent life, with your family, in an ethical manner. That you have the right to work, and consume and live with freedom – and to a certain extent happiness and joy".

This line of thinking about contemporizing traditions was one of the conclusions of a series of reports on *The Mind of Turkey* that

153

Haluk Sicimoğlu had written with anthropologist Mehmet Demiray. I met with Demiray a few days later and he told me that it was always important to look at the process of creative accommodation, never just simplistic categories like modern and traditional. Turkey now "has its most Islamic government ever, and yet this is the most modernizing".

Demiray thought that the Turkish mentality could be summarized by the word pragmatism. Pragmatism was the reason, Demiray claimed, why Turkey made such great entrepreneurs and yet such weak brands. The Turkish business culture would focus on distribution strength, on manufacturing, on making deals that brought immediate profits.

Demiray cited a meeting he attended with a company called Boydak Holding and an advertising exec who was very proud of having worked in the past with IKEA. The client told the account exec they were considering advertising in national magazines. She expressed surprise that they could afford to compete with IKEA in this way. The client countered that he had 60% of the whole Turkish furniture market, whereas IKEA only had 3%. That his products were sold in 86 countries. That he was actually one of IKEA's biggest global suppliers. That they had huge businesses in places in Africa that IKEA didn't even reach. The reason few would recognize Boydak's size, said Demiray, was that it was not one big brand. It was made up of lots of different tactical and local brands – like *Sultan* for Greece. And white-label manufacturing for others. A similar story is Vestel, the Turkish electronic company. This single Turkish manufacturer accounts for 21% of all the TVs sold in Europe. The reason you haven't heard of it is that many of their sets are rebadged as "Hitachi", "Sanyo" or "SEG".

The pragmatism, Demiray said, was far more than just a disdain for fancy advertising or design. It was because they thought contextually. Knowing that things could change from one minute to the next. For instance, if you built a strong export business in Syria, with recent problems you might want to switch these last few years to Iraq, where brands like Ulker (chocolates and ice cream) had been booming. "They always have a second plan." Hence brand strategy could be meaningless – because it was too long term, too inflexible, the antithesis of keeping all options open. The Turkish business culture also tended not to encourage the sort of mind-set that fostered brands in Western companies. There was usually a strong patriarch, a very strict hierarchy and culture of "obeying" – and a focus right through on profits and margins, "making money from your mind, not your brands". By looking to the context, Turkish firms could always adapt very quickly, and were brilliant in chaotic markets and crises.

The only drawback in taking too much notice of culture in a country like Turkey is you have to recognize how fast it is changing and how that relates to creating brands. That while five years ago the internet scene was still in its infancy, it is already by now producing some of the world's leading start-ups and challenger brands.

Markafoni was recently named MENA's hottest start-up in the 2013 Europas awards (Cinemoz was a runner up). And if it is about still adapting best practice, it is doing so on steroids, employing 650 people. Sina Afra, the Markafoni founder, showed me around the offices – a mix of modern glass partitioning and raw, Soviet-style concrete slab walls. He said it was an old industrial plant. The previous owner had made belts. After an order from America for a million belts fell through, it stood empty for four to five years, until the new industrial revolution arrived in the shape of Markafoni.

Afra grew up in the Netherlands (his father was Turkish ambassador) and then studied in Germany and Switzerland. He worked at eBay in strategy and corporate development, and was on the management board in Germany, and later of eBay Europe. Then in 2006, eBay posted Afra to Istanbul. And – after persuading Klaus Hommels, a Swiss financier and previously an early stage investor in Skype and Facebook, that Turkey online was the next big thing – Afra started Markafoni.

This is the essential detail that is missing from some of the debates about whether the "Middle East is cloning Western innovations". Someone like Afra isn't importing other nationalities' ideas, he is bringing his own knowledge and experience home. It's what many described to me as a reverse brain drain. You saw the same process in 2001, when many software engineers in Silicon Valley who had happened to be Indian nationals were laid off after the dotcom crash. So they went back home to places like Bangalore. This is one reason why ten years later Indian companies like TCS (a $10-billion revenue IT company), Unisys, Wipro and Redington are world leaders in IT.

Having said all of this, Sina Afra was very straightforward about his strategy; which was to adapt the flash sales model (as pioneered by Gilt Group and One Kings Lane) in national markets where it did not already exist. This explains why after Turkey was up and running, Markafoni launched, not just in neighbouring territories like Greece, but in Ukraine, Poland and even Australia. "We just opened an atlas and marked all the countries that didn't have flash sales," explained Afra.

The real leap of imagination was going international as a Turkish internet company. This had never been done before, and local players just didn't have the confidence. Whereas Afra, fresh from eBay (and with an amazing global pool of contacts to call upon), thought it was only natural.

Markafoni lives up to most of the media stereotypes for a dotcom start-up. The average age of employees, Afra told me, is around 25. And they are among their generation's top graduates, who would have become lawyers, investment bankers, consumer brand marketers and consultants in a previous era. The directors are handpicked by Afra who commented that "we don't hire too many buzzwords people". But the impression of being a style egalitarian "open collar" Silicon Valley style employer could be misleading. I asked Afra if this was a democratic company and he laughed. He told me that he worked with the nine directors, setting clear tasks and targets. Then they were 100% responsible for delivering on execution. And clearly it has worked, as they had taken the company from zero to being one of the top e-commerce companies in only a few years (and it may not quite be as brutal as its sounds – since "we've only had one change of director after 12 months"). Afra thought that the key was "hiring good guys who bring in even better guys".

Markafoni was founded in September 2008. It was the first flash sales company in Turkey. The flash sales model is based on two key elements: getting older stock that manufacturers are willing to shift at a steep discount (for instance, last year's range) and offering it for a time-limited, typically two-day "buy it now or never" sale. The stock is almost never purchased by Markafoni, rather it is "ring-fenced" within the brand owner's warehouse for the period of sale. It is a membership club model, giving it a feeling of exclusivity. All this is entirely common to any flash sales site. They were, however, the first fashion e-commerce site, at a time when e-commerce in Turkey was dominated by electronics. And the first site mainly targeting women. And from the start, it has enjoyed what Afra described as "hyper hyper growth" – making eBay (once the fastest-growing large company in the world) look slow by comparison.

Markafoni spent no money on marketing up until well after they had a million customers. It was pure word of mouth. Friends would ask members for an invite to join. When I probed Afra on how exactly they got that started, he said that each member of his team sat with all of their friends, with a laptop open and said "please join – here do it now, I will help you" and then "please invite your friends – here do it now, I will help you"! The process is familiar but the sheer determination also shows.

They grew so fast that by the time competitors launched only seven or eight months later, they had a huge first-mover advantage. They then started launching internationally. And when they ran out of countries that were flash sale virgins, they started launching their own verticals; three brands that they sell through their site alongside

157

other people's brands, offering fashion, shoes and cosmetics.

The name Markafoni means "brand symphony". And there is an ecosystem-like pattern to the business model that begins to explain why it is so deeply successful. What I mean is that every part of the business and every stakeholder is benefiting from each other. You might have thought that brand owners would hate people selling off their stock at 70% discounts. But actually it is a huge benefit. They get to shift old stock fast – rather than distributing it to discount outlets across the country to wait a year to see if it sells. And it insulates your brand (whereas if you constantly see cheap branded goods in discount outlets, you do start to question ever paying a full price).

Today, Markafoni is the leading brand in Turkish e-commerce, and has been hotly tipped by global publications and awards as a world-scale success. By now they advertise their brand on television, but Afra told me the real success has always been what he has witnessed at dinners; women asking other women to invite them.

I asked him how it was different to e-commerce in other markets, and Afra explained that it actually is a very different scene when you get into the details. For one thing – going back to the "no qualms" issue – if you launch in the UK and have a bit of success, you will probably find yourself with two or three challengers. But in Turkey, you will have 60. And they won't be trying to do something different to your model, but exactly the same. Because of the capital-intensive nature of businesses like Markafoni, that 60 will soon dwindle to 10, and later probably to two or three. But it is clearly competitive in a way that is quite unknown in the West. You'd be in big trouble fast if you launched with a good idea but weak funding, or something else that slowed your growth.

Afra said that the Turkish culture was important in the Markafoni consumer success too. Turkish people are especially attuned to getting a bargain. They almost enjoy the discount or the low margin more than the purchase itself. Whereas he told me that in Poland they had found the flash sales part of the offer was weaker – "people just want Gucci, and they don't care what they pay". The credit card penetration being as high as the UK certainly helped, as did people's willingness to pay up-front. The same model in the Middle East (a site called MarkaVIP) would always be hampered by the fact that people there expected to pay cash on delivery, and might then change their mind. The logistics helped too – with seven or so cut-throat competitors having developed such efficient infrastructure that it was no problem for Markafoni to deliver within 24 hours up to 600km away (and within 48 hours to any destination) at volumes of 40 to 50,000 items a day, and with almost no hitches. The Turks hadn't had a catalogue sales culture and so if a dress didn't fit, they don't have the culture of just sending it back (like in Germany or France), but will rather ask around relatives to see who wants it. For fashion e-commerce, returns are the make-or-break number; Markafoni's at sub-30% is quite low (over 50% would be more typical). Their key issue instead, because the market is so competitive, is margin.

As I sat listening to Sina Afra, I remembered conversations I had in Turkey only five or so years earlier, when people told me that e-commerce would "never be that big in Turkey". The internet penetration was low, connection speeds were slow, people loved going to the shops, most women didn't work (it's still only 25%); this was after all still a traditional country and the retail sector was ruthlessly well developed and competitive. Five years later, I listened to Afra set out why the international media now sees Turkish internet ecosystem as the number one investment destination in the world. There are now 25 million Turks online (34% of the population) i.e. still pretty low (the UK has 70%, Sweden 85%); so lots of strong organic growth to come. It's a very young population, avid consumers of new trends and new technologies.

For all of these external factors, Afra felt that the key element in their success had been the quality of their own processes and execution. It had been important that they had not outsourced many functions, but rather got them working for themselves. It was about taking full responsibility internally, really being close to operational details that are make-or-break, sometimes inventing your own systems from scratch.

Afra also said that Turkey was a perfect working culture for the internet, because "Turks learn very fast", are very comfortable with speed, change, chaos, trading on the edge. They have a very pragmatic mind-set. If you want a set of rules tested to destruction, then "give it to the Turks in the office to test". They are really creative at solving practical problems, optimizing. And the speed of execution meant they could afford to make and fix mistakes. So he was echoing what Demiray had told me led to Turkey being good at business yet rubbish at brands (but Markafoni did win a Superbrand award too; so maybe one doesn't preclude the other after all).

The drawback with Turkey's internet scene when Afra joined it was its lack of confidence and international experience; "people would think so locally". Afra guessed that might have something to do with past decades of economic isolation.

At the heart of the Markafoni success, though he wouldn't say so himself, was a founder who found all of this "second nature to me". After six years at eBay and at the heart of the internet scene, *of course* you scaled at breakneck speed, *of course* you went global within your first year, *of course* you refined and tested your process so meticulously that by the third or fourth country you could hand them a manual and say "there's your first six months". Afra, I am guessing, would never take the credit himself – he sees himself as simply getting a great team together and "managing our chances well". And in a way, he is right. There is nothing "magic", "talented" or "heroic" about learning to do a fantastic job in one part of the world, then coming to another part of the world and teaching colleagues to do it too. But it requires a culture that values the collective, the work, the results… That takes a self-belief as well as a certain amount of humility. And the more entrepreneurs I met on my travels, the more I started to think that it was the cultural factors that gave them such an edge.

The egotism that lies behind Western branding – what I referred to as the egonomy – means that we seem to think that ideas and technologies invented within our collective borders (quite often by teams of brilliant people from all over the world) somehow "belong to us". It is clear in the case of something like science or mathematics what a nonsense that is. Having come from a country that proudly claims to have invented everything from the steam train to television to football, I am rather used to the idea that inventions are part of the common stock of humanity and often taken forward most successfully in different places than they originated from. Soccer today is a Brazilian game. Maybe tomorrow an African one?

In that sense, the West is a kind of mega ego brand, the brand behind all others from that part of the world. When we copy each other, we think this is smart; for instance, a matter of being up with the latest fashions and trends. But when others adapt our best practice for the emerging markets, we call it cloning. That's fair enough in cases where people copy every detail of a site, only changing the language. But in the case stories in this chapter, we have seen a deeper process of internalizing and developing the model.

The practitioners are fortunate if, like Fadi from SEEQNCE, they have no qualms (no ego inflation) about learning from, adopting and adapting the best. The people who will look narrow-minded in the long-term are those who accuse the Arab web of "just cloning" Western models. As if Europe should have avoided using algebra or surgical anatomy because it was invented in the Middle East. The same sort of hubris landed on American soil in the form of the Japanese car and hi-fi – Japan whose products were once thought of as cheap copies – taking over the US car and electronics markets.

In the case of a senior executive of eBay Europe, who then launched

161

one of the world's most successful recent e-commerce start-ups that happens to be based quite sensibly in the booming market of Turkey, those sorts of slights are already past. What any seasoned internet pro like Sina Afra would tell you is that the internet is all about hitting the early mainstream. That the winners like Facebook were not the first to try a concept (that was Friendster, then MySpace) but the first to get it exactly right, at a time when the user base was booming. It's a total misunderstanding of the interaction between capital and market opportunity to think that most mainstream internet successes globally have been the products of heroic and unprecedented originality.

There is an internal implication from this "no qualms" mentality, which is: if in London you'd have three competitors, in Turkey you will have 60. Any classical economist will tell you that this is ideal for developing really competitive, robust, fast-growing global challengers (the last thing you need for commercial innovation is a quasi monopoly in a quiet backwater). It's one of the reasons why – as in construction – it seems like one year in these cities is like five years in London.

There is so much confidence and energy in these cities and clusters I have been visiting that it is palpable. It's the feeling of an emerging market when you look at the level of people's lives. Demiray told me he moved into a cheap and dodgy area in Istanbul five years ago and now it is becoming one of the upscale, luxury, fashionable districts. One of the earliest findings of economics – from Adam Smith – was that it is not the incumbent economies that are dynamic and confident, but those experiencing the most rapid growth. In Smith's day, his example was that upstart Poland was rampant, while France was moribund.

Adaptation also takes real application. That's the difference between cloning and really adapting. For the latter, you have to deeply understand how the whole thing works, whether a technology, a business process or a new paradigm in the creative arts. If you clearly understand how something works from the inside, you can always reinvent it. If it is received wisdom, you will never have a clue. Preferably you will have lived in its community, absorbed all the intrinsic know-how, the way of doing things. But then you have to adapt it. In California, a new start-up accelerator could post an announcement on a blog and get 1000 applicants. In Beirut, it took six months to build enough of a proto Silicon Valley type community to get to critical mass.

The other thing to realize is that all of this would be different if the technologies and associated markets had reached some sort of final form maturity. But the world is not at the end of history. New paradigms are opening up in mobile, e-commerce, cleantech and financial services. Given what many have called a second industrial revolution, these emerging market players if anything have an edge: with lower cost bases, less legacy assets committed to old technologies, a more pragmatic and collective management mind-set, with an energized and aspiring workforce.

With all of that social change and business dynamism comes strong brands. It's the hidden truth of Western marketing. It isn't advertising and design that create breakthrough success. Rather, behind every great brand is usually an early trailblazing history and context. VW rose like a phoenix from the ashes of post-war Germany with the small, affordable people's car. Coco Chanel transformed the way that women dressed at the time of the Suffragettes. Nike invented jogging (their founder, coach Bill Bowerman, wrote a 1-million bestseller that started the craze), not just running shoes.

It seems that even when the Interland is adopting Western technologies and "best practice", they are doing so selectively. But the process doesn't have to be so one-sided as adapting makes it sound. There is also the opportunity to create new fusions, which go beyond (are more universal than) their sources in either East or West. Which brings us to the next chapter...

163

> *Turks learn very fast, are very comfortable with speed, change, chaos, trading on the edge … if you want a set of rules tested to destruction, then give it to the Turks in the office to test.*

Sina Afra, CEO of Markafoni
Photograph & permission supplied by Markafoni

FUSE WITH

Synthesizing "East" and "West"
to create transcendent, universal ideas

4. FUSE WITH

Once in a city faraway in the desert, a local sheikh was very fond of racehorses. His horses were haughty, fine, proud and as fast as an arrow. Unfortunately, they were also sensitive and lacking in stamina.

One day, he was riding outside the city and was overtaken by a farmer on his wild and scruffy-looking horse. Outraged, the sheikh raced after him to teach him a lesson. He easily caught up, but then the farmer who was as proud as the sheikh raced after him. They ran for miles. And miles. And eventually the sheikh's horse pulled up with exhaustion. The farmer's horse seemed barely out of breath.

The farmer was too proud to sell his horse, although the sheikh begged him. But after haggling long into the night, they reached an agreement. They would breed their horses. The farmer would run a stud farm and would keep the income from that. And the sheikh would continue to race the horses and keep the income from that.

Their plan was a big success. The crossbred horses won race after race for the sheikh. And the farmer became even richer than the sheikh, by breeding horses for all the disgruntled owners that had lost to him.

These stories are about how brands Made With syntheses of East and West are bringing something more human and rooted to modernity. We see how the Interland is a state of mind, a commitment to "and" (rather than "or"). As explained by Elif Shafak, the novelist; by designers at the Lost City of Arabesque event; by the authors of a report on The Mind of Turkey; and by Serdar Erener, its leading adman. Also as epitomized by the AKP party of Turkey, and by Nada Debs, the Beirut designer who combines Japan and Arabia into a new fusion that makes poetic, universal sense.

167

East and West are often used as if they were mutually exclusive categories – static and eternal. There is, however, one city where you quickly learn to mistrust the two concepts. In Istanbul, you understand, perhaps not intellectually but intuitively, that East and West are ultimately imaginary ideas, ones that can be de-imagined and reimagined.[37]

Elif Shafak, who wrote these words, is a Turkish novelist, born in France, raised jointly by her modernist diplomat mother and her traditional, religious grandmother. Shafak writes her novels by a process of "commuting between languages"; a typical book would be written first in English, then translated into Turkish. She then corrects this translation, and from that goes back and corrects the English version. Shafak is fond of quoting a saying of Rumi that one should be like a compass, with one leg rooted in the local, and another traversing a broad circle of the universal. And this mixing of languages is more than a stylistic device:

> I believe in the depth and beauty of syntheses. When I am writing fiction, I like to combine the heritage of women and the oral culture with the foundations of written culture, which is more male-dominated. In a similar way, I like to combine Eastern and Middle Eastern techniques of storytelling with Western literary styles.

That kind of synthesis is the subject of this chapter. Many of those featured do have a foot in several cultures; and not necessarily only West and East. But before we explore their work, we need to pause to understand what these syntheses are *for*.

In postmodern art, we are used to creation without any purpose or meaning – rather that clashing combinations are being used for effect, or out of irony and distance. The overriding message being "take your pick and mix". Academics Georg Stauth and Bryan Turner (1988) wrote this about the postmodern condition:

> Since we live in a world of mere perspectives, the absence of stability in ethics and values results in a certain loss of direction which in turn leads to pessimism, disenchantment and melancholy. The world has become unhomelike, because we have lost all naivety and all certainty in values... a collective sense of homelessness.[38]

The creators in this chapter do not share this homeless worldview. They do still have roots. They are committed to both the truth of their traditions and the new realities they have to face. This implies a positive role and meaning of the syntheses: *Revitalization* (a term from anthropology) meaning a deliberate, organized and conscious effort by members of a group to recreate their shared culture.

The point of syntheses within a revitalization process is to join old symbols and customs to new lifestyles. The result is liveable because it has continuity with existing culture; that vast rambling storehouse of heritage, habits, symbols, recipes, power words, rules of thumb, motifs... And workable because it is adapted to new challenges and opportunities arising from the current environment. Revitalization places these *Made With* brands as first sketches of a possible future; as symbols of *becoming* rather than just adaptation. It is not about outside cultures learning to fit the West, or trying to catch up, but rather being able to lead beyond the West in a new direction.

Let's head now to Istanbul, the city Shafak evokes as a kind of cosmopolitan crossroads of all humanity. The first person I met there on a recent trip was Haluk Sicimoğlu, strategist at advertising agency Alice BBDO and co-author of a series of reports on *The Mind of Turkey.*

169

You don't have to Westernize, you just want to be modern. You can enjoy the merits of life, the high standards, but still be a Muslim. You don't want the lifestyle of the West, just its comforts.

Sicimoğlu was recounting to me the narrative he felt had made the current AKP Turkish government so popular and successful. And he told me "when people hear that, they relax; become more comfortable and open-minded".

The AKP is an Islamist party, a close relative of the Muslim Brotherhood. The Prime Minister's wife wears a hijab (in a country previously so secularized that wearing a veil was banned in university and in parliament). The AKP is not remotely reticent about speaking out for religious traditions and the glorious heritage of Turkey's Ottoman past. And yet this government brought ten years of stability, creating the base for an economic boom. Haluk Sicimoğlu told me that their synthesis involved more than just resolving the tradition vs. modernity split. The Muslim world, Haluk told me, was in quite a confused state; "trying to find ways of dealing with consumerist culture and fate – how the two can go together". But he said that Turkey was learning very fast how to survive and "compete as a soft power within a modern capitalist world".

Another key dichotomy where the AKP's best of both worlds narrative played out, Haluk told me, was that between individual and collective. In developing countries and especially in the Muslim world, he told me, family and community are central; "we are very much a 'we' people". Hence you live among the lives of those around you, you are expected to help each other, and that's seen as just the way of life. There is also a very paternalistic culture, with men as the head of households, and organizations like families tending to have a patriarch who should be obeyed. "But," Sicimoğlu pointed out, "that has to be juxtaposed with every human being's need for individualism, and for an individual identity." And the opportunities for individuals to develop and thrive had tended in the past to be quite limited; "whether in sport, in your profession, in a passion or hobby: there hadn't been the sort of infrastructure for people to learn, develop, grow, try things for themselves". And so while Turkey was very adequate in providing all the basic needs of food, shelter, community, security, when it came to self-actualization, then the problems began. This is where the AKP party and also Muslim civil organizations like Fethullah Gülen had been so strikingly successful in playing what Haluk described as "a new chord" – by weaving a different story between self and others:

> You have a great potential, you could be a great lawyer, doctor. I know you are working hard but there is no-one holding your hand – it is up to you to grow and excel but with our path the community will support you – the community that you thought could hold you back will actually prove the best path to self-actualization.

Sicimoğlu told me that while constantly reassuring the people about continuity of traditions, the AKP party in government (now they had been in power for ten years) had become adept at scanning international policies and models and picking out the pieces that would work in Turkey. And at avoiding imposing any Western models that could jar. Also, the government itself was so relentlessly hard-working that even its critics could see that it was struggling to deliver on its promise of a strong community to empower individuals. This was an impression reinforced by senior members of the government coming not from intellectual elites, but from the heart of the country.

A concrete example of this political narrative in action is the FATIH project, bringing 21st-century IT to every schoolchild in Turkey. The acronym stands for Movement to Increase Opportunities and Technology (F.A.T.I.H. in Turkish). But, as every Turkish schoolchild would hopefully also know, Fatih was the name of the conqueror of

171

Constantinople (now Istanbul) and hence the founder of the Turkish Empire. Prime Minister Erdogan spoke at an inauguration ceremony to mark the delivery of the first computer tablets at a school in Ankara:

> As Fatih Sultan Mehmet ended the Middle Ages and started a new era with the conquering of Istanbul in 1453, today we ended a dark age in education and started a new era, an era of information technology in Turkish education, with the FATIH project.

The project will cost billions and aims at the elimination of textbooks, in favour of digital texts. As well as computer tablets for every schoolchild, the programme will include digital whiteboards in 570,000 classrooms and regional teleconference facilities, to help educate the educators. It's a big cost, but also an investment in the Turkish economy. Firstly, these electronics supply contracts will also provide a huge stimulus for the Turkish manufacturers. And secondly, it stands to create a level of computer literacy and competence in the workforce to rival other leading IT nations.

Serdar Erener, Turkey's most famous advertising creative, founded Alametifarika, the biggest independent ad agency. He is also a leading public intellectual. Erener was intrigued by my book. He told me that the Turks in general did not regard themselves as part of a broader region. Yet in his experience, they had much in common with places like Egypt, Lebanon and North Africa and "any place the Ottoman Empire tried to rule". Erener comes from a family steeped in religious tradition – some of his ancestors having shrines and museums devoted to them – but his father was a staunch secular modernist, a dogmatic Republican lawyer who sent his son to the American school. Serdar quoted a Persian poet to illustrate his position: "I am not within time exactly, nor out of time either". He said that today he feels very much in touch with his traditions, and at the same time totally removed from them. And it's this dual perspective, he thinks, that has been helpful in producing advertising that touches a nerve. The key contribution he feels that he and a group of others have made is in changing the underlying presumption that the advertising in Turkey is based upon:

> Before us, the ad style in Istanbul was quite pretentious. It represented the world view of a pro-West cultural business elite who think Turkish people should look the way that people look in their commercials. What we did was put the real face of Turkey into our advertising; folk people, women with veils, Kurdish kids, people who speak broken Turkish.

While tapping into folk culture, Erener's agency is also committed to creating instant fame and modern appeal for its clients; as with its Pepsi commercials, featuring a famous transvestite singer. I was intrigued to know how that had come about.

Serdar said that Pepsi adverts in the past had featured American style pop stars drinking from little glass bottles and cans. Whereas the reality was that Pepsi was bought in huge supermarket multipacks of large plastic bottles, by housewives that wear veils (as 70% of women in the country do). So it needed a bridge, a way to connect with people. It was never going to be "local" but it could be populist.

Pepsi had lost ground thanks to a previous client of Erener's agency – Cola Turka (the local challenger). This had hit a popular note of what Erener called "positive nationalism". Their commercials featured American actor Chevy Chase, who every time he sipped Cola Turka would speak Turkish, break into a Turkish children's song from the 1930s, or start eating doner kebabs. In one ad, Chevy Chase even sprouted a bushy (typically Turkish) moustache. Quoted at the time, Erener had said, "You are drinking America, rather than a soda". These ads were controversial because they aired in 2003, the time of the

Iraq war, and there had been clashes at the border between American and Turkish troops. Cola Turka belongs to Ulker, a multibillion confectionary company that exports to over 100 countries and recently purchased Godiva. The founder Murat Ulker was a pious, frugal and hard-working Muslim famous for his incredibly fair, trustworthy and generous dealing with partners, suppliers and even rivals. His hard-working family went on to build an efficient distribution network and a dynamic modern FMCG company. They certainly had the resources and reputation to mount a challenge in the local soft drinks market. And it worked. Cola Turka made a serious dent in Coca-Cola (who were reported to have dropped their prices by 10% in response). But it was Pepsi that most lost share and position. Little wonder that eight years later, Pepsi would go to Erener to see if he could work his magic and help them regain relevance in Turkey.

Alametifarika's first campaign for Pepsi had featured Seda Sayan, singer and TV personality, who Erener told me was the Turkish equivalent of Oprah Winfrey. Sayan, blond and bubbly and dressed in a Pepsi-branded uniform, travelled through the back streets and villages of Turkey, driving a Pepsi truck and giving away money and mobile airtime minutes while singing the catchy tune "Pepsi makes your day". The campaign continued in a similar vein the next year, with popular actor Kenan Imirzaliogu, who was later joined by actress Hulya Avsar. The campaign toed the line between tradition (holding a Ramadan dinner with friends) and modernity (giving away Toyota cars). For the next phase of the campaign, Erener and his local Pepsi client had been keen to use a famous Turkish-Kurd folk singer. A strong statement indeed, given that music with Kurdish lyrics had in the past been banned in Turkey. It was Recip Tayyip Erdogan, the Prime Minister, in a gesture of unity and reconciliation, who had overturned the Turkish government's 30-year campaign to obliterate Kurdish language, television, literature and music. The American parent company at Pepsi, however, blocked this casting choice because the singer, although respectable today, had in his past gained a criminal record. The local Pepsi team were outraged at this interference and urged Erdogan and his team to find someone else who would be as scandalous, progressive and populist. Hence Azra. A glamorous classical Ottoman-style singer. Exiled to Germany by a previous military government. And incidentally, Turkey's most famous transvestite. When the campaign broke, it created a huge stir, with its risqué running gag of the three naïve boys next door who keep popping round for Azra's help and advice because (apart from being stricken by her beauty and sex appeal) they have run out of Pepsi, or mobile minutes.

Erener told me that in recent years, things had been changing fast in Turkey. Nowadays his "folksy, street life" style of advertising was not a new thing anymore because it was widely imitated, in execution if not entirely in spirit. He said that the Muslim sensibility once under political repression – labelled "Fundamentalist" – was now free to become mainstream. While from the outside it might look like Turkey was enjoying an economic boom, from the inside it was much more of cultural shift. Erener described the effects as being like "a nation coming to its senses and realizing who we are. No-one even knows where this will lead".

Serdar Erener had recently been asked by some financiers from the West what was going to happen. And Erener had told them: "Expect a future that is more modern, and more Muslim." As he explained:

It's really similar to my own position, because the Muslim tradition has no objection to salesmanship. In fact, it promotes it very strongly. The Prophet himself was originally a merchant. And doing business in a good way, working as hard as you can, is seen as a virtue. People forget that while Muslims put their faith in God, they are not fatalistic, but rather that they do so under a principle which says: you work

175

very hard and you do everything you can; and then and only then do you leave the rest to God.

Serdar Erener showed me an article he had been reading that day by a friend of his. It was about the rise of a new bourgeoisie. Contrary to the expectations raised by phrases like "New Middle Class" in Western books about the developing Islamic world, they happened also to be rooted firmly in traditions. Erener contrasted this with the old elite who had been brought up with a Western education, who still constantly read, watched and slavishly followed whatever intellectual fashion happened to be in vogue in the West. And yet the new elite was also modern and modernizing. The author of the article, for instance, was a woman who headed a national business association.

Erener told me that the former pro-West elite still accounted for the majority of those who I would meet in the ad industry.

You will hardly find anybody who is unbiased about our Prime Minister. I am probably still the only person who has openly declared what good the governing party has done for this country in last ten years.

And Serdar Erener told me that their opposition, as if expecting a return to the old days, was probably a mistake. Erener told me that the new establishment – in perfect rapport with the values and aspirations of the majority – was by now so established that the elite minority would have to start to get the message. "It's like in Tahir Square, when they held up the sign saying GAME OVER."

The situation in Egypt was similar, he told me. Despite all the controversy in the media, 56% had said yes to the constitution. The only opposition was from Cairo where the majority said no. He told me that there was a similar opposition between the cities (Istanbul, Ankara and Ismir) where a Westernized lifestyle was more prominent, and here you get vocal opposition to the government. Whereas in the rest of the country "you will see no opposition in terms of cultural values and what governs people's lives". Erener told me he was planning to shoot a video to make this point, by filming a crowded street, but then digitally replacing the head of every man and woman with that of Mr & Mrs Erdogan.

Serdar told me that he still meets opposition to this point of view, not only in his industry, but among Westernized clients. He told me of a recent client (a microcredit organization) request that at least 50% of the women featured in their recent publicity materials were unveiled. The national average said it should be only 33% unveiled. And in terms of the (rural, poor) population who would be likely recipients of microcredit loans, it would probably be more like 1%. The politics of representation in such advertising are always fraught, because there is a balance between perpetuating stereotypes and also presenting images that appeal to the donor or supporter population. But Erener has a point; if nearly all your rural poor client population wear veils, it is strange to hide this. His advertising for years has – in contrast with the Westernized prejudices – been trying to show life as it actually is, veils and all.

Not that walking this line between traditions and modernity was always easy. The Pepsi account had been "realigned" by the global brand owner, he assumed (besides the political machinations of the international agency group) because the campaign featuring Azra, the transvestite Ottoman singer, was seen as going a bit too far. It is interesting that what was deemed perfectly acceptable in the paradoxical traditional-yet-modern Turkey, might be blocked by a more conservative American corporation.

Erener felt that the real debate among a generation experiencing such rapid change was about "how to be a good Muslim when facing a shopping mall civilization. Do we really want to define ourselves through Jeep Cherokees and Prada?" While the debate between the

Republican nationalist secular elite and the new guard was effectively long over, the new elite had yet to fully work out its own identity. And that was where the symbols and signals of his work could play a role.

In Turkey, outside the world of dotcoms and ad agencies with trendy offices, there has been a phenomenal rise of more traditional Anatolian entrepreneurs – an example of the new establishment Erener was describing. Covering this story, the BBC interviewed entrepreneurs from Keyseri in Anatolia – an "Islamic heartland" whose population tended to be devout, conservative Muslims. The BBC interviewed the former mayor, Sukru Karatepe:

> People in Kayseri also don't spend money unnecessarily. They work hard, they pride themselves on saving money. Then they invest it and make more money. In fact, in Kayseri, working hard is a form of worship. For them, religion is all about the here and now, not the next life. Making money is a sign of God's approval, and this is also similar to what Weber said about the Calvinists.[39]

Gerlad Knaus of the *European Stability Initiative* think tank, who produced a report on these so-called *Islamic Calvanists*, told the BBC:

> Those doing business in Kayseri themselves argue that Islam encourages them to be entrepreneurial. They quote passages from the Quran and from the sayings of the Prophet Muhammad, which read like a business manual. They tell me it's important to create factories, to create jobs – it's what our religion tells us to do.[40]

This thoroughly modernist and entrepreneurial and, at the same time, religious traditionalist spirit is very close to the heart of the Turkish AKP ruling party. As the Deputy Prime Minister, Abdullah

Gul (himself an Anatolian) explained to the BBC:

> The most important thing to ask is what kind of modernism do we want? Are you living in this world, or are you dreaming? The people in Kayseri are not dreaming – they are realistic, and that's the kind of Islam we need. They go to the mosque, they lead pious lives, but at the same time they are very active economically. This is what modernism means to me.

Turkey sees this as a unique national development, but the same Islamic work ethic will be familiar to anyone who has close contact with the waves of immigrant Muslim entrepreneurs that settled in Europe from South East Asia and Sub-Saharan Africa. A classic paper in the *Journal of Psychology* by Abbas Ali also found a similar work ethic in Arab countries, which he defined through a basket of 17 key attitudes that are quite evocative (and seem relevant to numerous case studies in this book):

Islamic Work Ethic Scale (from Ali, 1992[41])

1. Laziness is a vice
2. Dedication to work is a virtue
3. Good work benefits both one's self and others
4. Justice and generosity in the work place are necessary conditions for society's welfare
5. Producing more than enough to meet one's needs contributes to the prosperity of society as a whole
6. One should carry work out to the best of one's ability
7. Work is not an end in itself but a means to foster personal growth and social relations
8. Life has no meaning without work
9. More leisure time is good for society
10. Human relations should be emphasized and encouraged

11. Work enables man to control nature
12. Creative work is a source of happiness and accomplishment
13. Any person who works is more likely to get ahead in life
14. Work gives one the chance to be independent
15. A successful person is the one who meets deadlines at work
16. One should constantly work hard to meet responsibilities
17. The value of work is delivered from the accompanying intention rather than its result

There are two points to note here in passing because they play a big role in this book.

Firstly, joy, happiness and personal development are placed together with work in this scale. The Western image of happiness is that it is found outside work, in escape from work, and that we need to seek a "work-life balance". Meanwhile, the Islamic ethic, while acknowledging the value of leisure time, is also attuned to the happiness, development, fulfilment and joy to be found through achievements within work.

Secondly, the ethical side – working not just for yourself but for "others" and "society" – is central. Not that there aren't also strong explicit ethics within this Islamic tradition of giving something back over and above work. But the integral responsibility to do good work in every sense puts this culture in an advanced position relative to the Western "CSR" as all too often an afterthought.

Back to the theme of cultural fusion, a group of creative industry professionals met up in Dubai for an event in 2012 called *The Lost City of Arabesque*, to discuss the place of Arabic culture in their work. The event was organized by Nuqat, a Kuwait-based organization founded by leading figures in advertising, PR, digital and design, whose aim is to revitalize the local creative industries. The speakers were a mix of local leading lights, plus creatives from across the Middle East and North Africa, and beyond. I wasn't at the event – but thankfully local design blogs were, and I am indebted to their note-taking, especially that of khaleejesque.com whose session-by-session write-up and interviews from the event I have drawn from below.[42]

Nuqat's aim with this event was to bring together the Arab creative community to consider the revival of the lost heritage and artistic forms of Arabesque; not in a nostalgic way, but reinvented to fit with modern lives and identities. As their website explains:

> A culture that is unique, not copied or duplicated from other cultures, a culture that interprets our past, and speaks out in a modern voice, ahead of change.

Twenty-three creatives spoke at the event, representing various disciplines including architecture, interior design, fashion, jewellery, graphic design and typography.

Kameel Hawa is director of the Al Mohtaraf design house with offices in Beirut and Saudi, known most of all as designers of exquisite Arabic fonts such as that used for the redesign of Saudi Newspaper *Al Jazirah*. The agency's recent work also includes brand identity design for ZSL, the Saudi Football League, and naming and branding the Sülaymaniyeni development in the historic centre of Istanbul. In developing the name, the agency combined "yeni" meaning new and Sülaymaniye being the old name for the area – referring to Süleiman the Magnificent. Interviewed at the event, Hawa talked about how modern and Western are not necessarily the same thing:

> Modern culture today is more about the mechanism of human life, rather than the cultural content. One might say that modernity can be summed up as the "worship" of change.

Given this, the task is not just to adopt modernism wholesale but also to tackle some of its dilemmas. Hawa pointed to France and

Italy, which have also attempted to counterbalance the engulfing nature of modernity by cherishing some of their traditional ways of life. The challenge for Arab societies was to step into the modern age, preferably in a way that was unified economically (to match the strength of the EU and other such blocs), but could still be diverse in their cultural contributions. It was all a matter of being open to global influences and tastes, but also valuing your own contributions as "inheritors of a great culture and members of modern society at one and the same time." Hawa spoke about how his own agency, Al Mohtaraf, had taken this duality of cultural authenticity and modern design values into the heart of its work and practice. Although he added that good creative work was never the result of some strategic intent or rational analysis, but "honest, original and enthusiastic practice. We do what we really like, and strongly feel for".

Another speaker at *The Lost City of Arabesque* was Salem Al Qassemi, founder of Fikra, a design studio specializing in bilingual typography and identity creation. Al Qassemi in a talk entitled "Arabish" spoke about the way that numbers and letters were being used on the internet to Arabize. After founding Fikra in 2006, Al Qassemi had worked on several bilingual branding projects; i.e. brand identities that are represented in both Arabic and English. He became fascinated by this bilingualism as a kind of key to the culture of UAE. To explore this subject, he undertook postgraduate research at the Rhode Island School of Design. More recently, Al Qassemi had been working with a think tank to map the collaborative networks between designers in the Arab world. He is also working on the rebranding of the UAE pavilion at the *Venice Biennale*.

Mixing languages in the way Al Qassemi describes (Arabish) has long been a staple of futuristic fiction. In Anthony Burgess's novel *A Clockwork Orange*, the teen subculture had developed a language called "Nadsat", which is peppered with borrowed Russian words as well as creative twists of English slang. Burgess, a keen linguist, would have been fascinated by the emerging culture of 3rabeezy, as Arabish is known among youth in Lebanon and across the Gulf. It is used as a kind of slang in social media and chat rooms – for example, as in this forum post:

al7een a9ln tlagi kl mjmo3a laha 6reegt klam mo3ayyana or words mo3ayyana mn e5tera3hom ... y3ni 7tta fe almkan alwa7id t5tlif feeh al-lahjat...

How this works is a mix of transliteration, where the Arabic and Latin letters have a similar sounding equivalence (for instance aleph and a) and introducing the numbers when there is an Arabic letter with no direct equivalent, for instance the 3 in 3rabeezy is a letter "ayn" (the Arabic letter looks a bit like a 3, only mirrored).

3rabeezy was originally needed in forums like IRC chat that didn't support alternative character sets. But lately it has come into more general usage as an informal way of sending short messages among young people. Because of its very widespread use, Google Translate, Microsoft Maren and other similar tools will automatically convert text written in 3rabeezy into Arabic characters proper. Of course, with this being the way that youth communicates, it has now been incorporated into branding too. For instance, Sami3ny is a mobile phone service that allows people calling you to hear music of your choice in place of the usual boring "ring ring" sound. Sami3ny is slang for "let me hear it".

Another speaker at *The Lost City of Arabesque* whose work explores contemporary re-expressions of Arabic culture was Rana Salam, a designer well known in London for images drawn from her enormous archive of Arabic Pop Art. Her work has featured well beyond Arabish brands – working with Paul Smith, Liberty, Harvey Nichols and Itsu. Salam's signature is her flamboyant, confident, emotional (almost

183

tropical) use of colour. In an interview on a design blog with Sophie Maxwell, Salam said that:

> Despite being in London for over 25 years, and having had my design training in the UK, Beirut and the Middle East still remain a source of inspiration for me in all aspects. This is done when I design, cook and how I feel. Colour is very natural to me, and it's a language I feel speaks stronger than anything. It sets the mood for everything, and therefore it's a valuable tone that I use in my work. Colour is very powerful. It is also an attitude.[43]

At the *Arabesque* conference, Rana told the designers to be more confident about their heritage. That there was a real interest and currency to Middle Eastern-rooted design in the West.

Rana Salam has since returned to Beirut and now faces the challenge of not being the only Arab-accented designer in town. Doubly so, since while Rana was away, her signature style has been much copied; even if she is "the original". In her most recent work, Salam has been exploring the local diversity and specificity of the culture of her client projects. For instance, her designs for Ayamme, a Kuwait restaurant, drew upon research trips to local markets making apparent the influx of cheap, brash, plastic Chinese goods. Salam set out to adapt this global design kitsch:

> The floral design comes from the trays that the Sha'aby use in the streets and markets and we glamorized it for the high-end consumer. But the floral design is a Chinese design and this is what the locals use. And although the Kuwaiti ladies would usually avoid this, I am saying, no, we must celebrate it. We call it Sha'aby Chic.

This touches on a truth at the heart of this book. Many traditional folktales point to the idea that to find something of great value, you have to look in humble places. Cinderella, for instance – from the prince's point of view. That is a creative truth that might be general to emerging markets themselves, of looking to their own roots which may seem humble but offer better foundations than the gleaming West.

One of Salam's collaborations on her return to Beirut was with furniture and interiors designer Nada Debs, who is the perfect example of synthesis, revitalization and brands *Made With* a very different sensibility to those in the West. After a long exchange of emails, and missing each other in Beirut, I finally caught up with Nada Debs on that epitome of modern communication: Skype.

"Islamic design is pure geometry" Nada Debs told me after I explained some of the themes this book was about. "It has nothing to do with the ego. It is about the universal part of being human." Debs readily agreed that this was a tradition of working from the Self, not working from the ego:

> If you look at the tradition, the great designs of the past, nobody knows who actually made all this work. There isn't one name. In the West, you know who the architect was, or that the artist was Da Vinci. Our culture wasn't about ever about the person who made it, it was just the craft.

Nada Debs' own work, she told me, was born out of a fascination with patterns. The more she studied them, the more absorbing and rewarding she found them. Nada told me she is still at an early stage of her apprenticeship with Islamic geometry. For now she is comfortable with simple geometric shapes – with triangles and polygons. As the years and decades go by, she "hopes to progress" to fuller patterns.

The fascination and universality, she told me, had something to do with "having no beginning and no end". And it is also pure synthesis. "It is not about this or that, it is about this *and* that." It was the *and* that fascinated her most. Perhaps because it connected with her own

185

background. She described how she found what was for her:

> ...a personal *Silk Route*. Picking up ideas in the same way as blue and white Chinese porcelain was brought to Istanbul, or learning how to make silk brocades, or the inlay work I use now, and damasks, originally from China and India – all of it part of today what you'd call the Ottoman style, the basis of the furniture of the Ottoman Sultans.

Debs told me that her personal Silk Route had started when she grew up in Japan, where she absorbed a deep sense of minimal purity. Educated in the Rhode Island School of Design in New York, she then absorbed the beauty of functionalism – "you know, like Shaker furniture, nothing irrelevant or decorative in the design". Nada had also absorbed their modernism combining the plastic potential of new materials like Plexiglas, with new ways of working with old materials like metals. Then Nada moved on to England where "all you see is crafts and antiques". By now making her own furniture, Debs started using craft techniques like marquetry, but doing so in a modern way. And then finally she moved back to Lebanon, her home country, and found it awash with emotion and ornament, but also with the Islamic geometry and the very detailed and developed craft.

As she tells it, Nada Debs then just "put it all together in my work". But it can't have been easy to do. On the face of it all, these styles contradict. Furniture is either starkly modernist and functional, or it is florid and ornamented. How can it be both? As Debs' work shows, it can be both and more, but through creating a hybrid that allows the spirit of all to combine.

Nada told me that more than anything what she had come to value was the craft element, working with artisans, the magic they worked with materials. And with this as a kind of anchor, the other accommodations become possible.

I came from a school of thought that said ornament is a big "no no". That it is just a surface element. But then it kept touching me emotionally. People are so attracted to patterns. They have no beginning and end. You get mesmerized. I'm sure there is a scientific background to this. You can take a child and put them in a desert – and they will probably draw circle. A child in the snow in Alaska will do the same. It is the most universal element in a human being.

Being surrounded by and also carrying so many cultures, Nada felt that what she was really doing with patterns was "bringing parts of myself together. It goes deeper than what we see. It's about emotional design". In working with patterns, Debs had held back, taken a minimal line. "I do work with patterns but only as far as going into a polygon – square, circle, triangle. That means I keep it as pure as possible. Then from that I will probably start recreating the shapes, layering them, shadowing, or superimposing."

Debs told me that her company, her first collection and what she thought of as a big part of her ethos was contained in the name: *East and East*. Both Easts she had grown up with – the Arab East and the Japanese East – were very rich within their own culture. And together they represented "a whole side of the globe that was relatively unexplored in the West. At least in a deeper way of (not just picking up an accent) but really deeply understanding from the inside what it meant and how it had evolved".

Nada Debs told me that she liked the explanation of her work given to her by an architecture critic and friend:

In this East, we think about the Afterlife, like the infinite patterns, our souls going to the next world. It's all born out of Islamic philosophy. But when it comes to Japanese Zen philosophy, it's all about the moment. You know that you

187

are going to die. By taking the feeling of both, the infinite and the moment, you can find balance between your heart and your mind.

Debs thought this type of synthesis was "of our times". But she said it wasn't that the universal nature of the work meant that everyone saw it the same way. More that it had something for everyone.

Europeans look at my work as exotic. The Japanese would say it just fits their homes, as it is both rectilinear and organic. In the States, they see it as very practical. Here (in the Arab world) people will emotionally relate to the patterns and through them to their own past.

I put it to her that it was therefore a kind of "design Esperanto" – a combined language designed to have familiar notes for all of its hearers. But she said in a way that the "made-up language" feeling was the kind of problem she was trying to resolve.

It's the whole problem with me, that I needed to relate to everyone. I'm an Arab and I'm Japanese. It was so confusing. Who am I? What's my identity? I found the answer in my work. And became fine with myself. I could be Arab and Japanese at same time.

Nada Debs told me about being in the American school in Japan and being told she was a *Third Culture Kid* – like the children at the school born to mixed-race parents.

If you have more than one culture then you are always seeking to look beyond. Being this and that. "And" rather than "or". That is the whole key. If people accepted this more generally, it would prevent wars. I am just creating work that is representative of the truth of the world which is that only with the best of both, a bit from here and a bit from there, can we ever move forward.

Debs told me that her idea of holistic ways to join opposites had become a more general theme than just *East and East* cultural fusion. For instance, a new piece she was working on was called *Lightness of Being*. This combined a huge concrete slab of a table top with deceptively thin-looking legs and was covered with live materials – wood and mother of pearl inlay – in the shape of butterflies. She was fascinated with the contrast and the fusing of weight and lightness, inert industrial materials and emotional living ones. I told her it sounded more like a poem than a table. But as well as the craft, Debs told me that this kind of design took a lot of work in engineering, pushing the boundaries of materials, exploring new types of resin. So the modernity and tradition fused ran the whole way through the process and the story.

Nada Debs told me that what was most important in her work was the human element. Someone would tell her that there was a new machine that could do some of the inlay work. But she would reply that then "where is the love of a human being? And where will their minds go if they don't have this kind of work to do?" She described watching her craftsmen at work. How although they might be unconscious of it, it was meditative, spiritual. She loved how absorbed and attuned they would be; the way they would focus on something for hours. Nada told me that she felt that this kind of work was healthy for the mind. That the way the Machine Age had taken it away was unacceptable.

We will disappear if we go on like this. That's why the Eastern spirituality has been creeping into the West. Because it is so powerful. And so needed to be human. And craft is a big part of it.

189

As an example, she described a scene from the film *Samsara* where Buddhist monks paint mandalas with powdered inks on the stone floor, in intricate designs. "And then at the end they brush it away. Because it is the process that is important. Not the result." That was the feeling Nada told me that she had, why she loved watching craftspeople work.

This chapter has been about people taking different parts of their own upbringing – none of it "other" or "foreign" to them – and creating new hybrids. The resulting syntheses are more universal. But they also help them and their audiences reconnect with opposites and polarities in more of a spirit of "and" than "or". This requires getting inside the work, absorbing its meaning.

The resulting hybrids can be paradoxical, but are chosen because they work and make sense. I loved the story in an earlier chapter of the AKP party in Turkey scrapping school uniforms; allowing liberal kids to dress more freely, while traditional kids would also be free to dress more conservatively. As Erener says, it is hard to know where this will lead, but there is a sense of the culture working out its identity and its own version of modernity as it goes.

The examples of synthesis are not only serious (in not "taking the piss" but genuinely exploring the power of "and" – and not retreating from emotion). They are also warm, human, authentic, witty – as a design team called Bokja will say in the next chapter, "a smile in the home". In this coming section, we will explore how layers of story and heritage can make experiences and products that have positive humanity (rather than just being less artificial)....

190

> *We will disappear if we go on like this. That's why the Eastern spirituality has been creeping into the West. Because it is so powerful. And so needed to be human. And craft is a big part of it.*

Nada Debs

Craftsman Working on Nada Debs Furniture, photograph by Mansour Dib

REMAKE WITH

Layers of heritage, creating an
archaeology of the future

5. REMAKE WITH

───────────────── /\/\ ─────────────────

Once in a city faraway in the desert, everyone was arguing over who would lead the annual procession. Unfortunately, in the grandparents' day, few records were kept. So when an ancient patriarch had passed away, nobody could agree who was next eldest.

The schoolteacher, who was the daughter of a weaver, had an idea. She got the children to interview all their grandparents about what they could remember from their earliest childhood. They found only one grandmother who remembered being alive during the time of a famous earthquake. So she led the procession that year.

From these stories, the teacher made a tapestry with a map of the city showing the history of its people – so it would never be so disputed again. Visitors used to ask for copies of the map to look around the city. And the teacher would send the children once a year to gather more stories, which would be added to the tapestry.

───────────────── \/\/ ─────────────────

These stories continue the fusion theme and explore how ultra-modern developments are being Made With layers of historical heritage, rather than ripping it up and starting again. The Interland is a treasure chest of heritage; its key cultural resources. We tour the new downtown of Beirut, walking its Heritage Trail with Amira Solh from Solidere. We talk about their "archaeology of the future" with hip lifestyle designers Bokja. And we get a glimpse of the Seven Wonders of the World II (this time it's a theme park) and other amazing edutainment productions from Randa Ayoubi of Rubicon.

Solidere's rebuilding of Beirut is one of the most ambitious plans to reconstruct a landmark city since Christopher Wren's plans for London after the great fire of 1666. Wren's plan was not only to build St Paul's Cathedral and its precinct, but a whole new district, stretching from the Tower of London as far as Blackfriars (the whole site of the current City of London financial district). It was, in modern terms, "a master plan". Wren's plan was geometrical; massive octagons with radiating roads at each end are connected by more conventional grid street plans in-between. Wren's plan comprised piazzas, markets, warehouses and churches. The spirit of the whole master plan was symbolized by the two illustrations on Wren's drawings; the venerable figure of Thamesis (a classical "God of the Thames") indicating continuity, heritage and the inevitable contribution of topography; and the Phoenix indicating a city (literally) rising from the ashes in a new and glorious form. And you know what? Wren's plan looked a lot like Solidere's Downtown Beirut. Similarly geometrical, graced with radiating boulevards, five or six-storey (imposing, but not too imposing) classical buildings that remind you of Paris, via the Ottoman Empire, faced in classic light stone. Perhaps they have this resemblance because it is a similar brief – both working within the constraints of rebuilding a classical city, in a modern style.

I was shown around the Solidere development by Amira Solh, their Cornell-educated senior urban planner. Amira told me her friends in the US would hardly recognize her working for a large corporation, when once she had been their fellow activist on the streets of New York. But Solh, also a film-maker, felt that her day job at Solidere was where she had her best chance to make a difference; contributing to new ways in which the ancient past of a city – and its future – could be reimagined.

Amira Solh was particularly keen to show me around the *Heritage Trail*. The souk that we started in (a modern mall, but with a recognizably classical and open form) was built to conform with the old souk's street plan, dating back to the Roman market that once stood there. There is a preserved Canaanite wall and gate, Roman and Crusader fortifications complete with a moat and remains of an Ottoman citadel. We paused while Amira complained about the Roman pillar laid on Crusader city walls; out of its proper context. She was getting it moved, Amira told me; a stickler for archaeological authenticity.

One ancient attraction that looks to have a lot of potential is some excavated Phoenician Harbour ruins, right under the streets and shops of the souk. We peered in at these remains in their raw state. Amira had also shown me the detailed plans to make this a modern interactive exhibit, the creative proposals being developed by Rem Koolhaus' studio (but yet to be approved or funded). Solidere seems to have its pick of the most creative and innovative global architects. From my part of the world, they are working on new buildings for the North Souk (the next phase of development) with Zaha Hadid and Rogers Stirk Harbour + Partners.

The *Heritage Trail* is annotated by informative posters, printed on huge lava stone slabs ("Ten years of quality in the Mediterranean sun," Sohl told me) and bronze plaques. There is also a walking map. We talked about the potential for virtual architectures to be overlaid on the real ones. I showed Amira some art projects I knew such as the Arne Quinze *Rock Strangers*, which used augmented reality to bring out details (the Statue of Liberty torch being lit) that could only be seen by phone camera. She in turn showed me a massive Arne Quinze statue, right outside her office.

The legibility of the city, the way it discloses its layers of history, strikes me as quite unique. London has some architectural interest and oddities, but you have to find them. Here, a totally new development is being built and layered in a way that integrates them. Not just telling people that once on this site stood so and so, but peeling back the layers of architectural time so that you can walk through the past.

Amira told me that the integration of archaeology with architecture was a result of the nature of the reconstruction. Beirut is one of the oldest cities in continuous use in the world; dating back 5000 years. For most of its history, it was not a capital, but rather a minor seaport serving the capital of the region, which was Damascus. In the 1990s, after the civil

197

war when the centre of Beirut was completely wrecked, it became the largest architectural dig in the world. The city being laid bare like this created an unparalleled opportunity to excavate the underlying remains. Usually, this may happen piecemeal in old cities as new foundations for single developments are dug. But here was an opportunity to excavate and map an entire integrated old city centre, using the latest techniques. As a result of this phase, it was natural to integrate exposed ruins, historic buildings and sites of interest into the master plan.

"The story of Beirut is a story of layers," Amira Sohl told me. "Throughout the whole timeline, each period built on top of the other." And this layered approach is key to the planning of the new centre. Nowhere else in the world, Amira told me, was there this focus on showing the multilayers, integrating the heritage of a city into its present. Amira told me this was a different concept of "historicity; not as a horizontal timeline, but as a vertical one, being able to look at who stood in your footsteps before".

A conceptually central part of the development is the *Garden of Forgiveness* – built on the old Green Line that separated the two sides in the civil war. The concept of a *Garden of Forgiveness* came from the vision of psychotherapist Alexandra Asseily; that lasting peace could not be attained unless the culture was able to commemorate forgiveness, in a concrete way, giving it a place in their collective memory. The *Garden of Forgiveness*, currently under construction, has been designed by award-winning landscape architect Kathryn Gustavson (who created the *Diana Memorial* in London's Hyde Park). It is intended as a place of peace and reflection. But it is also rooted in other times and remains, with at least 15 older civilizations sharing this site. Amira told me that a major intersection in the main Roman street, the *Carda Maximus*, was located here. It is also the location of a Christian shrine and an ancient heart-shaped well, believed to be a site of worship of the Goddess Astarte. It is hence an ancient site of meeting and contemplation. And these historical echoes give the new-built garden a depth of context and feeling which just a bit of "parkland" could never have. There is also a current reminder of the need for peace and reconciliation, in the form of an olive tree planted by three women who lost husbands and sons in the 9/11 attacks in New York. In the neighbouring plot is the tomb of the assassinated Prime Minister Hariri, the man who was widely credited with leading this whole reconstruction. His death united the people and sparked the *Cedar Revolution*, resulting in the withdrawal of Syrian troops from Lebanon (Syria having been held responsible for the assassination) in 2006.

With so much history in one square of this city, how could you not memorialize it? And that act has to be seen within a broader artistic and social effort to archive events from the war, retell its stories and also try to piece together a positive national identity. Creating a shared history that runs much further back than the present conflict and any of the factions is also a way to seed this identity. And it's a bold step to go from being reduced to rubble to such a grand architectural rebirth.

Another foundation of a future shared identity would be creating space for children to come into this city centre (rather than growing up in divided districts). There are many attractions for children and teens, including the *Planet of Discovery*, a museum targeting children with interactive science and technology exhibits. Walking through the souk itself feels like being in Monaco or Cannes, with luxury and designer stores and restaurants reflecting the fact that there is a wealthy population of residents, returning expats and tourists from the Gulf to attract. Beirut is in general a hugely expensive city, where even a coffee costs $7. But the Solidere development is not planned only to cater to people who shop for expensive handbags. Amira told me to boost the visits into the area by younger people, they are about to open 18 cinemas.

The heritage trail is only the visible tip of a much bigger project to create peace, prosperity and community in Beirut through cultural means. *Souk El Tayyeb*, Kamal Mouzawak's farmers market (with the slogan *Make Food Not War*), is currently held in an undeveloped lot in the North Souk. The whole development features a high proportion of public space and attractions, its vision being one of city making, with its mixed use creating a vibrant milieu. A place for living, and not just working or shopping. Solidere has of course faced controversies, compromises and challenges. There are ongoing wrangles over what different religious parties will allow to be said. But in a way, it is all the more admirable for having taken those on board, yet progressing and not becoming a thwarted by the same old conflict.

Amira Solh told me that with the building phases well advanced now, the focus had to be on bringing the community in much more: "Showing that the city is not the divided city it was during the civil war. Encouraging people to come and walk the sidewalks, get them dirty, appropriate the space."

Let's now explore this theme of layered history in a more intimate context, in the company of Beirut designers Hoda Baroudi and Maria Hibri – founders of Bokja, the uber-chic design brand (best known for their chairs, but rapidly extending into "Bokjadizing anything"). The word Bokja comes from old Turkish and is used across the region to mean the heavily embroidered fabric used to cover a bride's dowry. Hence it touches as a theme on the two creators being women, on memory, worldly goods and much besides. Bokja designs are usually made from assemblages of vintage fabrics, often adding another layer of embroidery to give the pieces another dimension and more contemporary edge. While the fabrics may be traditional, the objects that they cover are usually modern in style. An Eames chair picked up in a state of disrepair from a flea market or even a dumpster would be a typical frame. Bokja describe their work as "one-of-a-kind pieces that offer an explosion of colour, pattern and a richly textured sense of history". For Milan fashion week, they covered a VW Beetle. Where did this eclectic mix come from? Partly their backgrounds. Baroudi was a former economist, who collected antique fabrics. Hibri ran a flower shop, with retro furniture on display.

Bokja say that the purpose behind their work is treasuring the textile heritages that have been central to the history of their region, and marrying these with the influences from the West or at least its modernity and today's aesthetics. As the pair explained to an Italian design blog:

> You cannot forget your past and you have to really try to understand it and honour it. We have to move on and moving on is just to adapt. Geographically Lebanon is a recipient of many cultures, there is a richness here. But few people understand the meaning of Lebanon and how it is unless they come here; they will see how the East is open to the West, or actually, how its arms are wide open to the West. Somehow in this country we were able to make the best of both and this is why it is so attractive nowadays, and if we have peace it will be even more attractive.

As if to confirm the point about their arms wide open to the West, the duo's design was picked up by Lidewij Edelkoort (or Li, as she is known), who was named by *Time* magazine as one of the 25 most influential global fashion experts. *Li* made Bokja an example within her 2008 show *Archaeology of the Future*; based on the premise that modernity's idea of a break with the past or clean sheet is a myth and real design innovation comes from recombining and recasting ideas from the past.

Bokja's work is well composed and controlled, and yet witty, exuberant, emotional, vibrantly colourful and as they say "designed to bring a smile to any home". Having seen their work, and read so many of their interviews, I finally tracked down the Bokja studio team to talk about their work. In true Bokja style (a brand that seems to have a life of its own), the following answers were given to me as representing the views of "Bokja" as a whole team. So I will report it that way:

201

John: *You have talked about Bokjadizing as a verb, what is its meaning?*

Bokja: We see Bokjadizing as a way to re-interpret something that already exists, to give it new life and create a new meaning for it. So Bokjadizing is like a new way to see things. It's adding to the overlooked a twist, a sense of humour and even a new life.

John: *Where does your work come from? And is it art or design?*

Bokja: It's Beirut and yet not! We feel we belong to this niche group in design that is a relatively new phenomenon, it's not Western, it's not Oriental. It is a group that subscribes to certain values and aesthetics that are freer and more expressive than what is ordinarily expected of design. It is a trend that has started in the wake of the financial boom of the nineties. People needed to react to the excess and commercialism of that period with going back to the basics, to things that connected with them and made sense. Design had to answer some questions and automatically you had the two worlds merging: art and design. In Beirut in particular, because the urgency was felt more in the wake of the 15 years of war. The excesses of the nineties were more flagrant and contrasted with our tiny tired destroyed bubble. And therefore the need to come up with something different was more crucial. Bokja is the result of that, it is an amalgam of things, it is layers and layers of reacting thoughts. We like to call it social design, an idea that prospered because it answered all the immediate concerns of the moment: sustainability, recycling, social entrepreneurship. All this while putting forward a new aesthetic that is unique and individual. The cherry on the cake was that it also spoke to the cultural and civilized part of people's psyche as it dealt with layers of old traditional and ethnic embroideries from all over. It is an explosive mix that has made an impact and we hope it continues as we do.

John: *Sufi inspiration is referenced in your latest work. Is it a more general backdrop, and where does your inspiration come from in general?*

Bokja: The Sufi inspiration came during a time when the chaos around was growing. We began reaching for the teachings of Sufism as a way to cleanse and beautify ourselves and our work from the inside out. We have always been two, and that's at the very least. We work with artisans, carpenters, designers, there are 14 hands behind every design. Things really get interesting with many different perspectives. We gather and take and source and then we edit. The result is always a surprise, and it's much more interesting that way.

John: *How does your working process of making/creating shape the ideas?*

Bokja: It's constantly mixing and changing and evolving. There is never a definitive end result in mind when things get started. A lot of work is based on intuition, daily inspiration and sometimes whimsy. We also respond a lot to the materials at hand. It's a lot like working on a puzzle, the textiles talk and really dictate the next move.

John: *What are your future plans?*

Bokja: We're thinking big, expanding our product range into a lifestyle brand, more art exhibitions, outdoor installations. We are never at a loss for ideas, we have a lot of passion and really believe in what we are doing.

203

John: *What misconception about your work would you like to correct?*

Bokja: We seem to have become easily known as the company that takes old furniture pieces and reupholsters them. True, that is how we started out, but we have grown so much since then. We are really trying to communicate the stories and ideas behind the pieces now. We have also started to not only reupholster, but redesign the frames of the furniture we work on. But even more than that we are working on installations, artistic exhibitions, collaborations. Not only has Bokja become a verb, but we think it has also become a lifestyle, a distinctive style, or a strong personality. We are making items to complete the story.

John: *If your work could speak, what would it say?*

Bokja: Most importantly we want to communicate the rich history and complexity behind every piece. Everything we make comes with its own passport. These pieces have been places, they have a complex and multi-layered history. But at the same time they are also going places; they start conversations, they cross borders. We sell to countries that some people have never even heard of. There is a cultural barrier being broken with the work we make. While we as Lebanese citizens cannot always be allowed to, our pieces travel the world.

John: *Tell me how your work with Arab Spring and Fall came about.*

Bokja: We like to think that the foundation of our work is built upon connecting, or combining separate ideas, or materials. Our entire artistic installation was inspired by the Arab Spring, we wanted to find our way to interpret and talk about what was happening. By using the materials and techniques we know best, we used our voice, which is strong yet feminine, to offer people a new way to look at the events happening around them.

Arab Seasons, a Bokja exhibit at the *l'Institut du Monde Arabe* in Paris, represented something of a departure, in that the duo are concentrating now more on commissions – i.e. what in the West we would regard as art – while their studio takes forward the more commercial design of furniture and lifestyle products. The centrepiece of the Arab Seasons show and the source of its title was a pair of hanging banners (a traditional format, resembling the European wall tapestry), one representing *Arab Fall* and one *Arab Spring*. Each is a map of the Middle East region.

The *Arab Fall* map is full of references to the era now passing, when the Middle East was nothing but a canvas for Western crass commercial culture. The seas in this map are made from blue jeans, while the country-sized fabric cuts hold a rich and clashing set of stereotyped images including petrol for Saudi, camels, Aladdin's genie (holding a packet of French fries). Most eye-catching of all is a flying elephant, based on a linguistic pun (in Lebanese "flying elephant" means a lie or exaggeration, especially in politics) referring, as Bokja said, both to the duping of the citizenry and to their subjection to an inundation of inane slogans and plasticized culture.

In contrast, the *Arab Spring* map covers the same geography more hopefully. The sea is a destroyed Persian carpet (a heritage that has to be the start of moving on). And the images representing countries are more hopeful and progressive. Saudi is represented by a woman riding a horse. Perhaps this is referring to the activist women in Saudi who are driving cars and posting their pictures on Facebook. Or maybe to the ladies of the early history of Islam who fought alongside the men in battle? The overall effect of these maps is thought-provoking; far from political, dogmatic or lecturing; but rather light, funny and slightly crazy.

What artists and creatives do is not simply react to events, or package them like the news, but digest them, rework them, force us to experience and consider them from a much more subjective, insider viewpoint. The story *Arab Seasons* told also suggests that finding a replacement for imposed brands from the West is a key dimension of the broader *Arab Awakening*. It also cleverly gave the *Arab Spring* term a whole new richness of meaning, by contrasting it with an *Arab Fall*.

As Maria Hibri of Bokja once put it (in an interview with *Brown Book* magazine):

> Being from this area of the world, you have so many things inside yourself you want to express.

It is all about lightness of touch. In 2005, they made a collection that responded to the anti-Syrian demonstrations. A key to this was when and how they would engage. As Baroudi told Beirut newspaper *The Daily Star*: "As long as it was a social movement we engaged in it, but once it became political, we backed out."

Where Western brands are based upon Cartesian (either-or) distinctions, Made With brands like Bokja revel in the power of "and". Bokja's core creative operation is this "and" – the juxtaposition of modern furniture shapes with traditional embroidery, of pieces of textile that contrast and together weave a story. Sometimes there are other layers of meaning too; like a recent series of "fairy tales" (featuring a hijabi red riding hood in Japanese manga-style illustrations).

The original idea was to take the embroideries that they loved from their childhood and, by presenting them in an edgy, contemporary way, make them appealing to new generations; make them edgy and sexy. To treasure the past, but in a way that revitalizes the present. Bokja point out that fabrics more than perhaps any other medium do encode and carry the traditions and heritage of times and regions.

And that Beirut, like their work, is layered with so many civilizations and their stories; Phoenicians, Romans, Byzantines, Arabs, Crusaders, Arabs again, Turks, French....

Along with the functional mingling of fabrics, the attitude is so important. This is not some Western postmodern collage, designed to shock and clash. The emotion that goes with this "and" is love. As Tunisian film director Nacer Khemir explains about the Arabic letter "Waw" (which in Arabic also means "and"):

> The Sufis call it the letter of Love, because without it, nothing can come together. We say "the sea and the sky", "man and woman". The "Waw" is the meeting place, thus it is the place of Love. It is also the letter of the traveller, because it gathers together things and beings.[46]

Clearly it is also the letter of Bokja too. And their latest exhibition in Dubai in March 2013 was based upon the *Sufi Seven Stages of the Heart*. As the Bokja blog explains:

> This collection is rooted in Sufi teaching and, through the creative application of fabrics to seven of Nochi's iconic iron chairs, the installation illustrates the journey from the material to the spiritual. Each upholstered chair represents a stage in the journey of life – to shed oneself of all material possessions and earthly desires. When thinking about the impact of recent events in our region of the world, we found ourselves looking inwards, trying to make sense of things. Intuitively we were drawn to the words and teachings of Sufism to help us understand, spiritually, what has been happening.

Like the legible city of central Beirut, the annotation of Bokja's work, the way they ensure its meanings, histories, components are understood is very important to them. Each piece that they sell, as they mentioned in my interview, comes with a "passport", explaining the origins of its constituent parts.

Our next subject is also a stickler for creating content that enriches people's knowledge and outlook. Randa Ayoubi, CEO of Rubicon, a former E&Y Entrepreneur of the Year, was also named Middle East Businesswoman of the Year in 2010. Randa Ayoubi's Jordan-based company Rubicon produces animation and other content, and her watchword is "edutainment". As she told Ernst & Young's *Exceptional* magazine:

> You will never find a Rubicon product that is anti-culture, anti-religion or violent, or that doesn't promote tolerance. It is entertainment with a purpose – we call this edutainment.

Rubicon is perhaps best known in the world of entertainment for taking on global franchises and giving them a new richness and depth. Not just in a preachy, teachy way. But within catchy, funny comedy that kids love to watch. Their *Pink Panther and Pals* remake of a classic series won four Kidscreen awards in New York, including Best Animated Show for Preschool, and the Preschool Viewers' Award. Launching soon is their *Postman Pat* 3D movie. These represent the kind of gentle, mind-nourishing, good old-fashioned storytelling that any parent would want their kids to grow up on. They also represent the cutting edge of animation production which Ayoubi says people are sometimes surprised to hear is made in Amman, Jordan, rather than Los Angeles (although they have facilities there too).

More overtly in line with her vision of "moulding young minds" was Rubicon's breakthrough show, *Ben and Izzy*. Ayoubi told newspaper *The National* that "September 11 happened and I felt obliged to mesh the original idea – of two cultures meeting – with what was happening in the rest of the world."

The premise of *Ben and Izzy* is that an American kid called Ben and a Jordanian kid called Izzy learn to overcome their cultural differences. Ben was described in the show's publicity materials as "a symbol for his country", "big", "energetic", "on the negative side, he is a bit xenophobic, self-centred, needs-to-win competitive". And "like his native land, he sometimes blunders into situations without thinking". Izzy by contrast is "slight of build, sinewy and studious", but "can be a little too serious, self-righteous, superior, even devious". The two initially fight, but later learn to be a team.

The show won the support and funding of the Jordanian royal family. American producer of *Family Guy*, David Pritchard, was drafted in and he described how during the development of the show he met occasionally with the King. His main advice though, Pritchard told the *New York Times*, was "make sure it's funny". The show was a creative and commercial success, and importantly for Rubicon led to a series of further partnerships with MGM.

Rubicon is an important example of how challengers from emerging markets can find a niche USP. In their case, a blended value proposition; with studios in Los Angeles, Amman and also the Philippines to get the best in state-of-the-art animation, but also a compelling price point. "As a value chain, we capitalize on the best output," Ayoubi told EY on the occasion of her Entrepreneur of the Year award. "We are cheaper than the West, although more expensive than the Far East. The model is sustainable because we offer quality, not quantity."

Interviewed about her vision, Ayoubi has talked about wanting to contribute to an *Arab Renaissance*. And this seems especially relevant now that the company is also programming the content of an educational theme park. And this is where their edutainment approach has brought them right into the same territory as Solidere, finding new ways to reconnect with the past.

Rubicon led the initial conceptual design of the Red Sea Astrarium, a 184-acre educational theme park celebrating both the heritage of the region and culminating in futuristic attractions including (as part of its role as an Astrarium) a *Star Trek* experience. The educational contents of the park will include a Wonders of the Ancient World tour and content from the American Natural History museum's *Silk Road* exhibition. The theme park will also use innovative technologies, such as spherical domes filled with projections. It also includes luxury hotels, botanical gardens and some state-of-the-art roller-coasters within the $1.5 billion development.

Umberto Eco described Disneyland as the epitome of how America had lost touch with reality; invented, Eco joked, to make the rest of America seem real by comparison. This Red Sea theme park seems designed to have the opposite effect – to add richness and depth to your own appreciation of the region around it.

What all of Solidere, Bokja and Rubicon exemplify is some shared assumptions and ideas about the role of the past in creating a shared future.

Their starting point is that culture is ideally supposed to be for the public good – that entertainment and consumerism are only components. Secondly, that the way past the "fast-food" version of culture is to also provide experiences which are more cognitively and culturally healthy, natural and "nutritious". Thirdly, that it is the combination of the two – what some call edutainment – that ensures both popular (not elitist) appeal and effective engagement. In this, storytelling is key; weaving a narrative through the experience is how you are able to bring other layers, of learning, understanding, empathizing, reflecting.

When applied to brands, this is the difference between buying something for ego reasons like status, social currency and aspiration, and buying something you appreciate deeply, through a kind of connoisseurship. Appreciation doesn't have to be elitist either (there are connoisseur communities for jazz, comics, even LEGO).

There are parallels with "pre-modern" brands; food and drink labels often being built on provenance, knowledge, artisanal processes (with the modern branded alternatives appearing "cheap" by comparison). But it is not to say this is a "falling behind". Rather that most culture progress takes a step back and two steps forward. That when we find a line of progress is blocked, then we need to step back a few generations to the last time things worked better, before taking that forward.

Another key theme is that the modernity that makes a design or place relevant and appealing today does not have to start with a "blank slate", obliterating the past. Rather that it can only be fully meaningful and authentic if it has continuity, selectively reworking human traditions.

Developments like the Red Sea Astrarium, along with whole complexes of museums and cultural attractions being built by Abu Dhabi and Qatar, could begin to become emblematic of a new Middle East; characterized not by superficial glitz and consumerism, but by a cultured, civilized and deeply rooted (if thoroughly modern) approach – one that makes the West start to look shallow.

Examples across this chapter are *Made With* a living connection to the heritage, the past continuing in the present. And not just out of respect, familiarity and habit. But because, in the words of the trends forecaster Li, it is the *Archaeology of the Future*.

The project of reclaiming history is what any culture experiencing surging growth and new confidence will always do. The Chinese have entertained the world for the last decade or two with lavish epic movies about their golden ages. The oil and gas-rich Arab states are now building museums of Islamic art and culture. And one group in Qatar has funded the development and production of a movie about the life of the Prophet Mohammed with a reported budget of $1 billion.

The importance of encountering layers of history is that it makes your environment legible. The uprooted communities that were once moved into modernist tower blocks lost the crisscrossing community ties that distinguish authentic from artificial urban developments. And they lost something of their soul, the feeling of being at home because you live among the ancestors. Quite a few of those I interviewed who had returned from the West did so not because there were better jobs and prospects at home, but because of this feeling that they get in Istanbul or Cairo, that it wasn't "born yesterday". They had felt a kind of restlessness in places like California where the oldest building is barely from their great grandmother's time.

Anyone who travels the world and goes beyond the Western hotel or backpacker loaded trains will tell you that there are two whopping big mistakes in the current Western worldview. Firstly, it is not a small world. It is a VAST world. Unimaginably big, and varied, and teeming with cultural, geographic and natural biodiversity. Despite our growing knowledge of the space outside our atmosphere, this may very well be it as far as humanity goes – the ultimate expanse we will ever meaningful know. Secondly, the same goes for our lifetimes. Life isn't short. There are only 600 human generations stretching back to the invention of farming. You have number 601 and you have so much more to draw upon than the last 600. But that means the here and now, of our own lifetimes, at so many turning points in human history, is not fleeting. If you see yourself from the outside as a little ego – like an object or doll – then of course you are born, work, marry, have kids, retire and die. But if you look at the world from the centre of yourself and see what's around you, like a child does, like a good poet does, then you will find the space and time to operate.

That is the real point about living with a layered awareness of time. It gives us a broader perspective. Everything in this chapter is hence like an antidote to the ego centre perspective of Western culture. It gives a broader view.

Now we turn from history to history in the making – with the (often internet-enabled) trends that make the idea of "emerging" markets doubly meaningful....

It's Beirut and yet not! We feel we belong to this niche group in design that is a relatively new phenomenon, it's not Western, it's not Oriental. It is a group that subscribes to certain values and aesthetics that are freer and more expressive than what is ordinarily expected of design.

Bokja

Loveboat chair by Bokja. photograph & permission supplied by Bokja Design

EMERGE WITH

The power of networks to create
awareness, movements, change

6. EMERGE WITH

———————————— M ————————————

Once in a city faraway in the desert, business had been going so well that all was actually not well. There was such a problem with crowding and congestion at the great covered bazaar that people – the rumours said – were starting to stay away.

Some of the elders went up on a roof to take in the situation. One pointed out that the four gates at each corner were where the blockages happened. Another suggested it was made worse by people trying to come in to catch early bargains, just as porters and donkeys were heading out after deliveries. A third said it was not so bad queuing, it was when people lost their patience and tried to push in that it went wrong.

"I've got it!" exclaimed Nasruddin, the local wit. And he rushed off.

The next day, the market crowds flowed perfectly. All that had changed were four brightly painted signs by the four gates. The first said, "ONLY A FOOL WOULD ENTER HERE!" The second, "PEOPLE WITH MANNERS ARE MOST WELCOME TO ENTER HERE." The third said, "DONKEYS AND CHILDREN ONLY." And the fourth, "THIS GATE IS RESERVED FOR NASRUDDIN."

Now that entrances, exits and trade routes were so clearly marked, the crowds moved easily. Except at Nasruddin's Gate, where nobody minded the crush at all as it was clearly another one of Nasruddin's excellent practical jokes.

———————————— W ————————————

These stories are about communities and movements Made With *a real sense of participation. It's about emergent social processes with creativity, spirit, camaraderie and joy – and an openness to new ideas that emerge at that level. Case stories include a Syrian activist who explains why humour was the key weapon in the Arab Spring; Burak Arikan, an MIT-educated Turkish artist, whose medium is digital networks; and some founders of the hip Hijabi fashion scene in Indonesia that went from a small social group to burgeoning global community, thanks partly to online and mobile platforms.*

Libya, according to BBC news, has "a new love affair with ice cream". Before the revolution, there were only a handful of Italian style gelato shops in the capital Tripoli. But now, the BBC reports, "gelato shops have been opening up in almost every busy street – with names such as *Buenissimo*, *Limona* and *Gilati Italia*". The founders told the BBC it was a product of the revolution, of wanting to celebrate a new culture of freedom, to mark a new phase in the country's collective history:

> "There's a market for it here... Libyans are proud of things like this because we didn't have it before," Hussein Bannour, Buenissimo.

> "After the revolution, many guys wanted to open up Libya – the new Libya – with new shops and new cafes," Ruweida al-Rayes, Gilati Italia.

It also helps that Libya had strong ties with Italy. And that the population has a sweet tooth. But this new "love affair" is an example of how the new freedoms brought by social change can find unexpected expressions that just "emerge" and make emotional sense.

What is this social change? It seems to have something to do with being "swept up". Dr. Ammar Alani, a prominent Syrian activist, told Aspenia Online[49] that:

> I was never an activist myself until the social media phenomenon came along, so the definition is changing to include me, a film-maker and musician who has never been involved in any political or social activity in his life.

Alani says that this new phenomenon needs to be separated from the top-down organizations like trade unions, political parties and governments. It starts when one "e-nabled" citizen is able to connect with another, e-nabled to share, to become active. The communities that this creates are something quite new – "a new breed of citizenship". Within this freely associating community of e-nabled citizens, Dr. Alani describes creativity and humour as a "weapon". As he explains:

> The regimes in the Arab world are dictatorships we inherited from the previous century.... And while they can claim supremacy in force, finance and media ownership, the one thing they definitely cannot offer is creativity, freedom and innovation. That is why the young generation is using these specific tools to alter the rules of the game, leaving the regimes unable to keep pace, at least in terms of winning the audience.

Alani went on to give numerous examples from Syria. Including:
- Protestors marching carrying blank signs, so that when the armed forces broke up demonstrations they were made to look very foolish on the news
- Protestors responding to accusations from State media that they were being paid to demonstrate, by carrying signs offering their services for sale
- A village in the middle of nowhere called Kafranbel that published weekly slogans on Facebook, holding up signs that were photographed, for instance:
  Forgive me my love; I mentioned your name in the interrogation.

Dr. Alani cites this last example as showing how in social media people cross a line, no longer passive consumers of information, instead becoming participants, even sources. He said that traditional media by contrast seemed to be (in the words of another slogan) "aiming for zero credibility". People could now check what everyone was thinking more directly. Hence public opinion was increasingly being shaped online, rather than by broadcast traditional channels.

Western reports on social media's role in the Arab Spring have tended to look for linear cause and effects. So that the mass media incautiously rushed in and declared these to be "Twitter Revolutions". And they focused reporting on figures like Wael Ghonim, a Google employee and the (then anonymous) blogger who had first posted a suggestion to protest on 25th January (originally his idea was to hold an ironic Celebrating Egypt's Police Day). Wael Ghonim became a key figure in Egyptian media after crying during a TV interview when just released from 12 days in prison and shown footage of protestors who had been killed. Ghonim was hailed in the West as an icon of the revolution, despite his protestation that he certainly wasn't any kind of leader, having spent the build-up to the uprisings blogging safely from Dubai, and most of the actual revolution in jail. But Ghonim did believe that the internet played a key role, as he explained to CNN on the day that Mubarak stepped down:

> This revolution started in June 2010 when hundreds of thousands of Egyptians started collaborating content. We would post a video on Facebook that would be shared by 50,000 people on their walls within a few hours. I've always said that if you want to liberate a society, just give them the internet. If you want to have a free society, just give them the internet. The reason why is that the internet helps you fight the media war, which is basically a game that the Egyptian regime were playing very well (in the past) and when the internet came they really couldn't. I plan to write a book called Revolution 2.0 ....[50]

Which indeed he did. Meanwhile, opinions vary in their assessment of the role of social media. A study by the University of Washington looking at the online traffic, in particular that which preceded and built up to events, concluded that social media had played a key secondary role, especially when from cell phones (which was how the majority accessed the internet in this region). Philip Howard commented that:

> Our evidence suggests that social media carried a cascade of messages about freedom and democracy across North Africa and the Middle East, and helped raise expectations for the success of political uprising. People who shared interest in democracy built extensive social networks and organized political action. Social media became a critical part of the toolkit for greater freedom.[51]

Author Hisham Matar, speaking at a UK public debate organized by *The Telegraph*,[52] agreed with some of the gains and tools brought by social media:

> What's really exciting is that it allows a new generation a new way of communicating. It is almost like a new language – it makes them feel empowered in a culture that is very disempowered, politically speaking. In Tunisia and Egypt, I think Facebook and Twitter have created a political discourse that is bypassing the old regime. Political dictatorships take possession not just of money and belongings, but of narrative.

Matar also pointed to the key role of ensuring that there was global coverage of events. He compared this to past uprisings in the Green Mountain area of Libya where away from the Western media's oversight Gaddafi had sent in helicopters and crushed protests. But it was still wrong to call these internet revolutions, he insisted:

> The people who have access and know how to use it are the elite. The Egyptian uprising didn't happen on Facebook

or Twitter because it couldn't have happened without the working classes, and they don't have access to those things. But it allowed the agile, internationalist elite to mobilize and play to the international media. That was very important.

And Matar too stressed that a key component was mobile phones and their cameras, allowing filming and reporting during protests, creating greater transparency and exposure – what London politics professor John Keane calls "Monitory Democracy".

An amateur video uploaded to YouTube from Tahir Square is a case in point. Footage of the "girl in a blue bra" – a veiled woman dragged and attacked by soldiers, in the process her clothes being half pulled off – became a rallying point for the demonstrations. It also drew condemnations from figures like Hillary Clinton.

There is no need to claim what happened was "caused" by the internet. There were clear grievances and sparking points in the real world. And people were putting their lives on the line. Social media, as Dr. Alani says, could be seen not as causes but as e-nablers. Making things happen that wouldn't otherwise have happened – with emergent properties and unexpected knock-on effects. But once again, these weren't the only tools. Activists spread the news of upcoming demonstrations by talking loudly about them on mobile phones in taxis. The drivers, the gossips of Cairo, would then spread the messages they had overheard. Another form of "social media"?

What I would particularly highlight is not the technology, but this tricksterish nature of the uprisings; with the use of humour, symbols and creativity to win the argument.

Dr. Alani commented that the regimes rely upon fear; among protestors or dissidents of losing their lives, among minorities of persecution under majority rule, across the region of spreading instability, in the West that Islamists would take over. The only way to fight so much fear, he said, was humour:

People take to the streets and make jokes, laugh, dance and sing, not because of any hope that the regime might comply with their demands, but rather to diminish and subdue its only weapon.

The creativity, quantity and exuberance of the user-generated content that is nowadays easy to make with accessible tools would make any past propagandist jealous. One example really worth checking out on YouTube is the series of Syrian finger puppet satires – *Top Goon, Diaries of a Little Dictator* – which are funny and sad in equal measure, even in subtitled translation and at a great distance from events. And they are beautifully scripted and made, each episode being rehearsed for weeks before filming. So far, two series of 13 episodes have been made – each 5-6 minutes long.

Top Goon is the product of an anonymous collective of ten creatives from theatre, journalism, art and film. The choice of glove puppetry was partly practical, allowing the group to film secretly and remain anonymous. But it was also cultural, as it represents the revival of a popular form of folk entertainment in the region. The leading characters include Beeshu, the paranoid, childish, neurotic and lisping dictator, Shabih his Goon, a menacing army-uniformed thug with a huge moustache and jaw, Rose, a TV news presenter/ prostitute who flounces her way through pro-State explanations of events and adulatory interviews with Beeshu, and the protestors portrayed as reasonable and peace-loving. The topics are wide-ranging, biting satire the only constant; taking in the piecemeal and bizarre reforms (like a new "Law of Gravity"), torture and violence, the collaborator businessmen who can always be relied upon, distortions by the media, a game show called *Who Wants to Kill a Million?* A personal favourite is Episode 13, where the puppeteer appears and confronts the dictator puppet – "What can you do?" Beeshu asks – "I can make you dance," he replies. Speaking to the *Global Post*,[53] the director Jameel explained that:

223

Laughter, irony and black humour were quickly decided on to be the most striking tool, as the Syrian regime put all its effort in suffocating the people's will for freedom and life. Comedy strips things bare and gives you the strength to fight. Of course, with black comedy the laughter gets stuck in your throat. It makes you laugh and cry at the same time. But we will not allow the regime to turn us into victims that just cry and stay at home all the time.

The humour is so sharply funny because it is drawn from true-to-life, recognizable scenes of the conflict, played out as little human dramas. The dictator can't sleep well as he has recurring nightmares of being deposed. A fiancé can't bear to leave his beloved and escape across the border. A prisoner under torture tells the guard that he is the real prisoner, because he is afraid to take his freedom. It's scenes like this that bring home what it might be like to live as a real person amongst such a conflict, rather than see it from the outside as graphic street scenes and battles. Apparently many of the scenarios (such as that of the guard and prisoner's exchange) were drawn from real life.

A powerful bonus episode (*Beeshu's Interview: Who's the Muppet?*) used footage that was lifted verbatim from an interview between the real dictator Bashar Al-Assad and Barbara Walters of ABC News. During this interview, Bashar Al-Assad makes statements like:

"They are not my forces. They are military forces belonging to the government. I don't own them. I am president. I don't own the country."
"How do you know if you weren't there?"
(*And when told there were reporter photos and footage:*)
"How can you verify those pictures?"
(*And about a damning UN report, said:*)

"They should send us the document."

(*And to conclude:*)

"We don't kill our people. No government in the world kills its people unless it is led by a crazy person."

As Jameel commented to *Global News*:

> We used to worry that people outside Syria might think the things we show in *Top Goon* are exaggerated. But after we saw Assad's interview we decided to run it on its own as Episode 5.5, because the interview was more comic than we could have imagined. We didn't even have to make something up.

Back in Egypt, as well as being a way to mobilize people, humour also provides a way to map what was unfolding; an evolving story, traversing the course of the revolution from the grim humour deconstructing a dictatorship (like *Top Goon*), to the jubilant humour of new freedom. It is fascinating to see how the jokes changed over time.

Firstly, a pre-revolution joke (from when the secret police state seemed omnipotent):

> Azrael, the angel of death, was sent by God to collect Mubarak's soul. After more than two months, Azrael returns, bloodied, bruised and broken. "What happened?" asked God. "Egyptian state security seized me. They threw me in a dark cell, starved me, beat me and tortured me for weeks and weeks. They only just released me." God turns pale and says, "You didn't tell them I sent you?"

And next, still in the Mubarak era but starting to question the whole system – especially the "official" media and its version of events – comes this joke:

Hosni Mubarak, Barack Obama and Vladimir Putin are at a meeting together when suddenly God appears before them. God says: "I have come to tell you that the end of the world will be in two days. Tell your people." So each leader goes back to his capital and prepares a television address.

In Washington, Obama says, "My fellow Americans, I have good news and bad news. The good news is that I can confirm that God exists. The bad news is that he told me the world would end in two days."

In Moscow, Putin says, "People of Russia, I regret that I have to inform you of two pieces of bad news. First, God exists, which means everything our country has believed in for most of the last century was false. Second, the world is ending in two days."

In Cairo, Mubarak says, "O Egyptians, I come to you today with two pieces of excellent news! First, God and I have just held an important summit. Second, he told me I would be your president until the end of time."

Then we move forward to the jokes and banter that emerged in that critical liminal stage in the uprising; the week and a half between Mubarak saying he would not stand for re-election (1st February) and finally resigning (11th February) – when a whole new class of humour emerged about Mubarak clinging onto power. Samih Toukan (Dubai-based founder of Maktoob.com) started a hashtag meme on Twitter, where (as on Ekşi Sözlük) people offered up definitions as if Mubarak was a new word in the dictionary. Toukan's own tweet (on the 8th February) read:

#Mubarak (n): a psychotic ex-girlfriend who fails to understand it's over! #Mubareked

Other tweets in the same vein soon followed:

"To Mubarek" meaning "to refuse to take a hint". "I didn't invite her, but she totally Mubareked and showed up anyway." #mubarek

#Mubaraked: to stick something or to glue something. ex "I will punch u and Mubarak u to the wall".

#Mubaraked: to get stuck to a chair when u stand up.

Finally, as the dust and jubilation settled, came the post-revolution jokes. For example:

Q: Why did it take so long for Mubarak to leave?
A: You think it's easy packing gold bullion bars into vintage Louis Vuitton luggage?

Meanwhile in Tunisia, an interesting post-script to the uprising came with a PR stunt from the Memac Ogilvy agency in Tunis, working for pro-democracy NGO *Engagement Citoyen*. It aimed at persuading more people to vote in the forthcoming elections. The centrepiece of the stunt was a building-sized poster of (fallen dictator) Ben Ali which was posted overnight in a public square. Crowds gathered the next morning in disbelief. Was he back, they asked each other? The mob lurched into action and tore down the poster, only to reveal another one with a hidden message underneath:

BEWARE, DICTATORSHIP CAN RETURN.
ON OCTOBER 23RD, VOTE

These events were secretly filmed and the resulting video uploaded on YouTube generated over a million views and onwards news coverage on all the Tunisian and international TV stations, with

227

members of *Engagement Citoyen* invited on to explain the campaign. It's impossible to isolate the effect of just one such campaign, but before it was deployed only 55% said they intended to vote, whereas on the day there was an 88% turnout. And it seems plausible that this campaign at least helped. It also became a celebrated example in international advertising award shows – showcasing an Arab Spring effect in transforming the creativity and confidence of the region. There were fresh calls to install local creative talent in senior positions rather than the usual expats. Similar effects were hailed in the cinema industry with a rush of new films from the region, some dealing directly with the uprising, many others with rights and freedoms.

Contrast all this with the portrayal of the Arab Spring in the West. Many a true word is spoken in jest. The following quip from chat show host David Letterman opens up the whole question of this being seen as a revolution aiming to become just like us:

> The good news is that Hosni Mubarak may step down. The bad news is that he may be replaced by his idiot son Hosni W. Mubarak.

In *The Arab Awakening*, Tariq Ramadan, professor of Contemporary Islamic Studies at Oxford University, argues that the assumed resemblance between pro-democracy demonstrators and Western societies came "at the cost of deleting religion, culture, history":

> They joined the advanced, civilized detachment of the Western-led onward march of history. No longer primarily perceived as Arabs or Muslims, they had attained the lofty status of subjects, legally and philosophically, of the Universal. At last they had overcome their backwardness and strode in lockstep with the West in its enlightened path of progress.[54]

228

It actually seems quite unlikely that most participants were "deleting" their personal religion. According to a recent large-scale survey by research agency TRUVIEW:

> 93% of the surveyed teens in the Middle East and North Africa region agreed that "religion is among the most important parts of my life".

However, there is also a general reticence about public declarations on religion within Islam, a tendency to keep it as a personal matter, beautifully expressed in an interview with a prominent Tunisian activist and blogger, Afef Abrougui:

> Religion, though important to me, remains a very private part of my life. I don't discuss it much in public. Since you asked me about religion's role in my daily life I would not mind answering you. People deal with stress in their daily lives in different ways by drinking alcohol, doing yoga, taking a walk or partying. For me the teachings and values of Islam [honesty, tolerance, patience, gratitude, humility, generosity…] is what keep my daily life less stressful and brighter.[55]

If they do not want to be more like us, what do Arab youth want? Remember that what the demonstrators from all the Arab uprisings were chanting was:

Ash-shab yurid isqat an-nizam
The people want to bring down the regime.

We've seen in many of these examples a return to folk culture – of stories, jokes and ideas that spread through crowds in a way that will never be fully understood, by recourse to *egonomic* structures like looking for the ringleaders. The crowd here is acting as a kind of meta-Self. Somehow it *acts as one*. This is a point Benoît Challand, a Middle East politics professor, applied to the whole of the Arab uprising – having almost a life of its own:

> Autonomy in Arabic is translated as *tasayyir daati* – that is the "self-impulse" or "self-drive". And indeed, once the initial spark was lit, it was as if the Tunisian people moved as a whole, into spontaneous protests. Egyptian, Libyan and Yemeni people called for the fall of their respective regime. The slogan "ash-sha'b yourid isqat al-nithaam" [the people want the fall of the regime], appearing across the region, captures this social cohesion and the unity in the project.

Some of the Egyptian jokes I quoted earlier were drawn from a blog[56] by Mark Peterson, author of *Connected in Cairo*. In his book, Paterson, an academic anthropologist, argues that Cairo can only by understood through realizing that globalization is not – as often portrayed – a movement to standardize the world with universal (i.e. Western) values, but rather a creative process of negotiation and adoption fusing some Western advances with local relevance, culture, religion and identity.

If asked what it was really about, many directly involved said that the key issue was economic frustration, born out of unemployment and corruption on a grand scale. Muslim Brotherhood policy adviser Jamal Hindan told greenprophet.com that 2-3 trillion dollars had been looted from the Egyptian economy by the Mubarak regime over preceding decades; many times Egypt's annual GDP. How did this work? He explained it by repeating a popular Egyptian joke:

> The Emirate kings gave Hosni Mubarak a billion dollars as aid for the Egyptian people. It was passed from different

government levels, and each shelf took a digit from the sum. By the time it reached the population, the mayor shook hands with the citizens and said, "The Emirate kings say 'hey'." And the money vanished in-between. That's how it was in Egypt.[57]

That joke encodes a sophisticated model of how a process of "trickle down" works. Or rather how it doesn't. It's like a map. And that is perhaps another connection between social media, humour and popular activism. Not only do they mobilize people, they also contribute to a growing public consciousness of how the world works. Where "facts" are expressed within, or understood through systems and patterns.

This leads us on to our next interviewee, Burak Arikan, whose work is also devoted to this kind of e-nabled public learning. "If you want to understand society today, you have to see it as a network", Arikan told me, saying that he is committed to revealing the world; mapping it rather than interpreting it. Burak told me that while other artists use canvas and paint, he uses "networks as my medium".

Arikan grew up in Istanbul, studied civil engineering and moved into web technical development and design in its early days in 1995. He moved to the US to work for a big Turkish language portal called mezun.com. And from there he developed a fascination with the work that was coming out of the MIT Media Lab. Burak applied to the school, but was told he didn't have the right qualifications. He spent the following year teaching himself advanced programming and building a portfolio of visual programs. A year later, MIT accepted his application on the basis of this work and he went to study for a Master's and work as a research assistant under John Maeda in the *Physical Language Workshop*.

Arikan's specialist area at MIT was studying the meeting points of economics and technology. One project that came out of that work was a long-term analysis of Burak's own Mastercard credit card

231

spending data, including an attempt to predict his future behaviour; a study that is now an art exhibit called *MyPocket*, which has been shown in New York, Berlin and Stuttgart. Arikan told me:

> I knew marketing companies can predict what you will buy. So I decided to make my own predictions out of three and a half years of my own aggregated data. I wrote a program to make a connection between the date, item information, price, running total, date, time, day of the week…

Burak told me: "I am conscious of doing work in the postmodern world. In the modern world, people say this is the reason for that. In the postmodern world, everything is related to everything else and the only way to understand it is to make what Jameson called cognitive maps. As a technique it is a bit like radar."

A recent example was Arikan's contribution to the 2012 *Istanbul Biennale*. Here he compiled three maps of Istanbul, each overlaid with a network of locations and interconnections. The first was a map of the mosques, with the connections showing which could be heard from each other. Burak told me that since childhood he had been fascinated by the way that the *Azan* (call to prayer) from Istanbul's 3000 mosques would subtly overlap, seeming to echo each other and creating a kind of aural atmosphere. The second map showed a network of Republican statues. And the third showed a network of modern shopping malls. The resulting work is called *Islam, Republic, Neoliberalism*. As the catalogue text at burak-arikan.com explains:

> The demonstration of physical relationships that these physical constructions establish with each other, via a network diagram, reveals a more powerful line of argument than simply designing a geographical map. Going beyond

their quantity and the frequency of their salutations to the agents of the city, it renders the spatial power and network pattern of these ideologies susceptible to analysis.

Burak told me that his work was not about rejecting modernist ideas but infusing them with a new awareness. "It's modernism plus more. Alternative modernisms." The tradition he told me of modernist art in Turkey had tended to be iconoclastic; perhaps for example showing Kemal Ataturk (the father of the secular modernist Republic) faceless (like portrayals of the Prophet Mohammed), or praying. While it may be shocking the sensibilities of both religious and Republican populations, Burak thought that kind of art had been left behind:

Icon breaking doesn't affect dogma. And that's because the dogma doesn't rely on icons but on systems. The control is a flow. It flows everywhere, from family to factory, from school to street. I try to visualize such patterns which are not much visible.

What attracted Arikan back to Turkey in 2009 was that he felt more at home here:

There are so many things that interest me culturally, socially and politically – whereas I realized that I was bored in Brooklyn and Chelsea. I had a more direct connection to what was happening here, through my friends, the social media, the news. I was engaged by the energy, the speed of development. Living in the US and coming here once a year I could see how fashion, architecture, everything was changing so rapidly.

And while his skills – in programming and complex networks – had been honed in the United States, they were universal, and could be used anywhere. Burak told me many of his fellow students at MIT

233

had been from China and he assumed by now most had gone back. The MIT Media Lab, he told me, still liked to think of itself as the centre of innovation and creativity in the digital world. But the first thing you had to understand about the digital world in the network age is: it has no centre!

Burak's ground-breaking first work on his return to Turkey involved a major political scandal: the uncovering of the *Ergenekon* network. His artwork analyzed a 2455-page legal document detailing evidence presented about its alleged members. The nodes of his network were the 500 people named in the evidence. And the strength and proximity of connection depended on analyzing sentences which connected them. Named after a mythical wolf (that guided militia through mountain passes) in a nationalist legend, *Ergenekon* was believed by some to be the "Deep State" – a shadowy plot, and possibly the basis of a new Republican coup. The government prosecutors claimed that it was a terrorist organization responsible for nearly every act of political violence in recent decades. Others countered, Arikan told me, that as well as high ranking police, army and public officials, there seem to have been quite a few government opponents, including journalists, targeted by the same investigation. Wasn't that just a bit too convenient?

Burak Arikan was scrupulously neutral in all of this. He simply wanted to map what the bill of indictment court evidence said. Display it as a map of relationships. He created a graphical display of this map, had the bill of indictment printed and pinned to the wall, and annotated with red lines connecting names, to show how the process had worked. This was all displayed on the walls of a friend's vacant flat in Istanbul, along with video animations shown on TV sets. It was interactive so that people could come, explore the data, and make new connections and discoveries of their own. Before the exhibition was even open, the national news station NTV came and asked what Burak described as "manipulative questions". This was followed by the police who came to check out if Arikan was doing anything subversive or "wrong". He told both that he was simply publishing the bill of indictment, and his computer program that had read this document. But he wasn't "saying" anything on top of that.

For future projects, Arikan told me he was very interested in the Islamic tradition of a *musca* – a piece of cloth that has been read into or blessed. He wondered about creating a digital *musca* that might glow different colours as people talk about you in social media. He was also starting to explore the world of *cemaat* – an Arabic word – the self-help networks that formed around mosques and other institutions. He described Turkish society as the product of "millions of these *cemaats*". He wanted to see what their characteristics were as networks, how they functioned differently, or not. A famous one that a number of my interviewees mentioned was the movement started by Fethullah Gülen. Burak said this issue was not without controversy – a journalist who wrote books on this subject had ended up in jail (officially because he was accused of being connected to *Ergenekon*). Burak told me when he was young, one of these *cemaat* networks had tried quite persistently to recruit him. He could see how for many people it provided camaraderie, help with education, useful contacts in business. But did it work that way within the police academy, or court system...?

It's clear that Burak's work has matured as he has combined cutting-edge mapping and analysis skills honed at MIT with traditional subjects, ones that are more local and personal to him.

Another network phenomenon I suspect Burak Arikan's might be fascinated to explore is the growing global *hijabi* community of young women who see cutting-edge fashion and modest Islamic dressing codes not as contradictory, but as two sides of a new identity. The Islamic veil has become such a complex symbol, the subject of so many projections from a Western point of view, that it is doubly fascinating to explore what this community itself thinks it is all about, from the inside.

235

Hijab is actually a term referring to general codes of modesty (in costume, but also in gaze, movement, speech and behaviour) that has also come to refer to the headscarf covering the head apart from the face. I think it would be fair to say that it is generally presented in the Western media as a sign of the subjugation of women in Islamic societies. However, this has become a point of debate among feminists, some arguing that actually it is a positive sign of resistance against the Western male gaze. Naomi Wolf, author of *The Beauty Myth*, wrote:

> Indeed, many Muslim women I spoke with did not feel at all subjugated by the chador or the headscarf. On the contrary, they felt liberated from what they experienced as the intrusive, commodifying, basely sexualising Western gaze. I experienced it myself. I put on a shalwar kameez and a headscarf in Morocco for a trip to the bazaar. Yes, some of the warmth I encountered was probably from the novelty of seeing a Westerner so clothed; but, as I moved about the market – the curve of my breasts covered, the shape of my legs obscured, my long hair not flying about me – I felt a novel sense of calm and serenity. I felt, yes, in certain ways, free.[58]

Sheila Ahmed, an Egyptian feminist academic based in America, wrote a book on the reappearance of the veil in societies like Egypt that she grew up in. In the 1950s and 60s in Cairo, Ahmed wrote, the veil all but disappeared among the women of educated families like her own, becoming associated with the rural poor. Ahmed was puzzled by the seeming backward step of young women choosing to wear the veil, both in Egypt and also in America. Her whole motivation to write the book started with seeing a group of women students enjoying a summer party at Cambridge, all wearing hijab. As she researched the book, a more complex picture of motivations emerged, some personal, some social, some religious, and some activist and feminist.

Afia Fitriati, a blogger and entrepreneur who writes for *Aquila Style* in Indonesia, helped me to understand the emergence of a positive trend for *hijabi* fashion – a community also known as the *hijabistas* (a play on fashionista). We discussed Sheila Ahmed's book and Afia said she thought its key finding – one that tallied with her own experiences – was that women in the Islamic world were adopting hijab for two reasons: "Firstly to please God and second as a symbol of activism".

In recent years, there has been a boom in specialist online and offline fashion media and retailing serving this growing niche. *Hijab Style* is the UK's leading online resource. *Ala* magazine in Turkey is more upmarket, being nicknamed "The Vogue of the Veil". *Hijabista*, recently launched in Malaysia, is stridently young, funky and cool. *Aquila Style* (who Afia writes for) claimed to be the English-speaking world's first comprehensive resource for cosmopolitan Muslim women.

Afia Fitriati very kindly volunteered to help me understand the scene both from her own perspective – and also through interviewing some of its founding figures in Indonesia. For a basic orientation, Afia pointed me to several articles in *Aquila Style*[59] that explained the emergence of the *hijabistas*. *Aquila Style* defines this term as pointing to "fashion forward hijab wearers". It had begun with a local meet-up in Jakarta organized by four fashion designers and bloggers. They decided to have an iftar (Ramadan celebratory evening meal) at a Jakarta mall. To their surprise, fashion designer Dian Pelangi (who was one of the four) reported "50 lovely ladies showed up! We didn't even have a reservation for that many people!" They agreed after the meeting to set up a *Hijabers Community*, and it was natural to use social media – blogs, Twitter and Facebook – to keep members informed. This community launched in March 2012. A thousand people joined on the first day.

I asked Afia Fitriati how much of a pivotal role social media had played in all this. And Afia told me:

237

Internet, social media and technology are the most powerful leverages in the spread of these communities. From my conversation with Jenahara, the Hijabers Community in Indonesia started off as a Blackberry group with 30 members. These members then held "offline meet-ups", posted their stylish photos on Facebook and personal blogs, and more and more people were interested to join. Because they were stylish, there was also a huge interest in how they dress and wear the hijabs. So they set up a Twitter account, some posted their hijab tutorials on YouTube, and things took off from there. Many members of these communities have become sort of public figures through the spread of their hijab tutorials, Instagram photos etc.

Once the simple community of shared interest took off, a more complex cluster could develop; including fashion labels, hijabi boutiques, photo blogs and magazines. And Afia contrasted this with the situation for earlier generations of Islamic fashion designers. In the 1980s and 90s, these were mostly solo efforts. Now you see many more collaborations; "between the designers and their families like Dian Pelangi, Ria Miranda, or among friends". Afia's hypothesis is that this is a cultural inclination: "Indonesians are a pretty collective bunch, and we have a strong herd mentality." But also she said there had been a dearth of positive role models for young Islamic women. This generation also had to cope with growing up in a world of confusing signals, caught between modernity and traditional Islamic values. "So when this community emerged, it's just like oil and fire. The young Muslim women need role models to look up to AND a community that they feel they could belong to."

Tracing the longer history and roots of the scene, Afia distinguished key phases. Firstly, in the 1980s Hijab fashion was a niche with a few players, for instance Ida Royana (mother of Jenehara, whose interview follows). Afia commented that: "At that time, hijab was still viewed as old-fashioned dress worn by old ladies or girls in rural areas." Then in the late 1990s, after the fall of President Soeharto's (secularist) regime in 1998 and the Asian financial crisis, Afia told me that more people turned to religion and also that more religious people adopted the hijab. From 2000, more hijabi designers emerged. And there was also greater freedom to publish media with Islamic values (thanks to the *Reformasi* or reform government). But these catered mainly for the over 30s, and there were few options for the young and fashionable; a key gap in a population that is young, booming economically and urban. Then came the turning point:

> In 2010-11, there were a few things that came together. The emergence of labels that cater to young hijabis, Facebook and Blackberry became popular in Indonesia, the emergence of *Hijabers Community*, Indonesia reached 20 million internet users (hence shopping online became a regular thing). And I think that's how it all came about, at least partly.

Afia told me that the scene was not dominated by any one style but a whole diversity; from subdued and conservative, to vibrant and exuberant.

> Maybe partly it's because we are culturally used to diversity. After '97, we are also a very democratic country, almost verging on liberal. This translates into different themes of creativity and identity in hijab fashion as well.

This statement incidentally suggests that for members of this generation – far from the veil being a step away from modernism, democracy and liberalism – it can be felt (after the oppression of a secularist dictator) as a flowering of new freedom.

After the Egyptian revolution, a similar sentiment seemed to emerge. Late in 2012, Fatma Nabil, a female news anchor, appeared on Egyptian state-run Channel 1 television wearing a hijab; the first time this had been done in 50 years. Explaining her own feelings on the subject, Fatma Nabil commented on Press TV:

> I think it's a great breakthrough and achievement and the fruit of our revolution on 25th January. This was one of the aims of this revolution, to achieve one's civil rights and freedoms and justice in our society. And we have been waiting for this day when we are not labelling people according to their appearance and thoughts.[60]

But while styles were diverse, Afia said that the underlying values remained cohesive:

> Contrasting styles, most definitely. Jenahara's style is bold and edgy, Dian Pelangi's is neon bright and tribal, Shafira is safe and conservatively stylish. Itang Yunasz's is opulent. But contrasting values? I don't think so. They are all modest and faithful, with different takes on style.

The first interview Afia conducted was with fashion designer Jenahara, the daughter of Ida Royani, a leading Indonesian actress and former wife of a Malaysian prince. Jenahara's mother had started wearing and designing hijab after she remarried. Keenan Nasutian, Jenehara's father, was an Indonesian singer and musician. Jenahara, Afia told me, was one of the most successful fashion designers on the scene, with a strong following not only in Indonesia, but also Malaysia and Singapore.

Sensing her daughter's interest, Ida Royani encouraged Jenahara to go to fashion school, and later to start her own fashion line. In

2009, her older sister introduced Jenehara to Dian Pelangi and Ria Miranda, and they decided to start a *hijabi* social club. Jenehara started a Blackberry BB group called "Hijabi". They also hung out in malls and would post photos of fashionable young women they met there on their blog. Because of demand, they started a Twitter account called *Hijabers Community* (HC), to allow more to join in. By the time HC took off, Dian and Ria both had fashion labels and were doing well because of the online community following. So Jenehara followed suit and started a fashion label with her childhood best friend, using initial capital of $1000 (their joint savings). This was because she didn't want to ask her parents for funding, but rather to succeed on her own merit. This is an interesting point given that many might assume she got to where she is through having famous and wealthy parents behind her venture.

Jenehara also has a very clear design philosophy:

> Simple, edgy, modern. Simple because that's what mom always emphasized in modest dressing. She said that being a hijabi already makes you stand out among others, so dress simply. I also want to dispel the belief that Muslim clothing is complicated and uncomfortable. It is not.

And Jenahara made it clear that far from being a trade-off, or halfway house, the hijabi movement is experienced by its members as being liberating and positive:

> Contrary to many people in the West think, Islam actually liberates a woman with its rules. We know the "lanes" where we're supposed to go.

As well as designers creating social media markets for themselves, this space has also been characterized by some interesting and successful specialist retail plays. The internet has always been the ideal place to serve specialist audiences; where you can mingle with fellow enthusiasts who may be geographically spread; whether selling fencing swords, buggies for triplets or vintage guitars. That's because the internet allows community and shopping to mingle to a far greater extent than most physical locations. But e-commerce is also tricky and is an area where many have got their fingers burnt. The fact that Diajeng Lestari, our next interviewee, had a husband already operating a local Amazon.com equivalent (called BukaLapak.com) gave her an inbuilt advantage. The couple were friends with fashion designer Nabilla Ayumi. Diajeng asked her if she needed any help with a blog or visual design. Nabilla replied that she already had that covered but what she really needed help with was a system that could process orders and handle the e-commerce end of things. So Diajeng and her husband set about converting his existing IT backbone to create a multi-brand retail platform for *hijabis* to buy their fashion online.

Already a member of *Hijabers Community*, Nabilla introduced Diajeng to other fashion designers with a similar need. And so Hijup. com was born, only one month after *Hijabers Community* and "things just took off from there". Since then, they have expanded from three employees ("and one of them was my sister") to 11. They have worked out issues to allow them to sell internationally. In contrast to the street fashion focus of other sites, Diajeng sees her key market as young women who – like herself – were working in offices and having to work out how to present themselves professionally.

> My boss once asked me: "What kind of *hijabi* do you want to be: the strict one or...?" I realized then that grooming was important in a cosmopolitan environment. So this is my personal motivation in HijUp: to provide a place for *hijabis*, especially office workers, to be proud to be Muslims.

This places her brand beyond fashion, as a service, helping people find new traditions and customs that suit them. It's a much deeper positioning than just selling fashion designers online. Naturally, given this positioning, Diajeng said that the brand is about much more than selecting clothes in current and fashionable styles, but also community, inspiration and empowerment. As far as her own inspiration goes, Diajeng says she was challenged by one of her university lecturers to think about how she could contribute to the development of Indonesia as a society.

> He left a strong message in my mind that each one of us can be an agent of change. The textile and garment industry is one of the areas where we have potential and can contribute to a value-added economy. Another asset of this country is the huge Muslim population. All of these are the inspirations behind HijUp.com.

And like others in the scene, Diajeng was keen to emphasize that wearing hijab was not a restriction but in many ways a liberating choice, and a right:

> Hijab is a human right. Just as some people choose to wear revealing clothes, Muslim women have the right to wear hijab. Undeniably, we women possess sex appeal. You can't control people's mind or their intention to harass you. Hijab is an expression of control over our sex appeal. In that sense among others, hijab is a form of empowerment.

Next, Afia interviewed Kavita Rezi – founder of the Kavi Indonesia fashion label and also a radio presenter. Kavi's philosophy is all about combining traditional fabrics with contemporary styles. Kavita started the brand in 2008 and originally marketed the label through the online batik communities on Facebook. (Batik is a traditional

243

Indonesian fabric, patterned and comparable in its refined forms for ceremonial wear to silks.) The brand really took off when she joined the *Hijabers Community* in 2009 and was featured in a *hijabi* fashion blog. Kavita's market is not exclusively *hijabi* though, but rather "all women who love batik and choose modern styles".

Kavita said that over time she had learned to be more open hearted, less worried about people copying her styles, more open to sharing. One issue Kavita still puzzled over was being identified with hijab wearers exclusively. They had become the bulk of Kavi's customers since the brand was featured on fashion blogs and took part in hijab bazaars. But her design philosophy was about modest dressing in general. Kavita, while a *hijabi* herself, felt that:

> On one side, you can find strength in numbers, in meeting and grouping with people who are similar to you (wear hijab). On the other hand, it can limit your point of view and makes you "exclusive". I'm trying to mingle with everyone and not be defined in one community. I'm neutral. I'm an Indonesian.

Another interviewee who – along with its many positives – expressed some concerns about a potential distilling effect of the *Hijabers Community* was Lulu El Hasbu, a *hijabi* model, who now also runs her own model management agency:

> There is a worrying excessiveness. And we [Hijabers Community] do contribute to this phenomenon. But that's not what we intended to do. As you can see, I'm dressed normally. But there are *hijabis* who buy a Dian Pelangi outfit off the catwalk and wear it as it is.

Lulu said the way to rectify this misunderstanding (that exotic high fashion would ever be suitable for everyday wear) was setting an example, and also education at events and talks.

Lulu El Hasbu comes from a traditional background that was strict and religious. And due to originally being forced to wear hijab, she came as a teen to reject it:

> I never went to the cinema until I was in college because we weren't allowed. I remember the first time I went to the movie I was very nervous. Even now my Mum doesn't go to the theatre. I went to madrasah [religious school] since I was in kindergarten, so hijab was a compulsory thing. But that's just the way I see it: a compulsory thing for school. So after school I took off my hijab.

Then her aunt, who shared her interest in fashion, introduced Lulu to a modelling agency. Although Lulu's first foray into fashion didn't turn out too well:

> I joined the agency with a caveat: I don't want to wear revealing clothes. Sleeveless is the most revealing type I can tolerate. I don't want to wear bustier-type dresses. I was booked for a fashion show and was lined up for the wardrobe. I saw my friend who went first got undressed and was dressed up by the designers – who were men. I asked them if I could change on my own in the bathroom. They said "of course not, you'll get my dress ruined". So I resigned from the show.

In 2002, when her father was sent through work to Saudi Arabia, Lulu's whole family undertook the "umrah" (or hajj – the pilgrimage to Mecca). Inspired by this trip, Lulu started wearing hijab again.

> That year, the first magazine for *hijabis*, *Paras*, was launched. One day my aunt told me that they published an

announcement that they were looking for models who are steadfast wearing hijab. I applied and was invited for a photo shoot. After that photo shoot there was another, and another because *Paras* also had other magazines in the same group.

After that, her popularity increased through word of mouth and repeat business from designers who liked working with her. Rather than join another agency, Lulu El Hasbu now worked freelance. At that time, there were several hijab-wearing models on the scene, including Dian Pelangi, who went on to become a designer. Her model agency grew out of Lulu being asked by designers for contacts with other *hijabi* models:

> Through Twitter I got to know other *hijabi* models and often referenced them to the designers. At the end, there were five or six of us who often work together in shows, so we decided to form a management. Our big break was in 2010. Irna Mutiara [a designer] asked us to handle half the modelling management for her two events: Islamic Fashion Festival and another at Kelapa Gading.

Lulu El Hasbu said that the fame that came from the *Hijabi Community* was different than just being a model. "Suddenly people on the street – *hijabi* ones – often stop me on regular streets like this to take pictures." Before that, "I was only known in fashion circles". The social media not only drove much wider recognition, it also became a key tool; "I got to know new friends, got new orders through Twitter and Instagram."

Another *hijabi* figure that Afia interviewed next was Ashfi, whose shared blog *fiminin* was one of the very first on the scene. Ashfi explained that she started the blog with two *hijabi* friends who by coincidence ("maybe Allah planned it that way") both lived in the same house as her and went to the same architecture school. *Fiminin* was a composite of their names. They started the blog because in mainstream *hijabi* fashion media, all the styles looked too old and they wanted to post fashion inspiration "for younger girls like us". Hani Hananto, a fashion designer and her Facebook friend, asked her to make some adverts (Ashfi is also a graphic designer and illustrator – and Hani loved her "doodles" on Facebook). This led to other work, as creative director of a scarf range for another famous designer (Irna Mutiara). And this in turn opened the door to Ashfi's current role as PR for Indonesian fashion week.

Ashfi (like Lulu) felt that the scene had led people to dress excessively and spend more than was necessary on fashion. But she saw her role as consistent with the ideas behind wearing hijab:

> I think it's an idea investment. There was a time when people raised eyebrows to hijab fashion too in the 80s. Now it's becoming mainstream. Same with being a *hijabi* model. I think modelling is an art. A performing art, just like sports. It's a form of soft da'wah about Islam. Hollywood is selling us ideas, we should educate others (too) in an artful way.

We've seen how blogs and social media apparently helped create a thriving scene (not just a community, but an industry with brands, retailers, shows) out of nothing. The time was probably ripe. But it is hard to imagine how the scene would have snowballed so fast (that some fear it is getting excessive) without social media. The same goes for the merry prankster Arab activists. And many others throughout the book. What all these examples have in common is this concept of being e-nabled. And this touches not only on community (the "with" in *Made With*) but also the content itself, what you make, how you make it, what your freedoms, challenges and possibilities are.

E-nabled is also the perfect word to stand between a techno-utopian

Western view – that "Facebook Revolutions" were caused by Western internet platforms – and the more traditional political view that social media had nothing to do with it, they were just visible displays of what was going on that the media latched onto. The e-nabled point says that social media could have created emergent possibilities, without being the sole or main cause.

Humour is highlighted as working – just like social media – to do two things. Firstly, to involve and energize people. To shake off fear, bring them out of themselves. And secondly, to create patterns that open up new understanding, to act as a container for new ideas, future possibilities, alternatives.

Burak Arikan's work is tracing such patterns and bringing them into public awareness. It moves beyond simple ideas like cause and effect, or there being one leader of a network. His work is also playful, thought-provoking.

These networks invite people to come and play a part. Come and mark up the sheets of the court document. Comment, tweet, turn up. They create great enthusiast networks as we saw from the *hijabi* example. Acting as a social form of business incubator, test market and critical mass. And with a real sense of sisterly joy, a good feeling vibe that radiates into the broader world.

Burak suggested to me that the key difference with what would be more typical in the West was his tolerance of open-ended ambiguity. There is no conspiracy theory denouement, no whodunit in his network maps. It is interesting to speculate that the Anglo-Saxon mentality possibly isn't as well suited to social networks (as opposed to building and funding them). Collapsing what could be nuanced understanding into simplistic heroic narratives.

That's often pointed to as a characteristic of the culture of places like Istanbul – more nuanced, less stereotypical, refusing to play by simple rational ordering or rules. It's a slight disaster when it comes to traffic, but a beautiful thing when it comes to digital networks. And I suspect that the avidity of its digital creators and followers has something to do with the fact that this more provisional, emotionalized, chaordic and improvisational way of relating is second nature.

There is a catch, which is that the internet can create too narrow tribes, with hard edges. While sisters and close friends might make different personal choices, the internet militates towards bounded, them-and-us style tribes. And it can incubate extremes of followership – as with the fashion victims mentioned. In the case of the scene in Indonesia, this is moderated by the fact that they do really meet. There is more to crowds than abstract word of mouth. And the physical factors (like waves of emotions, imitation, role models, pattern recognition and mirroring) need to be overlaid. The two together – crowd dynamics and word of mouth – are the "oil and fire" combination Afia referred to. Another *Made With* to add to our collection?

This combination – of sharing ideas, but also getting together – is even more vital in cases where it is not a case of very similar people clubbing together, but potentially conflicting groups learning to get on. Which is the subject of the next chapter.

> **❝** *I'm trying to mingle with everyone and not be defined in one community. I'm neutral. I'm an Indonesian.* **❞**

Kavita Rezi
Photograph & permission
supplied by KAVI Indonesia

CITIZENS WITH

Finding a common ground and purpose
in divided societies

7. CITIZENS WITH

—————————————————— ⋀ ——————————————————

Once in a city faraway in the desert, two farming families had been arguing for so many generations that nobody could quite remember who started it, or what it was about. But there would always be some fresh dispute to keep it going.

Then one year there was a flood that swept through the farmland of both families. Only one piece of high ground in the middle between their two farms was safe and dry. They used this to gather what remained of their herds together. And took it in turns to brave the storms and gather up more strays.

After the storm had passed, they worked together to build wide earth walls along the banks of the river, so that hopefully the floods might be averted next time. And as they worked together, they found many things in common, not least of which were the son and daughter on each side who fell in love and were later married. So that one day their children would farm all of these lands together.

—————————————————— ⋁ ——————————————————

These stories are about how peace, progress and tolerance can be Made With creative platforms that give people common ground and a common purpose. The literal ability to Make With *is central to this process. Case stories include Kamal Mouzawak, the celebrated venture activist behind "Make Food Not War" in Beirut; a hackerspace in Iraq; Pete Teo's 15 Malaysia film project; how BBC Arabic managed to overtake Al Jazeera on trust; and Fadi Ghandour, founder of Aramex and Maktoob, now promoting a new pan-Arab initiative called Corporate Entrepreneurship Responsibility.*

Kamal Mouzawak, founder of *Make Food Not War*, is a social entrepreneur. His initiatives have won recognition from the Skoll

World Forum, TED and Ashoka. He is a leader in the global *Slow Food* movement (he sits on their board; three other board members being Italian, and one Californian). Mouzawak has proved difficult for the media to categorize, prompting the applications of titles like "Culinary Activist". Mouzawak told me that the heart of his approach was about finding common ground:

> The question is, Christian or Muslim, East or West, can we do things together or not? If one is not stronger than the other, and telling the other what to do, can we agree to do things together?

To answer that political question, what Mouzawak had found was a practical answer. That people couldn't get along until they found common ground and a shared purpose. And the way to make progress is to create a piece of the world you wish for (rather than fighting the world you don't).

Mouzawak's own approach towards creating a common ground was based on his insight (as a former food writer) that while religious sectarian divides in Lebanon could seem insurmountable, one thing they could agree about was food. The food that people eat, Mouzawak told me, is mainly dictated not by religions but the places where they grow it. Christians and Muslims eat the same mountain food in the mountains. And the same kind of coastal food by the coast. And they give the same kinds of cookies to their kids for religious festivals like Eid and Easter. There is something deeply connecting about food and eating, with the cosmopolitan ideal of one global family. Philosophers like Kant and Derrida have long said that a cosmopolitan world would be born out of the human gesture of hospitality. And the archetype of this is welcoming someone and giving them food. But there was much more to this than creating a peaceable place for food consumers. It had to work for everyone. And Mouzawak was just as concerned for the struggling farmers, who previously had poor economic prospects and a low status in his society.

My first meeting with Mouzawak was at *Tawlet*, his restaurant, where a different amateur cook every day (in rotation) brings a different traditional menu from their village, region or community. Today, the cooking was by Zeynab, and there were several dishes (like salads made from a particular flower) even my own hosts hadn't tasted before, and subtle variants of ones they did know. The food was fresh, healthy, brightly flavoured and delicious. The experience, ambience and decor are natural but hip; an impression compounded by the constant stream of interesting folk who just wandered by – "he's a comedian on television", "she's an architect".... I asked Kamal how he would describe the place.

> I used to call this a farmer's kitchen. I hate the word concept. And I hate the word foodie. Anything we do here is about human development, never about food. How am I bettering me, through who I am and what I do? How am I perpetuating me and my history through the most central expression of me and my history; which is food?

Mouzawak told me that social ventures like his filled a space that should usually be taken by a State – "the father you can lean your head on". Whereas here in Lebanon, the politicians, religious and other leaders referred only to factions and groups, not society or the national good. In this sense, the country had never existed. To create a thriving community (given that vacuum left by the State) meant finding "a common purpose", a simple tangible reason why people should even enter the space. You then had to find "a complementarity". I asked Kemal what he meant by this, and he said it was like us two doing the interview; he talks and I write: "If we both talk, no-one listens." In the same way, there had to be producers and consumers in

255

that market space. If you only brought consumers, "what would they do? Eat each other?"

Kamal Mouzawak's first experience of the possibility of people from this fractured country getting together was working with Lionel Ghara, who had founded a cultural centre in a house called *Art e Culture*. Kamal said even getting to the house at that time was "like crossing four different enemy countries". And yet people used to flock there. From Lionel he learned the importance of creating a common project (in this case, showcasing the local culture); and also of having a real meeting place.

From *Art e Culture*, Kamal started to lead trips to explore the culture of the country. And that in turn led to him being commissioned to write a guidebook for Lebanon. This resulted in him touring the country for several years in the mid-1990s, thus discovering the full richness and diversity of its small village life. Lebanon was, he told me, a place where you could grow almost anything; from mountain food, to the edge of the desert, to lush valleys, to the sea. And the farms tended to be small, because the only sort of growing land they didn't have were the kinds of vast plains that encouraged large-scale agri-businesses, as in nearby Turkey and Syria.

The farmers' market that Mouzawak started in 2004 was called *Souk al Tayeb*; a play on words meaning "The Market of Good" and also "The Market of Being Alive". To make it economically viable for the farmers meant holding it in the city where the consumers were, as "no-one can create just a producers' market". Although, Mouzawak told me, this is a big burden of responsibility. Because if you ask a farmer to travel across the country with fresh food, then you have to fill the market with consumers to make sure there is a good chance of them selling it. Nonetheless, Mouzawak saw advantages to building a market where the consumers met the actual farmers. He said it was a little way of starting to redesign capitalism. Teaching people that food is not just a commodity you can buy in a supermarket:

It's something 50 years ago you would have had to know how to produce yourself. And if you have money in your bank account, that doesn't make you better than the people who know how to grow it. Each of you is bringing something the other needs, so you can meet as equals – as human beings.

This kind of exchange in Mouzawak's view is the foundation of a good society. And the market is a real place where that can start to happen. "You have to give back," Mouzawak explained. "And there is no point in being a donor if you don't have a recipient. It means nothing." He contrasted this with corporate CSR, which in his view meant doing all the bad you wanted in the world, and then doing a little good, as if to compensate. "It's just complementarity, we each need to be involved, we each bring what we can bring, be it a problem, some money, some skills, some time… "

One mistake, Mouzawak told me, would have been "fighting the monster" – to try to compete with supermarkets directly. It was better just to let them be a parallel system. People came not just for practical reasons or products, they came for an experience; to have contact with people, life and activity. There was hence no point trying to make it convenient like the supermarkets, to caddy park their car, carry their bags for them… because the whole point was they were "spending time here, taking so many different things from it, not just trying to hurry by". If you were a tourist, you could come here to experience the real life of the country, of the people, to talk with them. "You couldn't invite yourself to Zeynab's house, knock on the door and ask to have lunch with her family. Here you can get close to their real life, get a sneak peek." The market places since the Roman *Agora*, Kemal told me, had always been the beating heart of the city, acting as the space between private homes and public buildings where people exchanged not just goods but news, ideas, projects. "It's an economic alibi to get together."

257

Another of Mouzawak's slogans could have been *Make Action Not Plans*. He had started with only ten producers and they got the whole farmers' market started in only ten days from the first discussions. From there it had mushroomed into four markets per week in different locations. They had started touring a one-day festival through the producer regions, so they could find out what was produced, where and recruit farmers. And these tours led in turn to *Food and Feast* regional festivals. And the list goes on; leading to such a variety of projects and interrelated initiatives that Mouzawak gave me a thick press pack folder of leaflets and descriptions.

I asked Mouzawak how he had time to make it all work. He told me that he had learned to run it as "a proper business institution, in a really disciplined way". A key step had been bringing in his manager, Christine Codsi, with a background in business consulting. Christine helped him in ensuring they had proper management, finances, people policies, clear action plans. There was no difference in the operations between this and a big company, he said; only the aims were different, "you still have to pay the salaries".

I asked Mouzawak how spirituality came into creating *A Market of Good*. Mouzawak replied that yes, this was key, but it had to happen beyond the divided religions:

> Either I am wrong, or you are wrong, or we are both wrong – or maybe there is a bigger truth than our religions? I do believe in Life. I'm not going to call it God. I don't want to explain it, or understand it. But I believe in the wonderful energy of Life itself. Why am I so different from you? What makes us both go on? This amazes me. How a radish can grow and sprout from just a seed. What makes a human being? Are we stomach, blood, pancreas? Is that all we are? This is what should be celebrated. And this is what you have to bring it back to. To Life. And then the question is: what is your contribution to

Life? In Islam, they say each act is an act of adoration. So just do what you can do, in the best way possible.

Mouzawak said there was room in this view to accept being imperfect, have emotions, fears, make mistakes. Not to set out to do "the ultimate thing". But just to do something, whatever you can, today.

I asked Mouzawak how he felt about the future. He told me that he was innately quite optimistic. But in a way that wasn't quite the right question. His energy and drive came not from utopian hopefulness, but from a profound sense of acceptance.

Life is fair. Whatever will happen has to happen, even if it is the end of the universe. It's what must be. If I learned something in 43 years, it is to trust Life.

I asked Mouzawak about whether we can really expect everyone to be less selfish. He replied that the egoistic part of life was in general "totally uninteresting" to him – "like a TV soap opera". Except that when you heard the story of someone who had done something in their own lives:

It touches your own life, inspires you to do your own projects. It's not the story in itself; how they did it. It's the fact that they did it, and how that inspires you, how it fills you with energy, ideas, confidence, positivity and will.

I was also curious about how he felt about brands. It was evident not only from his own graphic design background but from the interiors, his materials, the beautiful art on the walls that he had brought some panache to his own work. And Kamal told me that – yes – this was a key difference in everything he tried to do:

259

Why don't I treat my eyes? The tree hugging days are over. With macrobiotic food you always eat something plain, and the place had to be disgusting too. But no, I want to enjoy it. So do most people. At *Tawlet*, it was a low-cost project, but still tended like a five-star place; in cleanliness, in every single detail.

Which gets us towards the core of what makes Mouzawak's programme unique:

> If each one of us is responsible, and if this is a real man or woman, then he or she will do what needs to be done. They won't wait for the police to tell them what to do. This is my contribution to Life. Instead of Zeynab being at home today, this is her contribution. If the cleaner didn't clean the floor well, we cannot have a good lunch. I may be the face of this institution but if the toilets aren't clean, or you aren't greeted when you arrive and looked after...? We are all building a dream project. That is what this place means. Not the food.

Another group thinking along similar lines is GEMSI, who raised $30,000 on Kickstarter to launch a pop-up hackerspace in Baghdad. As their Kickstarter appeal explained, GEMSI's approach is based upon more than just making things – but on creativity, problem-solving and public service:

> Imagine you are a young Iraqi student, just graduating college. Opportunities to work in the country are few, and working outside Iraq is difficult due to strict visa requirements. Your country still experiences violence weekly, while also facing many technical challenges characteristic of a developing country. You want to build the country, you want to share – but you feel isolated. You hear about a group of people who

have an open space near the centre of town where you can build almost anything. One day you decide to see what it's about. There, you find others like you: looking at the world around them and thinking about how they can start creating solutions. They are creating open-source medical devices, filling potholes in city roads, creating clean street initiatives, or making alternative energy products to fix the intermittent power issues of Baghdad. These are people taking initiative.

Bilal Ghalib, the Iraqi American who created this initiative, had previously worked on a documentary about the global hackerspace movement. This had started in Germany in the 1990s, providing social places to learn about and develop open-source software, hardware and building or fixing things. And it took off around 2007, as the idea of using social tools like wikis and crowdfunding helped it spread. There are currently over 1000 hackerspaces across the world. The funding GEMSI received so far enabled them to pilot a week of pop-up hackerspace activities in Baghdad, in October 2012. Group activities included copper (circuit board) etching as art, hands-on experience of 3D printing, creating a Google street view of a park, and an origami class.

Interviewed in *Wired* magazine, Ghalib described the project as based upon importing what had proved a really good idea to Iraq:

> This is a globalized positivity where collaboration and sharing are ideals that are acted on. I wanted to see how I can be a part of the changing tide by bringing in this concept at a time which seemed receptive for community and change.

Reaching out through social networks, Ghalib had connected with existing hackerspaces in Egypt. These in turn connected him with Yahay Alabdeli who started and ran TEDx Baghdad.

Yahay's family had left Iraq when he was four; he grew up in Sweden and now lived in Holland. Having attended TEDx Rotterdam, Yahay decided that he had to bring the concept to Iraq, 33 years after he left. He worked as a volunteer for TEDx Amsterdam in 2010 and managed to get a meeting with the organizer Jim Stolze (who went on to run the TED event in Doha). Two years later, Yahay finally achieved his dream and ran a TEDx event in Baghdad with the theme *Make the Impossible Possible*. More than 650 guests turned up, including the country's Prime Minister, and it was streamed, tweeted, followed and liked – with 1.2 million joining their Facebook page. His message to the world? Yahay explains on the TEDx Amsterdam site that "After so many years of wars and living in a dictatorial regime, facing challenges every day, I want to show the world that we have enough talent and energy to build a new future."

And Yahay Alabdeli helped Bilal Ghalib (who was born in the USA after his parents had fled) to visit Iraq for the first time and introduced him to existing communities of makers, such as speakers from the TEDx event who had worked out ways to keep heart rate monitors working during power cuts. One thing that impressed Ghalib about TEDx Baghdad was the way it created a common ground:

> None of them talked about divisions between Sunni and Shia, Kurd or Arab. Everyone around TEDx Baghdad was simply Iraqi. Just as they took pride in their designs, they took pride in their culture — one of the world's oldest.[61]

According to Ghalib, what the hackerspace culture could do is bring people together around the common culture of entrepreneurship, engineering and science that Iraq was famous for long before the current conflict. Iraq was known with some justification as a nation of doctors, scientists and engineers. And before the wars, it not only had some of the best universities in the whole Middle East but a self-image of being a centre of learning. As Iraq Studies academic Eric Herring notes:

> Iraqis tend to see themselves proudly as coming from a society that was the cradle of civilization in its ancient contributions to the development of writing, legal systems, libraries, mathematics, astronomy, medicine, technology and so on.[62]

So this was a common ground, a shared heritage and culture and also a positive memory of the times before wars and divisions, just as food had been in Beirut. As Herring noted:

> The culture ties us not only to each other, but to our common ancestry. It ties back to the days before sectarianism – an innovative, collaborative culture, a hub of science, technology and philosophy.[63]

The hackerspace idea in the West, like the 1970s homebrew movement (the origin of the personal computer), is mainly a group of engineering types that have a passionate hobby for making their own technology. That passes for idealism in Portland or Frankfurt because it's a non-corporate approach to democratizing technology. But in Baghdad, the social problems are a little more pressing than technology being open to user intervention. So it is telling that – an example Kamal Mouzawak would highly approve of – the first piece of "making" highlighted by GEMSI was fixing potholes.

The story concerns an individual called Murtadha, who took it on himself to go in the middle of the night and fill in a large pothole; one that caused huge traffic jams every day as his mother and brothers headed to school and college. He explains that this was a risky thing to do, as patrolling forces were known to potentially shoot on sight. And what he was doing could look suspiciously like planting a roadside bomb. When Murtadha headed out at 2am and started heating and laying some asphalt, a group of local teens came over to see what he was up to. They were suspicious at first. But after Murtadha explained what he was up to, they started helping him, even fetching more asphalt. After an hour or so, he headed home having patched up that big pothole. And when he drove past with his family the next day, they noticed all the smaller potholes had been filled in too – seemingly he had created a ripple effect.

That's the kind of social project, the initiative of a new generation who in a way don't see "why not?" that has become a core focus for my next interviewee on building common ground for peace. Farah Pandith is Obama's official US State representative to the world's Muslim communities (although she says she hates terms like "The Muslim World" that imply they are all the same). I interviewed Pandith and her passion turned out to be social ventures, social media and social change.

Farah Pandith told me that the (in her view, false) idea that the West is at war with Islam has not gone away. And that just one sound-bite on a story on CNN could ricochet everywhere and become "the biggest problem in my job" overnight. I spoke to Pandith at a time when a video on YouTube had sparked anti-American protests and violence across the region. And yet what Pandith was keenest to focus on was not this conflict, nor any misperceptions of the US, but positive developments. She told me that her role was about "interfacing in a respectful way" rather than communicating anything about America. Pandith instead spent most of her time travelling, not just to the obvious Muslim countries, but also to Ghana, Brunei, Kenya... and meeting young social entrepreneurs, to see what she could do to spotlight or promote their work.

What that generation are saying, how they express themselves online, what they are creating from an innovation point of view is so new. I am mainly saying to them that they should believe in themselves, even though they may be young, or struggle to be heard. They are articulating the answer to some global problems, whether it is to do with food, shelter, wealth, identity. They can express themselves online. They can tap into a global community.

Pandith calls this new generation of youthful e-nabled social entrepreneurs *Generation Change*. Pandith points out that the Muslim population is young (60% are under 30) and that this for this new generation "YouTube brings the whole world in", even if they hadn't travelled outside their own nation. This was making them much more open to other cultures and aware of new developments elsewhere in the world. "You see the same influences everywhere; in rap, art, graffiti."

I would add that you also see the influences of that same global connected Muslim generation in the West. The most common street food in New York is now halal. Social businesses like the *Khan Academy* – which Pandith, to be fair, mentioned when we spoke – are bringing something new to the West that is grounded in a different culture. *Khan Academy* is a web education programme started by an uncle (Salman Khan, a Bengali American, educated at MIT and Harvard) to mentor and educate his two nephews. Only Salman used YouTube videos, because the nephews actually seemed to prefer this to seeing him teaching them in person. The resulting free online collection of 4000 micro lectures now claims to have delivered over 235 million lessons. Forbes described his business as a "$1-Trillion Opportunity". The success may seem very American – Bill Gates uses *Khan Academy* to teach his kids – but the importance of the underlying social customs shouldn't be underestimated. This is the time-honoured way that family members would do things in cultures like Bangladesh.

Our next common ground example comes from Malaysia, a Muslim majority country. The population divides between the Malay (who tend to be Muslim), Chinese, Indian and other ethnicities. It is overall quite peaceful and prosperous, enjoying a steady but steep 6% annual GDP growth for the last 50 years. With a GDP per capita of around $15,000, Malaysia is the 28th biggest economy in the world and the third in South East Asia. High technology accounts for over half of Malaysia's exports and it is one of the world's largest manufacturers of semiconductor devices. It is part of the same emerging market success story as Indonesia and many other Muslim countries.

Peaceful, prosperous and integrated though Malaysia is, racial and religious conflicts still haunt the country. A recent online feud developed between Gardenia, Malaysia's favourite sliced bread brand, and its new rival Massimo. It started with a Facebook boycott group criticizing the "crony" company behind Gardenia. The group claimed that the new Muslim owners Bernas had pressured the company to stop buying from a flour mill under Chinese ethnic ownership, for racist reasons. The campaign urged people to switch to Massimo, which happened to be owned by the same Chinese group (FFM) that owned the mills in question. Both companies denied any involvement in this and the counter campaign that circulated in social media claiming that Massimo used pork fat and was not halal. To understand how upsetting and public this all was, you have to bear in mind that Gardenia was rated Malaysia's favourite domestic brand, in a public survey conducted by *Superbrands*.[64] It would be like a battle in America between Coca-Cola and Pepsi, where Pepsi accused Coca-Cola of being racist against Latin Americans. Malaysian newspaper *The Star* polled bread consumers and one commented: "It's bad enough that race is already in politics and our forms. But when it's in bread, it just makes me sad and angry."[65]

The Malaysian government responded to these ethnic tensions with a programme called *1Malaysia*. Announcing this initiative, the Prime

Minister called for an emphasis on ethnic harmony, national unity and efficient government. The government spent around $12 million promoting the concept. Applying this brand to social initiatives, they launched a grocery store franchise under the name *Kedai Rakyat 1Malaysia* (KR1M) that aimed to ensure low income groups could get affordable basics. They also funded 50 low-cost medical clinics, and mandated the use of multilingual hosts and actors from different ethnicities in television programmes. A particular focus of the programme is youth empowerment programmes.

The 1Malaysia policy has had a mixed reception. Anwar Ibrahim, the leader of the Opposition party, claimed that the 1Malaysia scheme was based upon a similar idea called One Israel. A survey by newspaper *The Malaysian Insider* found that the non-Malay public were equally divided between those who thought it was aimed to win votes and those who thought it a genuine attempt to unite Malaysia.

More universally positive in reception judged by the media coverage have been a series of campaigns by singer-songwriter, actor and film-maker Pete Teo.

In 2009, Teo released 15 short films on the internet made with a diverse set of collaborators entitled (not 1Malaysia) but *15Malaysia*. The first film featured a humorous sketch about a Chinese man (actually a famous rapper, called Namewee) worrying about what he might have to do to open an Islamic bank account. Could he still eat his mother's cooking, for instance? The films ranged in tone from slapstick (another, which reminded me of a Monty Python sketch, concerned misperceptions about how halal chickens are killed). Some films were irreligious, some very religious, some silly, some serious, some documentary style, one was a slideshow.

The *15Malaysia* films focused on prickly subjects like religion, race, corruption – and the general impression is that they struck a good balance, being thought-provoking and much talked about, but without causing any deep offence. It probably helped that so many

267

leading public figures featured in the films, including an Islamic spiritual leader – who spoke about ethics in business – and also the current Health Minister and deputy head of the Malaysian Chinese Association. According to the organizers, the popularity helped too, with 14 million hits in only the first two months, so that even hardliners didn't want to publically criticize the project. It also achieved serious artistic success at festivals across the world. Critic Jean-Michel Frodon even compared the series to the French New Wave of the 1950s and 60s.

In an interview with blogger Sin Chew,[66] Pete Teo said:

> There is nothing in the films that the public don't already know. It's just that people dared not speak before. People appreciate that we spoke on their behalf.

The aim of the project, said Teo, was to get people to think and debate; and with 50,000 blog entries written about the films, it seems to have succeeded. Teo explained that:

> Malaysia is our kampong [village]. There are many social political issues here at home and everyone has their own thoughts about them. My brief to the filmmakers is simple – pick what sickens you most, or things you feel most worthy of discussion, or the most beautiful things – bring them up. The most important thing is to be honest and truthful.

Teo had particularly wanted to reach young people, who had often grown up apathetic about politics.

> The reason that they disregard politics is that sometimes they feel their votes are useless and will not change things. In fact, this attitude is wrong. Even if it is only one vote, it is

important. Even if it is only one word, we must speak it. They are the individual manifestation of our collective strength.

The 15 films were not intended to be a definitive statement, but rather the opening of a conversation. On the website where they were shown, the public were invited to submit their own films, on any subject they choose – it could be the dirty drain next to your school, or your favourite Malaysian food – so long as they were about Malaysia.

I see this as an exercise – almost a national version of psychotherapy – of breaking the silence. The ethic that united the 15Malaysia films was intellectual and emotional honesty. It covered the topics that are never touched upon in Malaysian mainstream media because of censorship. And this censorship (whatever its other political uses) was always justified through avoiding any racial tensions or divisions. There had been race riots in the country in the 1969. And ever since then, the people had been told that any mention of race, religion or "sensitive subjects" was too dangerous. The trouble with this, any therapist will tell you, is that the silence itself becomes the problem; a repression that removes the only means to deal with the underlying conflicts. Repressed conflict also typically emerges in displaced forms; in political infighting, or wars between brands of bread.

The follow-up to this project was a music video that Teo released in late 2011 called *Undilah*, which means "Vote". According to the undilah.com website:

> Like all our projects, this is a non-partisan effort. It features common folk and quite a few famous people, including politicians, business people, musicians, actors, sportsmen, and one Star Wars character. It was shot on the streets of Kuala Lumpur but its spirit extends to every corner of Malaysia.

The singers are Namewee (rapper in the first *15Malaysia* film), and

Afdlin Shauki, famous R&B singer and comedian. Ku Li, Malaysia's longest-serving MP and its former Finance Minister, introduces the video. His script goes as follows:

> Greetings. I am a Malaysian citizen like you. And I love our country. Malaysia is a beautiful country. But there are many problems. I don't need to talk about them. We know what these problems are. What I do want to say is: Malaysia's future is in our hands. So if you haven't registered to vote, please do so as soon as possible. And if you are registered, let us vote…. Undilah.

When the video was released, it was immediately banned from television. The original reason given (in an email to the TV stations) was that it contained the message that the country had problems. And also because it featured opposition politicians. Two weeks later, the ban was confirmed but the reason now given was that the video had not been properly cleared by the censors. Later still, the Prime Minister stepped in and revoked the ban. By which time (in only a few months), it had become the most-viewed YouTube video in Malaysia of 2011. One of the politicians featured in the video was MP Nurul Izzah Anwar, none other than the daughter of the opposition leader (former deputy PM) Anwar Ibrahim. Nurul Izzah, as she likes to be known, told *Saudi Aramco* magazine that the video represented a wider coalition of artists embracing politics and "bringing us together at a level that was unheard of before".

Malaysia has made progress by creating an open forum for the conflicts to be aired and discussed. But what if instead of too little, there was too much conflict news, so much that it blotted out any other news? This seems to be the case in the Middle East; so tragically defined by its civil and regional wars, sectarian violence and conflicts with Israel. Fighting is a kind of combustible fuel for live TV news reporting and viewing. The graphic and immediate nature of TV war coverage, the gripping nature of scenes of fighting, casualty, statements of revenge and threats of violence is emotionally overwhelming. My father was working in Saudi Arabia during the Gulf War, and I remember how my mother back in the UK watched CNN almost 24 hours a day. Similarly, with friends from the former Yugoslavia, during the 1999 conflicts. If you have an emotional stake in events, they are almost impossible not to be glued to.

TV can also fantastically exaggerate the extent to which a country is embroiled in conflict. Some friends in America sent me messages of concern during the London Riots on Twitter saying things like "be safe". (Don't worry, I told them, even though it was going on several streets from my office; it's only a bit of shoplifting). The point was that there was constant footage of burning, looting, hurling stones at police. The reality in London (unless you lived above a shop in an affected area) was life just went on as normal. At worst, you had to cut around it. One of my interviewees (Fawaz Al Zu'bi) told me the same about Cairo. I was asking whether it was safe to go there at the time. "Oh yes," he said. "I was staying in the next street from Tahir Square a few weeks ago. It's quite safe, people are eating out, shopping, going to their office as normal. It's fine unless you actually choose to walk into the middle of the trouble."

The tragedy of course is that all this conflict in the news deters visitors, tourists and trade, so that the economy and tensions worsen. That's the story I've been hearing from places like Beirut (currently a no-go area for many from the Gulf because of Syria). It's the same for Egypt and Tunisia. What you need is a balance. I met some bloggers several years ago who created a site in Palestine called "the good news". What they reported every day was a simple, human, local story of something very normal. It could be a child winning a school competition, a new café opening, a social project to help the deaf. Their idea, the organizers said, was that without stories like this of

271

what the country would be like without conflict, there was nothing for the people to build upon; they could only imagine it being one way. Which was self-fulfilling.

In 2006, the BBC came to a similar conclusion when they conducted research into how they might launch a new BBC Arabic TV station. I remembered this because I had been consulting for BBC World News at the time. So I went back to interview Sanjay Nazerali, marketing director for news across the BBC.

Sanjay told me that the launch of BBC Arabic had turned out to be a big success. He was especially proud that in 2012 they had beaten Al Jazeera on public trust ratings. Even though the region isn't nearly so anti-West as we seem to think, given the context (of British foreign policy, for instance in Iraq), it had taken deft positioning and development to get to this point. And it had turned out that the key had been to create programming that addressed the audience's other interests than just conflict – in entrepreneurship, fashion, technology. Creating a common ground, yet again, rather than news serving only to keep people locked into what an expert interviewee described in their research as "common frames of injustice".

There had been a BBC Arabic TV service before, in the mid-90s, but this closed after their Saudi partner pulled the plug following a BBC programme broadcast in the UK that criticized the Saudi Arabia government. Many of the staff who formerly worked at this station went on to join Al Jazeera, which would now be the BBC's main competitor.

The research started by exploring news viewing habits in the region. In contrast with Europe and Asia, where news audiences tend to be "middle class", in the Middle East people of all income brackets watched stations like Al Jazeera and Al Arabiya. Further, the research found an implicit stance of being "neutral" when it came to religion and politics could not possibly work in a region where it is assumed all news is political. Most pan-Arab channels were assumed to be Islamic (and many do carry popular Islamic religious programming). If it said nothing, the BBC would automatically be assumed to be Christian (or Jewish). The audience for TV news in the region is very young; around 60% are under 25 (compared to 30% in Europe). Asked why they watched so much news, young people said it was partly because the conflict affected them – that you needed to know what was happening every day. But it was also perceived to be because there was simply a lot more news available (compared to restricted availability before), especially since Al Jazeera and the satellite TV channels.

A key difference the BBC had to take on board is that the tone of the news in the region is more visceral, gritty, real. It is described by the researchers as worlds apart from dispassionate European news norms. This corresponds to an audience that expects media to be emotional, because – they told researchers – "Arab people are emotional".

The research found that the great majority of viewers could be characterized as "Modern Conservatives" (outnumbering the "International Liberal" group by 10 to 1). This means that they are au fait and comfortable with 21st-century lifestyles and not traditionalists in that sense. They would be big fans of shows like *Millionaire* and *Star Academy*. But they would also be among those who wanted *Big Brother* banned because they found it demeaning. And interestingly, the research found that they regarded the BBC Arabic radio station positively. One reason they gave for this was the BBC's politeness, refinement and elegance – whereas they saw a more American style of broadcasting as bringing confrontation for the sake of it. They were all for radical ideas and criticism, but not rudeness as a kind of entertainment.

Analyzing the types of news available, the BBC researchers found that existing channels fell into three broad categories: the Hero (Al Jazeera), the Statesman (Al Arabiya) and the Propagandist (most state channels). The gap was for a channel that was emotionally motivating (like the Hero) yet neutral (like the Statesman). And it was in this territory that broader news needs (than just conflict) emerged: news with a social remit; news that was educating youth; looking at solutions; a platform for real voices; building a new Arab world; giving news more breadth, but also topical relevance; documentaries about life today, new developments.

They still wanted this to be news (not just leisure or the arts), but concerned with the economy, employment, housing, business; issues that affected young people's lives, today and in the future. The key request was for news about more topics than just conflict.

The BBC have gone on to produce informative content about these issues. But our next interviewee has a big plan to do something about them. Fadi Ghandour is best known for starting and growing Aramex (the "FedEx of the Middle East") into a $700-million business listed on the New York Stock Exchange. Ghandour was also an investor in Maktoob and described himself as a "mentor and friend" to the two founders in a blog post which also described the importance of the Yahoo deal that valued it at $164 million:

> The ultimate success story in a region long used to failure. For our younger generations, it is a wonderful example of how a dream can turn into a brilliant achievement through a combination of boundless creativity and down-to-earth business sense.[67]

Ghandour also drew attention in this post to the fact that, contrary to prevailing Arab attitudes, money counted for less than "education, smarts and determination" since the business was started in Jordan, "one of our area's more resource-poor countries – and, even when their company reached way beyond it, never left".

There is a demographic bulge of smart, qualified, energetic, optimistic young adults reaching their age of peak economic value creation. A similar bulge in Brazil has created a sustained economic miracle. The other side of this baby boom could be – just as in the USA in the 1960s – an enhanced tendency to idealism, dissent and rebelliousness. The question for the Arab region and the *Interland* as a whole is whether they can channel the energy of their young populations into an economy that creates satisfying jobs for the young and prosperity for all – or will optimism turn sour, if these aspirations are thwarted? As Fadi Ghandour argued in a recent speech at the Abu Dhabi Media Summit, it is a critical moment:

> It is a matter of fact that chronic poverty and unemployment have long been the twin hallmarks of most Arab economies. While poverty afflicts between 30 to 40% of the populations of non-oil producing countries, unemployment is denying legions of Arab youth a dignified and productive life. It seems evident, then, that unless innovative and bold solutions are deployed in the fight against these two problems – indeed in the struggle for our societies' socio-economic progress – they will haunt future generations, much like they have harassed and demoralized past ones. Now that the Arab world is contemplating a transformative leap, we, in the private sector, must seize the moment, recognize our vital role in the development of our region, tap into our huge reservoir of knowledge and experience and put vision and resources in action.[68]

In this same speech, he unveiled a new initiative, having stepped down as CEO of Aramex, which Ghandour calls *Corporate Entrepreneurship Responsibility*. I interviewed Fadi Ghandour about this new initiative and how he sees the connection between business, society and entrepreneurship creating a virtuous circle. Fadi started by explaining what CER was, and why he had related it in the name to CSR (Corporate Social Responsibility):

The key point of Corporate Entrepreneurship Responsibility is trying to move the talk of CSR to action oriented steps on the ground; trying to lay the responsibility at private sector, to develop and build an entrepreneurial system and society.

It's an interesting *Interland* type of positioning. On one side you have the Western idea of *Corporate Social Responsibility*, looking at ways business can contribute to tackling social and environmental issues. On the other side business, economy, entrepreneurs. What Fadi is talking about is a new kind of hybrid. He means taking action outside your own business operations, in your community. But doing so in developing entrepreneurship (as distinct from social or environmental programmes). What you could do includes mentoring, giving internships, investing, educating, providing workspaces, resources and facilities.

It means thinking of entrepreneurship not only as a private activity, but as a public good.

Fadi sees this as needing to come from the private sector. It's not something that will ever work if governments or educators try to foster it, as "it's just not their job and they don't know how to do it". Not only do the private sector have the skills and resources, they are also much more canny about where they put their money.

Why should business care? How would it benefit them to help new businesses? Fadi Ghandour has thought about this question long and hard, not only today but throughout his time at Aramex:

Economic stability, prosperity, affluence in the countries that companies operate in are integral to its balance sheet. If we don't realize that we won't make profit. So you need to move your brain and thinking from only seeing as far as the tip of your noses, from profit maximization, from the efficiency and productivity of your own business; to seeing that the affluence

in the whole of society is part and parcel of our profitability –
and that we're going to have to work on that part too.

In his blueprint for this CER programme, Ghandour sees it working
on a city-by-city basis, with local business leaders coming together
to work with entrepreneurs in their communities. And while this
is clearly a high-minded initiative to improve society for the next
generation, he thinks it is strongly in business' interest as well; to
ensure that the next generation of talent have the right skills and
attitudes as future partners, suppliers and employees.

Another of Ghandour's passions is "bringing entrepreneurship all
the way down to earth". Not that whole idealized thing about *doing
things different* you hear from business gurus, but it being about
people starting businesses that succeed and create jobs. After all, he
told me, it was only very late in his career that he started to think of
himself as "an entrepreneur". Previously he had just thought of himself
as "someone who is running and building a business". Nowadays,
Ghandour complained:

> It's a sexy word, everyone wants to get on board. But it's not
> that helpful as a myth. We need to humanize it. It sounds so
> inspiring, but it doesn't have to mean all this stuff. Make it
> practical. If you want to start a business, then change things and
> go and do it. We need to take the concept and break it down to
> its elements: like "here are ten things that you need to do".

The sexy myth that Ghandour is describing is that of the heroic
individual innovator with their dashing derring-do and flashes of
genius. As Ghandour pointed out:

> If you take the sexy element out, entrepreneurship is very
> tough. It's the hardest job on earth to become responsible for

277

your own life, for your family, for paying your employees. Even if you have one employee who you have to pay at the end of the month, you have to worry, it keeps you up for a long time at night.

Fadi's scheme, launched as a long and detailed blueprint and action plan, is ultimately all about practical steps on the ground to make a difference. For example, he told me:

Three months' experience in an internship is worth more than one year of study. There is nothing better than practice. And it is not just about skills; it is about culture, your work ethic, getting used to an open environment where you compete in a meritocracy. All of this you can only acquire by going into companies and working.

Fadi sees most of the opportunity for the region being in creating SMEs (small and medium enterprises). After all the opportunities to create businesses the size of his own, Aramex will be "few and far between". But he isn't talking so much about blue collar businesses as knowledge economy ones: "People leaving college and university and most importantly adding value to the economy."

To achieve a truly sweeping and transformative CER initiative, he thinks it is vital that Arab countries open up much more to Arab businesses from other countries. He also acknowledged that as it took root across the region, the programme would also develop, beyond his initial thinking, when put into practice.

I am a firm believer that the first idea is not necessarily lasting. It will evolve, because it is not an ideology, but rather a practical process, so it can be destroyed and recreated as it goes.

Fadi Ghandour told me that 240 volunteers from the corporate sector had already signed up to take part and that they covered multiple regions including Saudi Arabia, Jordan and Lebanon. And this was just the start. Another part of the initiative would involve putting together an extensive set of educational resources for entrepreneurs; in an online platform, with lots of video and practical tuition. He was funding this himself, bypassing existing educational institutions.

Alongside the local mentoring, Fadi also thought that local angel networks had to play a role, providing access to capital. With all these elements, there was a skill to doing it well and as "after all I am the most active angel investor in the region, so it should be possible to teach others to do it well, so that they can actually make money". That part of the programme was kicking off the very next week, with a session in Doha. Fadi had been invited to run this session, and was getting invites from across the region. People agreed with the principles, but needed help showing how you could make it work.

For corporates supporting this kind of initiative, he also thought that better ways to measure the impact, "what it does to P&L", would be key. This, Ghandour told me, was another real meaning of political changes brought about by the Arab Spring. Democracy was a means to an end. People wanted the leadership to be accountable; not just to make promises, but to show they were being delivered on. If not, they could vote them out.

Commenting on the experience in Jordan, Fadi explained there were three simple reasons why such a vibrant entrepreneurial scene had emerged in the last ten years:

> Firstly, for the first time ever you saw alignment of interests – public and private – and policy decisions made to actually support a programme. It started with the king; and then the public sector said "okay, this is no threat, let's give it the benefit of the doubt and let's actually do this".

279

Secondly, Jordan is a poor country. If we had oil, you would see zero entrepreneurship. Everything would be government controlled, there would be a national safety net; a socialist society. And you could get by in life without really thinking about it.

And thirdly, Maktoob when being built employed 400-500 people over a ten-year period. When it was sold to Yahoo, it's like you struck oil for the whole sector, because everyone walked out, with such a powerful learning behind them – and every other geek in Jordan said if Samih can do it, I can do the same thing.

Fadi Ghandour told me he knew that things were really changing when he heard stories about mothers encouraging their children: "This Maktoob thing sounds good, why don't you go and do something like it?" We also talked about the power of role models, and his conviction that talent isn't something innate, rather it is all about skills that can be learned, plus having the self-belief to try in the first place. It is in other words the opposite of the ego-based hero myth of entrepreneurship. It is rather about putting your whole Self (and particularly your back) into your work.

This thesis of the common ground strikes me as being really important. Creating a space that is open, inclusive, part of a potential shared future. Kamal takes this further and says it can't just be an entertainment, it has to have a common purpose and involve economics and the practicalities of life. Just as the BBC found; what people wanted was purposive content, about issues relevant to youth (like employment). This is the common ground that Fadi Ghandour and others plan to build on.

Another of Kamal's key points is that it is about human development, creating systems where people feel that they can and in fact should make a contribution. Whereas hackerspaces in many Western cities are places for homebrew hardware nerds to hang out, GEMSI took the concept further in Iraq – into mending potholes. People pointed out to me in Beirut that when you don't have a functioning state, it's actually healthier in some ways, as people learn they have to take more care and responsibility.

Then there is what Kamal called complementarity. Not "charity" but reciprocity, trading, exchange. That exchange might dramatically alter the image of farmers in society, as skilled artisans doing what we can't and vital contributors to our health and enjoyment (rather than the anonymous beleaguered suppliers of our supermarkets). For this to work, there has to be a human exchange, involvement and conversation. Middle-men can get you so far. But it won't create a thriving common ground community, with all the spin-off benefits, besides the central one of peace.

What's so important in these situations is to get inside each others' worldview. I can see that Zeynab or Pete Teo's artists have very different lives than me. But by sharing their food or madcap humour, I am invited into their world. And when we sit there together, we find that the visible differences like ethnicity, age, gender can be superficial. There has to be a common ground. And it seems to work better when this is a people's space, not a government programme with all the overtones (however well meant) of political spin, propaganda and control. Perhaps because people have to step into the space themselves, be citizens, not wait for others to sort it out.

In these cultures, being more emotional is a common theme. This is something highlighted by the BBC research but quite general across the various groups I talked to (even if they would tell me this was an Arab, or Turkish, or Indonesian ethnic trait). The function of empathy, of finding common ground, is much more of a feeling one than a rational understanding one.

This kind of thing always works better when it is profoundly localized. And when people actually meet up. Everyone made that point, from Kamal to Fadi Ghandour. In a way, that is the whole point, getting people back into a community. One that works at the street and community centre and market level.

An imaginative example I loved that came up in my background research was that of a Palestine artist, Mohamed Abusal, who invented a Paris-style Metro system for Gaza. Abusal took photos of fake Metro signs placed next to the tunnels in Gaza (used by smugglers and others). It's an imaginative common ground, a dream project, a vision. A real Metro would cost billions, but the art show version cost very little. Yet it was able to have a big communing effect. People approached Abusal as he was making the photos and asked if it would really happen. Because they thought it would be a good idea. If you want to build a peaceful, prosperous society, you have to take people there in their imagination. Show them what its pleasures and conveniences might be.

Finally, to create common ground, what all our examples have pointed to is a kind of unguarded, quite robust sincerity or honesty. There is too little trust to go around in areas that have suffered conflicts and tensions, so it takes a real commitment to truth. Conversely, the new truths that emerge from such places (like those of Mahatma Ghandi) can so often prove the ideas that take humanity forward.

I hate the word concept. And I hate the word foodie. Anything we do here is about human development, never about food.

Kamal Mouzawak

Amateur chefs prepare food at Tawlet, photograph by Giacomo Perasti

BRAND GEOMETRY

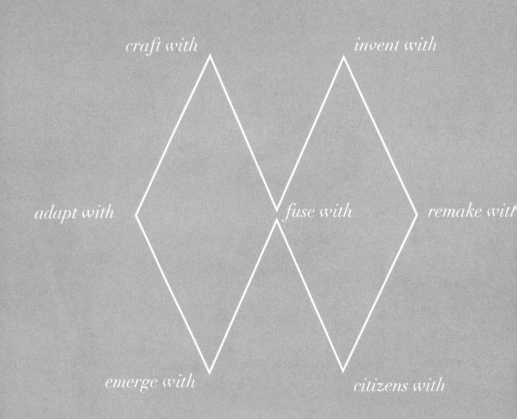

craft with

invent with

adapt with

fuse with

remake with

emerge with

citizens with

AN EMERGING MARKETS
MARKETING WORKBOOK

AN EMERGING MARKETS MARKETING WORKBOOK

Now, finally, we move from theory to action. Firstly, the different brand stories are related to each other, compared and contrasted. Then we look at how each could be abstracted and applied. We also draw from the case studies in the book to look at how by starting with one strategy, it is natural to develop by adopting another one.

How to Develop Made With Brands

I have written this book mainly for people who create and build brands. I understand it could be of interest to broader audiences of business owners and strategists, policy makers, investors, academics and so on. But even for these, I think the only way to really understand these brands is to have a "maker" perspective.

The way I have written the book has some advantages for understanding the case stories, but some distinct drawbacks for using this material to make brands:

1. The case stories seem too creative, too established or too much themselves to use directly in your own work.
   How can we Bokjadize our brand? would be quite a daunting question to most.
2. The categories are too close to the case stories to use directly in your work. And they aren't abstracted enough to draw general pointers.
   What a furniture maker, a TV producer, a lighting designer and an online food ordering start-up have in common is their commitment to small craft producers and placing these within a business and design system that appeals to contemporary markets. But if you

287

don't literally work with artisans yourself, what to do with this?

3. The categories stand alone, and are not seen as fuzzy categories that not only overlap, but have closer and further relationships with each other.

Some of the categories are more about making, some more about working with community, some about combining elements of culture. How can they be categorized, understood better, compared and contrasted?

It has really helped my own understanding of the different strategies to do some of this work of analysis. And some surprising conclusions have emerged. For instance: each one seems to have a unique sister category as a natural direction for its brands to be further developed, filled out and evolved.

And the analysis itself is recognizably off the Western grid. As it turns out, the natural way to analyze these categories is not a matrix. Nor a hierarchy. But rather a lattice of interconnections. I had already been using structures like "the brand molecule" to explore a more organic approach to developing brands. But most of my books have still been based upon grids and hierarchies. Whereas *Made With* seems to want to live in a network.

For those not familiar with Western marketing diagrams, here are the classics that account for 90% of marketing textbooks and say a lot about its reductive thought style:

The Grid

For example, a positioning grid might have *Emotion* vs. *Science* as the vertical axis and *Premium* vs. *Economy* as the horizontal axis. On such a grid you could map most car brands, washing detergents, breakfast cereals, even supermarkets. Another grid from marketing academic Peter Doyle concerns how to name your brands. You have *Same Audience* vs. *Different Audience* on one axis, and *Same Benefit* vs. *Different Benefit* on the other. Where both are the same, give it one name. With same benefits for different audiences, create grades (e.g. BMW 3, 5, 7). With different benefits for same audience, use sub-brands (e.g. Kellogg's cereals). Where both are different, create independent brands.

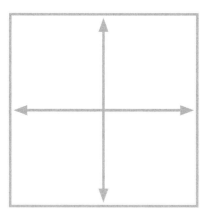

The Hierachy

The pyramid shape is used to express hierarchies that build upon each other; for instance, Maslow's *Hierarchy of Needs* is a popular staple for communication planners and brand strategists; used for distinguishing brands that satisfy basic needs like sustenance and survival vs. higher needs like self-esteem and self-actualization.

The concentric circles diagram is used to express qualities that are either core or peripheral as in the omnipresent "brand onion". Or from basic to higher, just like the pyramids. Philip Kotler[70] suggested a diagram where the centre is the "basic product" (an iPhone offers phone calls, a camera, email, web, apps…), the middle ring is that "actual product" (an iPhone offers desirable design style, ergonomics), the outer ring the "augmented product" (an iPhone offers services such as iTunes, MobileMe).

The hidden basis of all such analyses is the prevalence of either-or thinking. It feels logical and scientific. Almost like physics or chemistry. And it may be helpful at times to distinguish such factors and tendencies.

But the conclusion is that your thinking must be reduced to either-or choices. "Positioning is the art of sacrifice." Kenneth Roman[71] wrote. Whereas every working brand strategy consultant will tell you that their clients often occupy a grey space of compromise, special cases, merging, precedent and real-world indistinction.

A certain type of client – usually quite a corporate one – will spend hundreds of thousands developing sophisticated, logical, linear "brand architectures" that explain how every brand and sub-brand, value and message are related in a kind of "machine" that automatically makes decisions for them when it comes to design and communications. There will usually be an extensive library of "brand manuals" to go with such an exercise. The benefit is a consistency in diverse brand expressions. The disbenefit is it can quickly come to feel sterile, corporate, unresponsive to changing times. It only takes a new CEO or a new design agency for it to be completely overhauled. Add to this the bureaucracy of international brand management and you can quickly see why some growing up in marketing departments in the emerging world may have got the wrong end of the stick. You can't tidy something to brilliance.

But it's hard to kick the habit. When I was writing this book, I went through a painful "mid" period, when I tried (and tried) to analyze the strategies into some kind of familiar grid or hierarchy. But the best I could do was sort them into seven different headings, each of which seemed to me to be a distinct marketing model. Seven is a really awkward (prime) number whereas six (2×3) eight (2×2×2) or nine (3×3) would have been much more "grid-able". I tried to reduce it to five, because of the appeal of having "Five Pillars" in the subtitle (a reference to the Five Pillars of Islam). Any categorization is artificial. And if I had done different interviews, maybe I would have come to a different number. But for the purposes of my material, what emerged were seven stubbornly distinct strategic approaches.

Then a diagram came to mind. One that is a network or lattice of interconnections. Originally, this was to create an MW symbol (*Made With*). And after a lot of playing around with what category went where, it started to make sense.

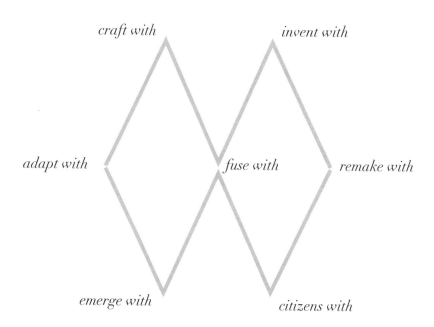

Lines of Analysis

The original reason for drawing the diagram this way was to spell out the letters MW. That's because we wanted to create a brand symbol: a bit like Chanel's interlocked Cs.

MW was originally the product of an earlier title, *Middle World*. This is the name for the *Interland*, as suggested by historian Tamim Ansary. Unfortunately, the phrase *Middle World* reminded people I tried it on of Tolkien (*Middle Earth*). But the idea of creating a logo using the letters M and W and some kind of geometry had been hanging around the book project and cover designs for some time. A Jungian would say that the Self knows where a project is going, months before your ego cottons on!

When I realized there would be seven categories, I went back to this diagram. And it helped me (once I had moved the categories around so the ordering had some sort of logic to it) to analyze the strategies into three levels:

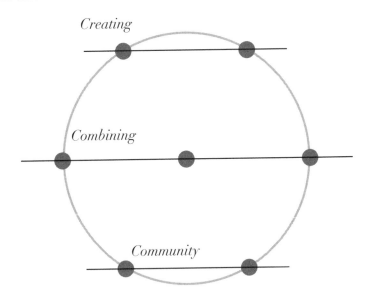

CREATING: *Craft With* and *Invent With*

Both of these involve making, producing, inventing and designing.

And they both address the desire for authenticity, humanity, familiarity, sincerity – at the same time as wanting something modern, convenient, a pinnacle of quality.

Hence overcoming a conflict – wanting modernity without the alienation.

Craft With: as a strategy, this involves taking artisanal crafts people (in the examples in the book; literal artisans with wood and metal workshops, but also cinematographers and local independent restaurants) and putting them into an accessible, convenient, custom-made, modern and sparsely designed system or aesthetic. Interestingly, what is done is often to invest a humbler field (delivery kebabs, mass TV drama) with brilliance, rather than choosing (as a creative ego) to enter a more "brilliant field".

Invent With: as a strategy, this is its paired opposite. It starts with a high-tech invention, something that has never been done before. And it then humanizes it through opening it to the audience; co-creating the *Ekşi Sözlük* site, making prototypes with *Little Bits*, audience voting on *Stars of Science, 1001*, an interactive touring exhibition, and interactive schemes from the digital agencies; OzU, swiping and practical jokes. It is humanized through participation but also purpose; all of these being little contributions to a better wellbeing (rather than alienated "pointless gadgets").

Both of these brand strategies tend to come from committed individuals; mentioned in the interviews as a feeling of vocation, or fate. They also involved subjective insight; creating from the knowledge that children love sitting under tables, or how cool it would be to make an MP3 player from bits that snap together. With these come a quality that is judged through sincerity; how "true" to life it feels.

293

The design thinking is also holistic and from the Self. For instance, .PSLAB's Demitri Saddi saying his own development helped develop the company; getting his teams to cook together; their whole bespoke approach to working collaboratively with clients. Or Ayah Bdeir developing *Little Bits* from her experiences of teaching.

What they are designing or inventing is not so much products as human interactions.

The "with" of *Craft With* is about forming a guild or network process of producers.

The "with" of *Invent With* is more about audience participation and co-creation.

Combining: *Adapt With, Fuse With* and *Remake With*

All three of these involve creating new combinations out of existing fields, which may be processes, stylistic components, contents, artefacts, designs.

They all address the same central function of the *Interland* of amalgamation: the combination of heritage and modernity, local cultures with imported ones.

This allows for modernity's advances without obliterating the history, meaning, identity and flow of daily life. It is about overcoming any inbuilt conflicts from living between the mall and the mosque (or other rooted traditions).

Adapt With: as a strategy, this starts with a model from the West, be it a start-up incubator or the green building standards, and selectively adapts it to be relevant and fitting locally. In the process, the original model may be reinvented beyond recognition. There is a real first generation attitude that goes with this, tenacious, pragmatic, flexible – modelling and remodelling – outsourcing nothing, taking full responsibility, getting it working in much less developed conditions. The protagonists need access to inside knowledge and experience of the workings to help in this.

Remake With: is the paired opposite. Starting with the region's heritage, so comfortable and familiar to the audience, and then layering it into a thoroughly modern production and context; be it the master plan for a whole city centre, the artsy and exuberant *Bokjadizing* of modern furniture, or the programming of a theme park. The modernity is brought into this frame – through cutting-edge architecture or rides.

Fuse With: sits between, and to some extent transcends the other two. It is the product of a mastery of both fields which are being amalgamated. And of the ability to create something new, which emerges at a higher level. Every level of the process from materials to what language you write in is drawn into this synthesis, which aims through this combination not to create a compromise, but rather something more universal. The perspective from a bridge being more complete; you can see both sides.

All three of these create an *Interland* hybrid out of modern and heritage elements. They vary in their starting point and also the spirit; the "no qualms" pragmatism to *Adapt*, the feeling for history to *Remake* and the cosmopolitan worldview to *Fuse* higher universals out of disparate parts of the human jigsaw.

All of them take confidence, tenacity and a commitment to see the job through. They all share the mind-set of those who are in it for the duration. It is their life's work. And often the very difficulties that they struggle with and overcome are what also add to the "hybrid vigour"; creating stronger models that outgrow their original reference points and prove to have potential to compete globally.

The approach of *Adapt With* is pragmatic, creating jobs, money and business.

The approach of *Remake With* is educational; making life legible and meaningful.

The approach of *Fuse With* is humanistic; creating signposts to a revitalized society.

Community: *Emerge With* and *Citizens With*

Both of these are about community; society, contexts, networks, movements, clusters and participation as the energy source and focus of the brand(s).

They both address public questions of how the world works, how I can be a citizen, make a contribution – and they both offer new freedoms and possibilities. Beyond the individualism and atomization of society – but also balancing ego and community.

They hence allow me to be myself fully, to live in a thriving society and community, by being part of something bigger than myself, which I throw myself into.

Emerge With: as a strategy, this concerns the many emergent possibilities that come from living in a network society where things can be done in a joined-up way, with new degrees of freedom; whether it's movements like *Arab Spring*, communities like the *Hijabers*, or a shared understanding and participation in networks. The individual experiences new freedom, identity and consciousness by participating in the whole.

Citizens With: is the paired opposite. Rather than starting with the whole crowd, it confronts the individual to work out what you can do to improve things; whether it is a farmers' market, speaking out and voting, or mentoring young entrepreneurs. This is the original idea of citizenship (not the representative version) remade for a network age.

Both strategies represent a *Made With* collectivism; the old spirit of the neighbourhood meeting the new infrastructure of the network. Both are redesigning society through action. Both are centre-less and while leading voices are influential, they aren't centrally planned, so much as unfolding and surprising.

But in other ways, they are opposites. *Emerge With* is Many-as-One ("the people want the fall of the regime") and *Citizens With* is One-as-Many ("be the change"). One creates friction, heat and discontinuous change; and the other peace, plurality, common ground. Citizens With is more planned as it needs the statement of a purpose, the creation of a space and activities. *Emerge With* is more of a chain reaction of unintended consequences. With more of a spirit of free-flowing enjoyment.

The collectivity of *Emerge With* assumes solidarity and creates projects.

The collectivity of *Citizens With* assumes projects that help to create solidarity.

Through all three of these layers, we do find that we have learned more about these brand strategies by finding the "similar opposites" that they live alongside in pairings. But it is not a simple hierarchy – rather a network. Hence there are two other lines of symmetry, and two other ways to draw out its mysteries...

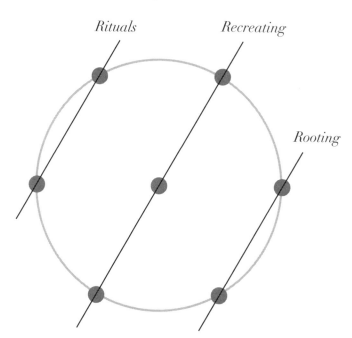

Rituals   *Recreating*

Rooting

Routines: *Craft With* and *Adapt With*

Redesigning the working process, adopting and adapting modernity into local forms. The common factor here is designing new systems, modelling, a fascination with process – creating brands that are "producer culture" led.

Recreating: *Invent With, Fuse With* and *Emerge With*

The shared experience of "recreation"; meaning new ideas, and also playfulness. The common factor here is the creativity that comes with freedom, and the freedom with creativity – we can invent a better world and we can enjoy doing so together.

Fuse With again sits at a midpoint between the inventiveness of the individual (inventor) and the collective (social media). For instance, an individual creative who may embody the impersonal collective traditions they are fusing (like *East and East*).

Rooting: *Remake With* and *Citizens With*

The common ground of heritage, and also a common purpose and meeting place.

The common factor here is the rooting of the brand leading to a shared identity (be it passing on experience to youth, or food, or archaeological treasures).

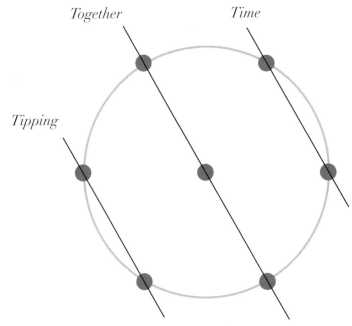

Together   *Time*

Tipping

Time: *Invent With* and *Remake With*

These are two ways of relating to time. The use of new inventions to tap into human universals. And the "archaeology of the future"; combining the past to create the future. The common factor is that these are two forms of futurism that don't jar or alienate.

Together: *Craft With, Fuse With* and *Citizen With*

Ways of helping producer and consumer be closer; the creation of modern systems to make crafts, farming and politics inclusive and accessible. The common factor is stripping away alienation and distance, getting together.

Tipping: *Adapt With* and *Emerge With*

Growing into the potential space that is implied by the internet and other social developments – adapting to local forms and adopting them into runaway movements. The common factor is that these are e-nabled; that doesn't predetermine the outcome, rather it sets the stage for other developments to occur.

How to Develop New Brands Using these Models

They are seven strategies that – while the cases often overlap – are themselves quite distinct as starting points for creating and developing brands. Within each one there is huge flexibility; it will be quite different if you run a café or a bank. But still it should be possible to choose which one feels "the most us". And it could be quite obvious.

What follows is a checklist of the key features and ingredients of each in case you wanted to work through them to find the best fit, but also to get ideas by trying some others on that aren't as natural (that might hence be less generic).

I've added some initial ideas for workshop-type exercises in case you want to explore them that way. These exercises are designed so your team can experience what it's like living and working inside these other strategies; helpful, as *Made With* strategies are full commitments to a way of doing things, not abstract rational choices. There are no rules though – and sometimes pick and mix is the best approach.

1. Craft With
The brand strategy (abstracted):
- *Be an aggregator for little crafts, artisans, specialists*
- *Bring a modern wrapper or design – add contemporary appeal*
- *Retain their humanity, quality, skill, difference*
- *Work with them to adapt to new processes, designs, commissioning*
- *Connect consumers with their work (and yours) through storytelling*
- *Connect them with new markets, consumers*
- *Add value through design, service, organization, sales and marketing*
- *Offer modern systems of quality assurance, support*
- *An ecosystems model; with benefits to artisans, consumers and you*

It's the same strategy whether you:
- Created a high-end range of specialist teas

- Created a global ethical label like Fairtrade
- Serviced a network of independent life coaches with training, marketing and support

You need to do three things well and they all need to benefit each other:
1. Meet customers' needs with unique, authentic crafted products and services
2. Recruit and develop a network of artisanal scale suppliers
3. Develop your own encapsulation model, shop front, added value

It's unlikely that there will be room in this model for too many partners, commercially. Since you started with a less industrialized and exploited production model, as soon as they add their margins, you will be too expensive. So the shop front and finding a market is likely to be the key early challenge. You can build an e-commerce site today (and a nice-looking one too) for €1000. But without bringing customers, that would be like opening a store in the remotest village in the world.

Another tip is that you don't just want customers, you want appreciators. They have to get involved in the story of how their (beautiful, crafted) products and services are made. Or be able to appreciate the difference at first sight (like Timur's productions).

A friend wanted to set up a business selling beautifully crafted shirts and ties made in his home village in Italy. My advice was to round up speakers and non-competing partners and host a series of "how to dress better" events for (presumably bachelor) men in London's snazzy private members' clubs; and follow this through into e-commerce, and partners like employers of investment bankers. Because there was no way to compete between (inferior, but cheaper) shirts sold through catalogues at one end and high-end tailors' shops at the other, without creating your own unique shop front that disrupted those two models and reached a middle audience.

301

Workshop ideas

One thing that's really enriching is to go and work with the artisans. Learn to do what they do. Not nearly so well. But get a feel for it.

Or if you work in a service or manufacturing sector, then find a way to spend a day making your product beautifully by hand. Get into a kitchen and make your own cosmetics. Or go to a market or souk and create on-street banking services, live.

The key dynamic of designing this sort of brand is a kind of negotiation.

WHAT YOUR ARTISANS NEED
WHAT YOUR CUSTOMERS NEED
WHAT YOU NEED

From my example before, what the artisans need is regular, large-scale orders. What the customers need is to learn to dress better. What you need is a unique channel.

Depending how well you know all three, you probably need to do loads of research. Research to identify artisans who have amazing skills, but either miss out on modern tastes, or have poor routes to market themselves. Research to identify customer groups and channels to reach them. There might be customer groups whose needs you haven't thought of (and remember the brilliance of bringing high quality to neglected niches). And also research into your own model. Even if you run "a cafe", there is no reason to be lazy in your assumptions. It could be a bike repair shop too. Or it could be a hub for local deliveries and collections. Or a centre for lifelong learning.

The creativity is in finding imaginative win:win:win answers. For instance, could you break through in home furnishings by renting, not selling? Or by selling high-end covers for IKEA sofas? (BEMS, a company in Sweden, did this.)

Whether you actually do a role-play, or get real examples of artisans and customers in the room to work through things with, or just play out the whole thing in your mind (like some of my interviewees seem to)… the thing is to keep trying on the different hats, while all the time exploring creative ways out of the blockages.

If you were helping a client run a larger workshop to redevelop this sort of model, my first instinct would be to find some kind of game version; suppliers and consumers roam tables, which develop different competing models to attract and keep them. This is how a bee colony chooses a new nest site; a democracy of gathering consensus.

2. Invent With

The brand strategy (abstracted):

- *Invent life-improving products that meet human needs*
- *But as that's hard to think up, start off with "wouldn't it be cool if?"*
- *Show users the earliest prototypes and see what they do with them*
- *Keep finding ways to involve users in conversation, all the way through*
- *Get to understand their wishes, habits, difficulties in situ – e.g. in their houses*
- *Make it open-ended so other developers and end users can invent too*
- *Build laziness in – for instance, try to find an easier way to meet the same needs*
- *Use technology to automate things that are inconvenient (not as an end in itself)*
- *Normalize the end product – make it friendly and familiar – in language, design, gesture*

It's the same strategy whether:

- You are trying to develop mobile banking's next killer app
- You are developing new ways of training teachers to teach better in schools
- You are looking to develop a diet system for office workers that actually works

If you were a corporate R&D department, you would have a pipeline of concepts based upon research into new technologies, consumer trends and occasions. The one thing you wouldn't have is the playful mind-set and amateur process of a true inventor.

A big trap can be getting stuck with your original objective or inkling. It is so often the case that you set out to solve one problem and actually find the solution to another problem. This even happens to medical researchers (did you know Viagra was originally developed as a heart drug? One that turned out to have side effects!) Not that you shouldn't be committed to stuff that you care about. You just need to be flexible. Sometimes you later come full circle – like Ayah Bdeir (originally an artist) inventing a tech start-up that succeeded in the art world (exhibited at MOMA).

You might be wondering "where is the brand marketing bit?" The answer is that your customers, influencers and advocates are insiders. And the brand is built through their input and word of mouth (amplified by media). With that kind of following, you don't need the old distant kind of brand building. As a founder of social network site Bebo told me "Marketing is the price we pay for getting the product wrong."

Workshop ideas

The big step is putting your whole person and imagination into the scene. Like Einstein whose thought experiments included imagining falling from the roof and noticing his tools fell at the same accelerating pace as him, and so seemed static (hence realizing that gravitation and acceleration might be tantamount to the same thing).

If this sounds lofty, I met a management consultant once who had sent the leadership team of a large delivery company on "the journey of a parcel" (brown paper and all). It's incredible the insights you can have when seeing a service or process from the inside.

It's the same trick Orhan Panuk plays in his *My Name is Red* novel (see Chapter 2); moving narration from one character to another, to a dog, even to a picture of a tree. The more viewpoints you look at the same subject from, the more you will see it. Don't get locked into the one individualistic perspective (the Western trap).

Research should bring you closer to real life. Not only other people's real lives, but your own. I ran a workshop for Kingfisher (a home stores group) and I got the participants, CEO, FD and all, to each bring a photo of their "most shameful storage area at home". Typical were garages so full of junk they hadn't had cars in them for a decade. As a result of which (the extremity of the need) it became obvious that people don't need shelves, they need clear-outs.

Here's one tip. Whatever you make or sell, open a pop-up shop (or create an out of hours social time if you have outlets), where people can come and try things out. There is nothing like a community who actually meet and play. Even Sedat Kapanoğlu, who runs a top five website in Turkey, invites contributors to a summer get-together.

3. Adapt With

The brand strategy (abstracted):

- *Find a model that works well in other markets (it could be a model that works in another geography or industry)*
- *Map it out into detailed components or steps*
- *Interrogate and understand how each element works, creates value*
- *Now map out which elements would not work in your market*
- *(Test any assumptions or "don't knows" with research)*
- *Select the parts that will still work, junk or adapt the rest*
- *Interrogate it over and over, finding better fixes for any blocks*
- *Prototype (if possible) and try it on audiences, fine-tuning as you go*
- *Be prepared to change your problem, not just the solution*

It's the same model whether you are:
- Applying insights from gaming apps to phone banking
- Creating a version of "Starbucks", based on local food tastes

- Applying the library concept to other goods that people need infrequently

This is the kind of work that whiteboards were invented for. Practical mapping of processes, with creative sparks of problem-solving or selective editing.

It's such a good model, I've been using it for years, for general purposes (outside start-ups) with any clients looking to innovate. There are two big gains. Firstly, you start with something that you at least know works in another context. It could be a "Buy It Now" button or a whole business model. Secondly, the creativity thrives by finding sparking points. "Buy It Now" might not work outside auction systems, but short-cuts (like Amazon's adapting this into "One Click") could do.

Another way to do the same exercise: take a successful brand or business from a totally separate market, then imagine they took over your company and tried to reapply the whole thing. And remember the real sparking points are where it doesn't quite fit, and you have to reimagine it (like that brand would) so it does.

You have to have – or get – proper inside knowledge. A management fad is the result of blindly applying process you didn't invent (or reinvent) that may have worked somewhere else, but in a different context. You end up doing something because it is "in", or "cool", or "recognized". And while some part of that model might fit you well, many others won't. It's the point Sina Afra from Markafoni made about making sure you don't outsource too much early on. Because then you have to take full responsibility for making it work.

The chances are that if you are copying something established and successful, it will just be much harder to make it work out of that context. You will have to be much more resourceful, patient, careful, tenacious. The result could be that you end up with something more efficient, or more effective, or both. Don't be too discouraged.

The key is to understand why it is "just so". Otherwise you will never know what needs adapting. Similarly you have to know the intended market. Usually that will be your home market, but even so – do you know every facet of regulation, competition…?

Get out there and try something. The experience will be worth a year of whiteboard sessions. A really crucial piece of the SEEQNCE story was the Cinemoz prelude. They knew how hard it was to recruit good people for start-ups in Beirut, because they'd just been through it.

Another tip is see if you can find a much smaller part-model. I met a start-up which is planning to launch an internet banking service. My suggestion for a first step (in a market where those services are new) was to try something much smaller – which is the service of giving people digital statements and balances; as an add-on to their existing bank. I don't know if that is a good idea, but it illustrates my point.

Don't forget that you are not creating a Frankenstein's Monster, but something beautiful. That it has to make sense as a whole, to people who have never met it before. And they still need to be wooed (remember the "night of the start-ups" party?)

One final tip. You want to copy the workings. The process. But your end result doesn't have to look anything like your reference point. It should be designed purely with your own market and audience in mind. I don't just mean the graphic design. I mean don't assume it will come out looking like the same service. You could, for instance, apply high-end concierge service learning to pizza home delivery; but don't expect silver service, or the guys and girls on bikes to start acting like butlers.

Workshop ideas
The strategy pretty much is a workshop, ready-made.

It is about breaking a model into chunks of value, steps in a process, elements in a network and asking – would this one work here? If yes – or no – why and how?

If it helps, write a list of the "top tens" and go through those in turn.

- The top ten features
- The top ten innovations
- The top ten things customers value

One thing you will notice is that – as a sociologist once pointed out – everyday life is very easy to do, but very complicated to describe. You'll be amazed how detailed even quite a simple service system is, when you look into the nitty-gritty. But the point isn't to map every detail, rather to understand in broader terms "what won't work here". The first thing I would have looked at in the case of Cinemoz is licensing content (Hulu who they modelled themselves on, got investment from NewsCorp, ABC and Disney; and hence they could access masses of US TV show content). Cinemoz cleverly changed the model to offer much less content, but indie films and high end.

4. Fuse With

The brand strategy (abstracted):

- *Take a field from one part of the world*
- *And a field from another part of the world*
- *Amalgamate them, to create something better, more universal*
- *Do so at every level, in the working process, through to final design*
- *Bear in mind what strengths each brings, and hence where it sits*
- *Look for moments when something more than the sum of the parts emerges*

It's the same process whether you are:

- Creating transnational brand identities
- Creating a recruitment and coaching company for women in the Arab world
- Starting a new concept in nursing care for the elderly based on local family traditions

The catch with this strategy is that it has to be a whole person subjective involvement. It's not about importing foreign stuff you think is exotic or cool. It is about having deeply lived-with experience of several approaches. An internal mixed marriage.

Of course, most of us don't have ten years, nor is it really something you plan for.

The easiest shortcut is to take two sides of your life that are quite distinct. One of my clients had a mother who was an artist and his father an industrialist. Having dabbled with becoming a writer, he had found one compromise working for a corporate in a fairly creative role. But there would be many other ways to bring his two lifelong paths together. My own suggestion was that he join the circus (shift to working with a brand like Cirque de Soleil). Or perhaps a Broadway theatre. Bringing business skills to creativity, rather than creativity to corporate business.

A common reason for starting a small business is turning a passion or hobby into your work. The opportunity, though, is not just to leave your old role behind. But to combine them in creative ways. It would probably start to happen naturally anyway.

Another shortcut is partnership. So long as your team is a hybrid, there is a good chance of constructive creative fusion. So long as the relationship is rich, communicative, curious and evenly balanced. I used to run "brand dates" to get marketing teams from two different brands around a table and it was amazing how many new joint schemes and ideas they would come up with in just an afternoon.

The upsetting bit is letting go of stuff you hold dear. You really have to have a feeling for both sides. That feeling is Love (or if you come from a less emotional culture, you could call it "unconditional positive regard"). If you are a copywriter from Bahrain who teams up with a designer from Holland, the prospects are good so long as you are patient, don't rush into one or other's comfort zones, or let one lead too much – and especially don't double guess what you think the other one will like. I've made it sound difficult, but actually we do this artful creative compromising every day in dealing with much bigger differences in family life (like dealing with a child, or a spouse!)

When I worked with a team of people last year partly from London and partly from Brazil, we did a lot of activities; like shopping trips, or slide shows of stuff we liked.

The most telling thing, though, was personal stories that explained "how it is different" from people that had lived in both cultures.

Workshop ideas

What you want to do is create a third space. Not here, not there, but here AND there. If you are too stuck in your routines (here- routines, or there- ones), these will dominate. A simple example is to try to create something in a different medium. If you usually work on design, start off instead working in film. If you are making a digital plan, start off making a paper version. If you are launching a product from one market, in another, take your joint team to a third country to workshop your plans. So your assumptions come with you but your habits less so.

And always make collaborations, even if you usually work alone. They will spark changes in you (often through misunderstandings) that may take longer on your own.

5. Remake With

The brand strategy (abstracted):

- *Start with the heritage of your region*
- *Mix this with a modern production, frame or development*
- *Ensure that the result is legible and layered – annotated*
- *Make immersive experiences to explore*
- *Let the process take its own course based on samples from the past*
- *But ensure it is future-facing, cutting-edge as a result*

310

It's the same process whether you are:

- Designing contemporary fashion or lifestyle products with a distinct provenance
- Trying to find a new form of digital charity by exploring models from centuries past
- Creating education exhibits that are rooted but richly augmented

I think the music industry is an object lesson in remaking (more than movie remakes that often just shoot the old script with new stars and production values). Talk to any music producer about the power of a sample. It is like the grit that the pearl can form around. It comes with a kind of mystique and authority that is able to dictate many other choices, styles and patterns. Of course, if you were a drum and bass producer you aren't literally trying to remake R&B. But the original sample plays a key role.

So it could be helpful to start any creative process with a few treasures from the past that will act like musical samples. It could be a pattern or motif (Gianni Versace seemed very fond of Roman Empire touches). Or a different way of laying things out. Like in older cities, designed to be walked around, not driven through.

The other thing about bringing in history is it never fails to animate, illuminate and entertain. History is a collection of stories. It's what we mean when we say a place has character; that it comes with stories attached. At every moment, when people are meeting something they don't really understand, there is always an opportunity for them to be curious. Where did it come from? How was it made? Whose hands did it pass through? Why this design? And it's increasingly possible to do this in layers, which are there to explore if and when people want to, with digital media.

Workshop ideas

One workshop idea would be to imagine you had a time machine. Travel back and let yourself imagine working on the same brief or brand hundreds of years ago. Then take the results forward 100 years from now and rework them again. And so forth in smaller time distances until you land at today.

For instance, if I was developing a natural skincare brand, I might start with the long traditions of the Turkish Hammam. Then whizz forward to a future when all skincare is done through ionized steams designed for your skin type and desired result. Then back closer to now to explore pre-modern ingredients; salts, muds, botanicals. Then...

One great advantage of this is that the *Interland* cultures really do have long unbroken traditions. If you are working on e-commerce, why not pay a day trip to a market, bazaar or souk and observe cooperation, comparison, communication (always asking, which of these patterns or models could we adopt or incorporate?). I think it could be really cool on an e-commerce site if you could haggle the price down a bit.

6. Emerge With

The brand strategy (abstracted):

- *E-nabled models that create a new kind of community*
- *One that thrives on the feeling of being "of one mind"*
- *A community that combines local circuits of rich human-scale interaction*
- *...with large-scale coordination and effects*
- *Creating a feeling of emergence, a fresh start, freedom*
- *A spirit of conviviality, brother- and sisterhood*
- *Making patterns visible and open to participation*
- *Raising literacy, opening up to ways of seeing things*

It's the same process whether you are:

- Building a business out of a tribe of fellow enthusiasts
- Developing new platforms that combine reporting and citizen journalism

- Creating a popular movement for change and sharing content to build that

The concept of emergence comes from systems theory. It says that when you arrive at a new level of complexity, then there are new rules and results. You can't predict how blood works in the body from its chemistry alone. Nor (despite ancient medicine's ideas about "humours") how we think and feel from our blood.

Arriving at a collective seemingly with a mind of its own creates a similarly emergent space. It feels freer to participants, not because they have more control, but because the controls that restricted them at different lower levels are less effective.

At this new level, new brands and (which amounts to the same think) cultural ideas emerge. In fact it is easier to be a new thing in this new context. People look for signs that how they feel is true – that the world is different. Even if that sign is just ice cream shops spouting up in Libya. Ice cream shops aren't just food outlets in that context – they make emotional sense.

So there are two potential brand avenues of thought:

- How can we be part of emergent developments, the ongoing flow of social patterns and potentials coming from mobile, social media and other developments?
- How can we be something that just makes more emotional sense to a generation experiencing the newfound freedoms to go with the flow, living in a more information-rich world?

An example of the first could be traffic updates that are created by the movement of the users' mobile phones (where its GPS says that a phone moves and then stops, then it might be stuck in traffic).

An example of the second could be emotional road signs; like a smiley face sign to tell you your speed is okay; as used in Scotland (and found to reduce speeding by 53%).

Workshop ideas

This model suits large-scale deliberation or "jamming". There are plenty of existing forums where you could pose a challenge, call for ideas.

And while the ideas themselves may not be what you use, their character is something you can definitely tune into and start to layer into your own work. Or try testing ideas "in public" and film how people react to them. My point is that you need to take your process to the next level; to that of the crowd-mind.

7. Citizen With

The brand strategy (abstracted):

- *Creating a common ground, a shared interest*
- *And a common purpose, something to achieve together*
- *Finding the reciprocity, who brings what and how do they match?*
- *Calling for individual contributions, creating space for people to take responsibility*
- *Creating multiple streams, each well managed – a central spine of organization*
- *A core circle of collaborators, role models as well as having roles*
- *Replicating tools, lists, how-to guides, mentoring and education*
- *That delicate balance; leading and letting it find its own initiative*

It's the same process whether you are:

- An emblem of unity
- Promoting plurality, the bigger picture, a shared sense of identity
- Projects focusing people on shared fortunes, on society

Those sound like they lie outside the commercial realm, but actually brands have often stepped into this space and prosper when they get it right (e.g. Dove).

Give people rights and responsibilities. I had a client who sold Fairtrade chocolate and coffee. And their model was "more than

Fairtrade"; investing half their profits in communities, being part-owned by the farmer. But the message never seemed to get through on a supermarket shelf. My suggestion was that they sell a few products online and get people to set their own price. By moving sliders saying "how much to the farmer" (people might be shocked to know how low the Fairtrade premium is, and might well want to set it higher), "how much to communities", and so on.

Find a higher purpose to unite people. It doesn't have to be ethical in the puritanical sense. It could be healthier food, longer holidays, cleaner streets. Why not ask people what their issues are? We put up with a lot when we assume it can't change, but some things are much harder to put up with than others. Find the pain points.

If it's a case of conflict (and arguably, business itself is a process of wars of competing interests), then find a place that is safe, that you can agree on, and preferably a real place to meet.

Workshopping the Model

- *Just do it*
- *Create a basic manifesto*
- *Get a core team together and workshop the details of this*
- *Agree who will do what next*
- *Get it off the ground and build the details as you go*

How to Redevelop Existing Brands Using these Models

The first thing to do would be identify roughly which one of my seven brand strategies best applies. And work through that "as if starting again" to see if it yields fresh insight.

But then – here's the remarkable thing about looking at cases through geometry. There is a simple pattern to how most case stories

315

in the book were developing further. And that was (in terms of our diagram): move two categories clockwise.

Why does it work like that? I honestly don't know, and wasn't quite expecting it.

There are some obvious factors because of the way things are arranged; like moving to a new model that is not too close, but also not too far. (But if that was it then moving two categories counter-clockwise would help too.) All I can say is that's how it goes.

There is a different answer if you start at the centre with the *Fuse With* strategy, so let's come back to that. Here's what I found for the other six brand strategies, moving around the whole polygon:

1. Craft With → Remake With

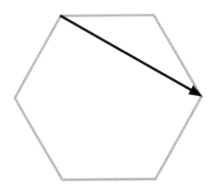

Examples:
- Timur Savci's big break into historical drama with *Magnificent Century* (and next the *Young Turks* and *Sufi*)
- Karen Chekerdjian's incorporation of nostalgic and familiar-looking elements
- Yemeksepeti's next venture being foodie and Turkish regional heritage-based
- .PSLAB creating space for the local heritages of their non-Beirut offices

2. Invent With → Citizen With

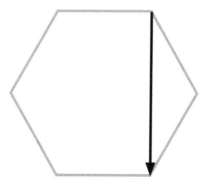

Examples:

- *Stars of Science* gravitating towards socially positive inventions
- *Little Bits* opening out inventing to the user
- *Eksi Sozluk* creating a forum for all views, with honesty (like Pete Teo, writ large)

3. Remake With → Emerge With

Examples:

- *Solidere* exploring using more interactive, digital exhibits
- *Bokja* moving into exploring the *Arab Spring* (and *Fall*)
- Rubicon edutainment moves from passive entertainment to theme park experiences

4. Citizen With → Adapt With

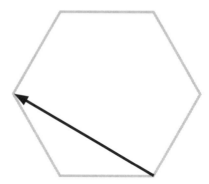

Examples:
- Kamal Mouzawak teaming up with his ex-business consultant partner
- Fadi Ghandour remodelling CSR
- Pete Teo's move from *15 Malaysia* to adapting *Rock the Vote*
- BBC News carefully researching, modelling and finding its adaptation for MENA

5. Emerge With → Craft With

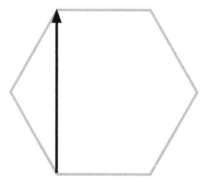

Examples:
- Arab Spring activists going back to jokes and taxi driver gossip
- Burak Arikan's next projects exploring the Islamic *musca* and *cemaats*
- The *Hijabers Community* leading to (guild style) group e-tail, events and blogging

6. Adapt With → Invent With

Examples:

- MAFP taking an interest in young social entrepreneurs
- Cinemoz starting to launch unique new Facebook sharing features
- SEEQNCE's ambition (to co-create by) franchising their model around the region
- Markafoni's starting to launch and host its own brands

7. Fuse With → Sub-Brands

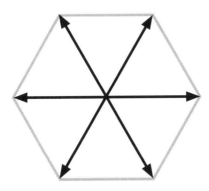

Examples:

- Nada Debs increasingly moving from their original pair of opposites (East & East) to other pairings (lightness and weight, natural and industrial...).

319

This is me extrapolating from other *Fuse With* brands that I know from client work. From those experiences, I think the more mature version of this model is to create one central parent brand that expresses this kind of unification, and then other strong sub-brands. Brands like the BBC and Natura Cosmetics, for instance, have done this. The BBC has an integrating ethos (part commercial, part public service) at the centre of a sprawl of positionings and offers. Natura is an eco-minded innovator touching on quite a few of these emerging market models with sub-brands too that happen to cover most of our six strategies. For instance, they have a range (Ekos) which is working with Amazon Indians to identify new botanicals; a kind of *Craft With* strategy, and *Invent With* ideas like soft packaging that you can transport 38× more of, in one truck, than standard rigid bottles.

I don't know Ulker well enough (to know for sure), but it strikes me as this kind of parent brand, with popular sub-brands like Dankek, Çamlıca, Bizim, Biskrem, Alpella, Golf, not to mention the acquired Godiva; these are very much satellites that are free to find the best model for them. For instance, the ice cream business in Iraq is probably playing on the *Adapt With* model, whereas Cola Turka was a *Remake With* Turkish heritage.

CONCLUDING THOUGHTS

CONCLUDING THOUGHTS

Imagine this book had been not about brands, but about food.

It is clear that the foods eaten around the world do relate to local customs and traditions. And these in turn draw upon the patterns of life in different societies, the climate and terrain, agriculture, the degree of urbanization, religious and other cultural factors. And there is also the sheer weight of historical precedent and the momentum of the habits that come from what people grew up eating. So that even if food differences are quite contingent, they can still be persistent.

It would also be clear that food is changing. We have new ways of cooking. We understand food differently. We are more exposed to other cuisines. We absorb huge amounts of knowledge and inspiration from media. This is not such a new factor either. The cuisines we think of as traditional are made up of previous innovations and imports – pasta from China, tomatoes from South America.

It is clear too that food is an example of something that expresses both human universals and cultural differences. Anywhere in the world, people tend to eat together and to offer food and drink as a gesture of hospitality. But the way that they eat, what they won't eat, who eats with who, how and when does vary. In describing brands in this book as "different", I have in mind that they are somewhat the same (still brands, still tapping human universals) as well as being somewhat different.

Like food, I would say that it is clear that brands have to be related to culture and context (what brands are made out of), to modernity and change, to global influences, media and information, and also human universals. As one who has worked in many parts of the world, it does seem to me that, not just their content or style, but what people actually mean by the word "brand" does vary between different countries. As indeed it often does between different industries.

It is also evident to me that the Western idea of having invented and somehow owning or dominating the idea of brands is passing. Whether brands originated in the West is debatable, when they owe so much of their origin to the moment when Renaissance Italy opened itself to imported ideas from the Middle East, from the classical world and from Asia. Whether they are "Western" (intrinsic to our hedonism) and could only come from the West is very doubtful. Just are there are alternative cinemas (other than Hollywood), there can be alternative brands.

It is hence entirely possible that alternative types of brands would emerge along with rapidly developing economies. And not just possible, but demonstrably something that can happen if we take the historical case of Japan and the rise of brands like Sony, Honda, MUJI and Issey Miyake. And just like Japan, what we have traced in this book is alternatives that are remixing and remaking ideas from the West, as well as drawing from their own different cultural and historical mind-set, sensibility and aesthetic. Initially making products that work better in their home context. But finding through their intrinsic difference, authenticity and relevance, they can quickly become globally successful too.

In the previous wave of globalization, we saw the spreading of Western brands and foods. Perhaps unfortunately, what travelled most was fast-food, chain restaurants, processed and packet food. That is an ongoing process, with global brands seeing their key opportunities for growth in emerging markets. McDonald's is opening vegetarian-only restaurants in India, while Kentucky Fried Chicken is already a leading fast-food brand in the Middle East.

But perhaps the tide is beginning to turn. While Pizza Hut chose Dubai to launch their staggeringly unhealthy "Crown Crust Pizza" (a deep pan pizza ringed with mini cheeseburgers), in New York the most popular street food vendors these days are the Halal Food Carts selling "chicken over rice", kebabs and biryanis.

And all across the world there is a growing appreciation of the local, the authentic, the healthy, the artisanal, freshly farmed, organic, handmade. While convenience, price and indulgence are still clearly still factors driving sales in supermarkets across the world, we at least now know that sugared drinks, processed foods laced with corn syrup and saturated fats, diets depleted of fresh vegetables are – together with lack of exercise – more deadly than smoking.

Generally speaking, the countries that have produced the most successful global brands (outside luxury and fashion) have tended to have the worst food. The USA takes a clear lead in this; on the evidence of author Michael Pollan and others. I don't mean that there aren't brilliant exceptions, I mean what the average citizen eats. And (if readers from countries including my own will forgive me) you could include the UK, Holland, Sweden and others in this list. The linking factor in my view is that in the last phase of global brands, it was precisely the "space age" excitement about breaking with the past, about image over content, that both created food deserts (a term coined to describe poverty and diabetes-stricken American city districts where there is little or no access to healthy fresh foods) and also global brands which are (in the words of Umberto Eco) "better than the real thing".

We are starting to see a phase in global branding where the countries that have the best food (quite a few of which, in my opinion, do lie within the Interland region) are starting to find the confidence to rediscover and reinvent their own traditions. And doing so in a world that is rapidly revaluing the authentic.

There have been numerous examples of food brands within this book; like Yemeksepeti, Ulker and Souk al Tayeb. But my point really is to use food to show how when I talk about "alternative kinds of brands", I mean that these are both the same and yet different to those in the West. The brands in this book are still brands. People's needs are fairly universal, even if then filtered through cultural conditioning

325

and personal circumstances. Yet it really is an alternative humanity that is emerging – both modern and yet not Western. The Interland is coming out from under the shadow of the West, which so long dominated global culture that it seemed (at least to itself) to represent not a partial view, but the universal one.

The best brands always come about in places and times of rapid social change. Coca-Cola caught the wind of an America at its absolute tipping point. Chanel was born into a world where the position of women was shifting further and faster than it ever had in the previous 20,000 years. And so many of the current "hot" brands have been born out of hot fault lines and rapid social change – from new markets like Google and the iPhone, to new (24-hour) lifestyles and Red Bull.

Most of the real history of the next 50 years is going to take place in Jim O'Neill's *BRIC* and *Next 11* countries. Not just because they are growing economically, but because they are young countries. And they are changing fast, socially and politically. The Arab Spring is just one indication of an irrepressible new spirit and truth. It is just the seed of what may follow.

When others have put forward the theory that strong brands are (in their emergence) almost the same thing as trends, they have made it sound a bit like it is just a case of being in the right place at the right time. I would only agree with that up to a point. What the case stories in this book show is that it is more a case of the right people, with the right mind-set, at the right place and the right time. There was nothing inevitable about Apple making geeky computing fashionable. Or about Nike making hot and sweaty exercise cool. Nor is there anything inevitable about experienced dotcom or design professionals adapting what worked in Silicon Valley or Milan into something that can work in Beirut. History isn't determined, it is made – and, as this book has tried to show, the next phase of history for brands could be a shift from being *Made By* to being *Made With*.

REFERENCE NOTES

1. The Story of the BRICs By Gillian Tett January 15 2010 www.ft.com
2. The Story of the BRICs By Gillian Tett January 15 2010 www.ft.com
3. http://www.ey.com/GL/en/Issues/Driving-growth/Strategies-for-success-in-emerging-markets---A-reversal-of-fortune
4. http://www.ey.com/GL/en/Newsroom/News-releases/News_BRICs-face-competition-as-globalization-creates-new-emerging-players
5. https://www.bcgperspectives.com/content/articles/globalization_growth_introducing_the_2013_bcg_global_challengers/
6. http://www.pewforum.org/the-future-of-the-global-muslim-population.aspx
7. http://www.forbes.com/sites/singularity/2012/10/15/how-indians-defied-gravity-and-achieved-success-in-silicon-valley/
8. Wilson, J. A. J. & Grant, J. (2013), "Islamic Marketing – a challenger to the classical marketing canon?", *Journal of Islamic Marketing*, Vol. 4 Iss. 1
9. http://www.ogilvynoor.com/index.php/meet-the-futurists-the-new-muslim-consumer/#.UUi5ZqW9blI
10. Giddens, A (1991) *Modernity and Self-Identity: Self and Society in the Late Modern Age*, Cambridge: Polity Press
11. Tamim Ansary "Destiny Disrupted: A History of the World Through Islamic Eyes", *Public Affairs* (2010)
12. Franklin D. Roosevelt, *Rendezvous with Destiny: Addresses and Opinions of Franklin Delano Roosevelt*, (2005) p. 130
13. Michael E. Eidenmuller (1960-07-15). "John F. Kennedy - 1960 Democratic National Convention Address". *American Rhetoric*
14. http://en.wikipedia.org/wiki/The_Hero_with_a_Thousand_Faces
15. Jewett, Robert and John Shelton Lawrence (1977) *The American Monomyth*. New York: Doubleday
16. Edward W. Said, "Islam Through Western Eyes," *The Nation* April 26, 1980
17. http://www.thedailybeast.com/newsweek/2012/08/26/orhan-pamuk-on-his-museum-of-innocence-in-istanbul.html
18. http://www.thedailybeast.com/newsweek/2012/08/26/orhan-pamuk-on-his-museum-of-innocence-in-istanbul.html
19. "The Life and Thought of Rumi" Translated by Aneela Khalid Arshed. (1999). All rights reserved. The Crossroad Publishing Company, New York
20. http://www.bbc.co.uk/news/magazine-20756247
21. Berger, John (2008) Ways of Seeing, Penguin Classics
22. https://wiki.brown.edu/confluence/download/attachments/74858352/FoucaultWhatIsAnAuthor.pdf
23. Pierre Hadot (1993) *Plotinus, or The Simplicity of Vision*, University of Chicago Press
24. Rumi's Discourses (Fihi ma fih, 24-5)
25. *The Glance: Songs of Soul-Meeting* by Rumi, translated by Coleman Barks
26. http://jan.ucc.nau.edu/~jsa3/hum355/readings/berger.htm
27. http://www.spiritualityandpractice.com/films/features.php?id=17822
28. http://world.time.com/2012/12/26/why-is-turkeys-prime-minister-at-war-with-a-soap-opera/#ixzz2KmOchGEP
29. http://www.wamda.com/2012/07/entrepreneur-of-the-week-bassam-jalgha-inventor-and-hackerspace-pioneer
30. http://www.1001inventions.com/doha
31. http://www.1001inventions.com/1001-Inventions-announces-Qatar-exhibitions
32. http://www.saudilife.net/life-and-society/personalities/29738-wake-up-early-says-founder-of-productive-muslim
33. http://www.saudilife.net/life-and-society/personalities/29738-wake-up-early-says-founder-of-productive-muslim
34. http://www.dailystar.com.lb/Culture/Lifestyle/2012/May-04/172288-rabih-kayrouz-designs-charm-beirut-and-paris.ashx#ixzz2Ms2jBg2V
35. http://couragetocreateabusiness.wordpress.com/425-2/
36. http://couragetocreateabusiness.wordpress.com/425-2/
37. Shafak, Elif (2006-07-31). "Pulled by Two Tides". *Time Magazine*. Retrieved 2010-12-10
38. Stauth, G., Turner, B.S., 1988. *Nostalgia, Postmodernism and the Critique of Mass Culture, Theory Culture Society* 5, 509–526
39. news.bbc.co.uk/1/hi/business/4788712.stm

40. news.bbc.co.uk/1/hi/business/4788712.stm

41. Ali, J.A. (1992) "Islamic work ethic in Arabia", *Journal of Psychology*, Vol. 126 No. 5, pp. 507-517

42. http://www.khaleejesque.com/?s=lost+city+of+arabesque

43. http://creativity-online.com/news/the-wild-east-the-inspiring-world-of-rana-salam/140887

44. http://hongisto.com/bokja-interview/

45. http://www.brownbook.me/fabricated-craft/

46. http://www.spiritualityandpractice.com/films/features.php?id=17822

47. http://www.ey.com/RU/en/Services/Strategic-Growth-Markets/Exceptional-CIS--September-2012-January-2013---Cartoon-heroine---Rubicon

48. http://www.nytimes.com/2006/04/30/arts/television/30stei.html?pagewanted=print&_r=0

49. https://www.aspeninstitute.it/aspenia-online/article/creativity-and-arab-spring-conversation-ammar-alani

50. http://edition.cnn.com/video/#/video/bestoftv/2011/02/11/exp.ghonim.facebook.thanks.cnn?iref=allsearch

51. http://www.digitaltrends.com/social-media/study-confirms-social-medias-revolutionary-role-in-arab-spring/#ixzz2NLJR4uJi

52. http://www.telegraph.co.uk/culture/books/ways-with-words/8629294/Ways-With-Words-role-of-Twitter-and-Facebook-in-Arab-Spring-uprising-overstated-says-Hisham-Matar.html

53. www.globalpost.com/dispatch/news/regions/middle-east/111212/top-goon-syria-puppet-show-bashar-al-assad

54. *The Arab Awakening*, (2012) Tariq Ramadan, published by Allen Lane

55. http://globalvoicesonline.org/2012/10/31/afef-abrougui-blogging-from-tunisia/

56. http://connectedincairo.com/mark-allen-peterson/

57. http://www.greenprophet.com/2012/04/greenwashing-egypt-brotherhood/

58. http://www.smh.com.au/news/opinion/behind-the-veil-lives-a-thriving-muslim-sexuality/2008/08/29/1219516734637.html

59. http://www.aquila-style.com

60. http://www.youtube.com/watch?v=Z0dsW9Fhg6g

61. http://www.wired.com/dangerroom/2012/09/iraq-hackerspace/

62. http://www.wired.com/dangerroom/2012/09/iraq-hackerspace/

63. http://www.wired.com/dangerroom/2012/09/iraq-hackerspace/

64. http://www.superbrands.com/my/index.php?option=com_content&task=view&id=107&Itemid=95

65. http://thestar.com.my/news/story.asp?file=/2012/1/8/nation/10225286&sec=nation

66. http://www.facebook.com/notes/15malaysia/pete-teo-interview-sin-chew-english-translation/194974343117

67. http://www.fadighandour.com/samih-and-hussam-maktoob-story-is-so-relevant-today

68. http://www.fadighandour.com/corporate-entrepreneurship-responsibility

69. Peter Doyle and Phil Stern (2006) *Marketing Management and Strategy*, Financial Times/Prentice Hall

70. Philip Kotler and Gary Armstrong (2009) *Principles Of Marketing* (13th Edition) Prentice Hall

71. Kenneth Roman and Jane Mass (1976), *How to Advertise*, St. Martin's Press